THE TRAVELLER'S HEALTHBOOK

The pocket guide to worldwide health

swimming shoes
repellant.

The editors

Dr N.J. Beeching, MA, BM BCh, FRCP, FRACP, DCH, DTM&H, is Senior Lecturer (Clinical) in Infectious Diseases, Liverpool School of Tropical Medicine. The Liverpool School was the first School of Tropical Medicine in the world and celebrated its centenary in 1998. It is a registered charity affiliated to the University of Liverpool and committed to improving the health of people living in the tropics through teaching, research and technical assistance. As part of its role in British-based healthcare, the School has daily clinics to provide pre-travel health advice and immunisations, as well as referral clinics for patients with possible exotic illnesses. Its website is at www.liv.ac.uk/lstm/

Jonathan Lorie is the Editor of *Traveller*, the UK's original travel magazine. Since 1970, *Traveller* has published the leading adventurers and explorers, many of whom now sit on the Editorial Board. It is editorially independent, and distributed to over 35,000 members of WEXAS International, the independent traveller's club. It can be accessed at www.traveller.org.uk

Also available
The Traveller's Handbook: the insider's guide to world travel offers expert advice and a comprehensive factual directory. Contributors include Michael Palin, Chris Bonington, Ranulph Fiennes, Clive Anderson, Eric Newby, David Bellamy, Dervla Murphy, Benedict Allen, Nicholas Crane, George Monbiot, Irma Kurtz, Esther Freud and many others. This is the most authoritative travel planning and reference book available today. Published October 2000, £14.99

THE TRAVELLER'S HEALTHBOOK

**Edited by Dr Nick Beeching
and Jonathan Lorie**

A WEXAS publication

This second edition published in 2000
by WEXAS International
45-49 Brompton Road, London sw3 1DE, UK
telephone 020 7589 0500
fax 020 7589 8418
email mship@wexas.com
website www.wexas.com
First edition published 1998 by WEXAS

ISBN 0-905 802-12-8

The views expressed in this book are those of the
authors. The authors, editors and publisher cannot
accept responsibility for any inconvenience, loss or
injury sustained by any person using this book.
Medical information in this book should always be
supplemented by individual advice from your own
healthcare advisors. The inclusion of product names
of vaccines or medications does not imply exclusive
endorsement, as the products and their trade names
differ in their availability in different countries.
Every attempt has been made to ensure that doses
and schedules are correct, but individual product
information should always be checked at the time
of administration.

Cover design by Wylie Design, London
Typography and typesetting by typoG, London
Directory research by Roger Crisp/Maria Coyle
Printed and bound by Legoprint SpA, Italy

COVER PICTURES *(clockwise from thermometer):*
The Photographers Library, Pete Turner/Image Bank,
The Photographers Library, Peter Holst/Image Bank,
Fritz Polking/Still Pictures, Bruce Coleman Inc.

Contents ❧

Introduction ❧

D<small>ON'T PANIC.</small>

This book contains the nastiest things that could ever happen to your health abroad—and explains how to avoid them.

Wherever you're going—ski-slopes or sun-kissed beaches, backpacker hostels or corporate boardrooms—we've got something in here that could scare you to death. But we've also got the experts who know how you can avoid trouble, stay healthy and enjoy any trip to the full.

Between them, the travel doctors and seasoned travellers in this book have probably covered more miles—and survived more diseases—than anyone else on the planet. They've been up Everest, down the Amazon, over the Andes and across the North Pole. Some have written guidebooks or lectured in travel medicine. Others have just soaked up the sun. They've all been out there and come back in one piece, inspired and refreshed by their travels.

Which is how it should be. And how it could be, with a little help from the expertise in these pages.

Then again, we're hoping you never need to use most of this. We'd like this to be the least-read book in history. If you take its advice on planning your trip and watching out for everyday ailments, it probably will be. We hope you'll wonder why you ever bought it.

But just in case you become friendlier than you'd like with a strange foreign disease, or find yourself in a survival situation… maybe you really should consider packing this little volume in that unused corner of your luggage.

And then, as they say in southern Africa, you will go well.

JONATHAN LORIE AND NICK BEECHING

Chapter 1: **Before you go** ❧

HEALTH PLANNING
by Drs Nick Beeching and Sharon Welby

THE MOST CAREFULLY PLANNED HOLIDAY, business trip or expedition may be ruined by illness, much of which is preventable. It is logical to put as much effort into protecting your health while abroad as you have into planning your itinerary and obtaining the necessary equipment and travel papers.

Unfortunately, it is not in the best commercial interests of travel companies to emphasise the possible health hazards of destinations that are being sold to potential customers: most holiday brochures limit health warnings to the minimum legal requirements, and some travel agents are woefully ignorant of the dangers of travel to more exotic climates. We have recently treated a travel agent for life-threatening malaria caught on the Kenyan coast. He had not taken malaria prophylaxis, despite the long and widespread recognition of the dangers of malaria in this area.

Happily, travellers' health problems are usually more mundane. Fatigue from overwork before a business trip or much-needed holiday, the stress of travel itself, exposure to new climates and over-indulgence in rich food, alcohol and tobacco, all contribute to increased vulnerability to illness. Short-lived episodes of diarrhoea affect up to 50 per cent of travellers, and up to one fifth of tourists on some Mediterranean package holidays will have mild respiratory problems such as head colds, 'flu-like illnesses or, rarely, more severe pneumonias such as Legionnaires' disease.

Sunburn or heat exhaustion are common, and accidents associated with unfamiliar sports such as skiing are an obvious hazard. But the most common cause of death among expatriates is road traffic accidents—not exotic infections.

Pre-travel health check-list

Starting three months before you travel, consult your family doctor and specialist agencies, as necessary, to:

1. Obtain information about specific health problems at your destinations.
2. Consider current health, medical and dental fitness for travel and current medications.
3. Obtain adequate health insurance (and form E111 if travelling to an EC country).
4. Check again that health insurance is adequate.
5. Plan and obtain necessary immunisations and malaria prophylaxis.
6. Plan and obtain other medications and first aid items and any necessary documentation
7. Consider need for first-aid training course.

Sources of information

The depth of preparation required before travel clearly depends on the general health of the individual and on his or her destination(s). In the last few years, accessible information on health for travellers has improved considerably. The sections in this chapter are intended to provide a brief outline of the steps to be considered.

Travellers to areas outside Europe, North America or Australasia are advised to invest in a copy of *Travellers' Health: How to Stay Healthy Abroad* (third edition, OUP) by Dr Richard Dawood—a guide containing a wealth of information on all aspects of travel medicine. This is updated by regular features in *Traveller* magazine (published by WEXAS), and is particularly recommended for those planning to work abroad or embarking on prolonged overland trips or expeditions in remote areas.

British travellers should obtain the booklet *Health Advice for Travellers Anywhere in the World*, prepared by the Department of Health and the Central Office of Information (booklet T5). This contains details of the documentation required for entitlement to free medical care and can be obtained from post offices, GPs' surgeries and vaccination centres, or by telephoning the Health Literature Line (freephone 0800 555 777). The leaflet is also constantly updated, on pages 460-464 of CEEFAX and on the computerised data services PRESTEL and ISTEL to which most travel agents have access.

Some useful web-based sources of information include the Department of Health travel advice (www.doh.gov.uk/hat/index.htm), the Foreign Office (http://193.114.50.10/travel/countryadvice.asp), the American Centers for Disease Control—Travel Health (www.cdc.gov/travel/), the World Health Organization (www.who.org), and Shoreland's Travel Health Online (www.tripprep.com/index.html).

When travelling outside Europe, it is wise to obtain information about compulsory immunisation requirements from the appropriate Embassy, Consulate or High Commission of each country that you plan to visit. However, do not expect their personnel to be able to give you general medical advice, and their information is not always as up to date as it should be. British travellers to exotic locations should also consult their District Public Health Department or one of the centres of specific expertise listed in the *Directory* for the latest information on immunisation requirements and malaria prophylaxis.

Those planning to work abroad should try and contact an employee of the company to ensure that adequate provision for medical and dental care is provided within their contract. If necessary, they should also consider taking out health insurance in addition to company policies.

Medical and dental health

If in any doubt about possible hazards of travel because of a pre-existing medical condition, consult your family doctor. People with heart or chest problems, recurrent blood clots in the legs or lungs, recent strokes, uncontrolled blood pressure, epilepsy, psychiatric disorders or chronic sinus or ear problems may be at risk when flying.

Late pregnancy is a contra-indication to flying, diabetics taking medication will need special advice, and the disabled will have specific requirements that may need to be notified to airline and airport authorities. People with chronic health problems or women who are obviously pregnant should ask their doctor to complete a standard airline form certifying their fitness for flying. This form should be obtained from the airline concerned.

Adequate supplies of all routinely-prescribed medications, including oral contraceptives, should also be obtained before departure. For short trips within Europe, these will be provided as NHS prescriptions. Those planning longer stays abroad should determine the availability of their medication overseas or take adequate supplies (you may need to pay for these on private prescription). It is also strongly recommended that you obtain a certificate from your doctor detailing the drugs prescribed, including the correct pharmacological name, as well as the trade name. This will be necessary to satisfy customs officials and you may need to obtain certified translations into appropriate languages. Some drugs readily obtainable in the UK are viewed with great suspicion elsewhere (codeine, for example, is considered a controlled drug in many countries, and tranquillisers such as diazepam can cause problems). Women working in Saudi Arabia should take adequate supplies of oral contraceptives and will need a certified Arabic translation of the certificate stating that the contraceptives have been prescribed for their personal use.

Those with recurring medical problems should also obtain a letter from their family doctor detailing the condition(s)—the letter can then be shown to doctors abroad if emergency treatment becomes necessary. People with surgically implanted devices are also advised to carry a doctor's certificate to show security officials. Artificial hip replacements often set off metal detection security alarms at airports, as do in-dwelling intravenous (e.g. Portacath) central venous lines. People with cardiac pacemakers are unlikely to run into problems due to electrical interference from British or North American airport metal detectors, but should try to avoid going through them and arrange instead for a personal body check by security officials.

Individuals with specific chronic health problems such as epilepsy, diabetes or long term steroid treatment, should obtain a 'Medic-alert' bracelet or similar, which is more easily located in a medical emergency than a card carried in a pocket.

Many countries insist on a negative HIV-antibody test before allowing foreigners to work. Some will not allow any known HIV-positive individual to enter the country (http://travel.

state.gov/HIVtestingreqs.html) despite advice from the World Health Organisation (WHO) that such regulations are ineffective as a means of controlling the spread of HIV infection. HIV-positive travellers should consult their medical specialist and local support groups about specific travel insurance problems and the advisability of travel.

Dental health is often taken for granted by British citizens who get a rude shock when faced with bills for dental work overseas. Those embarking on prolonged travel or work abroad, or planning to visit very cold areas, should have a full preventative dental check up before leaving. Spare spectacles, contact lenses and contact lens solutions should also be obtained before travelling. If you are planning a vigorous holiday or expedition (e.g. skiing, hill-walking, etc.) it might be a good idea to begin an appropriate fitness regime before you leave.

It is worth noting that expatriates taking up a contract abroad will often have to submit to a detailed medical examination as a condition of employment.

On your return

On returning from a long trip, most travellers will experience some euphoria and elation, as well as family reunions and the interested enquiries of friends. After this, as relaxation, and possibly jet lag set in, a period of apathy, exhaustion and weariness can follow. Recognise this and allow a few quiet days if it is feasible. There are usually many pressures at this stage, especially if equipment is to be unpacked and sorted, photographs processed, etc.

Another pressure for most people is the none too welcome thought of returning to the mundane chores involved in earning one's daily bread. If your travels have been challenging, then a couple of recovery days will probably make you work more efficiently thereafter and cope more expeditiously with the thousands of tasks which seem to need urgent attention.

After a time of excitement and adventure, some will go through a period of being restless and bored with the simple routine of home and work. They may not be aware of this temporary change in personality but their families certainly will be.

Having pointed out this problem, we cannot suggest any way of overcoming it except perhaps to recommend that everyone concerned try to recognise it and be a little more tolerant than normal. This may not be a sensible time to take major decisions affecting career, family and business.

Some will be relieved to arrive in their hygienic homes after wandering in areas containing some of the world's nastiest diseases. Unfortunately, the risk of ill health is not altogether gone as you may still be incubating an illness acquired abroad—incubation for diseases such as hepatitis or malaria could take a few months or in the extreme case of rabies, a few years. After your return, any medical symptoms or even just a feeling of debility or chronic ill health must not be ignored—medical help should be sought. Tell your physician where you have travelled (in detail), including brief stopovers. It may be that you are carrying some illness outside the spectrum normally considered. Sadly this has been known to cause mistaken diagnosis so that malaria, for example, has been labelled as influenza with occasionally fatal consequences.

Tropical worms and other parasites, enteric fevers, typhus, histoplasmosis (a fungal disease on guano, breathed in, making cavers particularly vulnerable), tuberculosis, tropical virus diseases, amoebic dysentery and hepatitis may all need to be treated. For these illnesses to be successfully treated, many patients will need expert medical attention.

Routine tropical disease check-ups are provided by some companies for their employees during or after postings abroad. They are not generally required by other travellers who have not been ill while abroad or after their return. People who feel that they might have acquired an exotic infection or who have received treatment for infection abroad, should ask their doctor about referral to a unit with an interest in tropical diseases. Most health regions have a suitable unit and more specialist units are listed in the *Directory*. All travellers who have had freshwater exposure in a bilharzia (schistosomiasis) area (see section on schistosomiasis) should be screened 3 months after the last freshwater contact or sooner if symptoms develop.

All unprotected sexual encounters while travelling carry high risks of infection with various sexually transmitted diseases in addition to HIV and hepatitis B. A post-travel check-up is strongly advised, even if you have no symptoms. Your local hospital will advise about the nearest clinic—variously called genito-urinary medicine (GUM) clinics, sexually-transmitted disease (STD) clinics, sexual health clinics, VD clinics or 'special' clinics. Absolute anonymity is guaranteed, and no referral is needed from your general practitioner.

After leaving malarial areas, many will feel less motivated to continue their anti-malarial drugs. It is strongly recommended that these be taken for a minimum of 28 days after leaving the endemic area. Failure to do this has caused many travellers to develop malaria some weeks after they thought they were totally safe. This is more than a nuisance: it has occasionally been fatal.

Fortunately, the majority of travellers return home with nothing other than pleasant memories of an enjoyable interlude in their lives. ❧

WHEN TO GO
by Paul Pratt and Melissa Shales

CHOOSING WHEN TO VISIT A COUNTRY can affect more than your suntan. In many places, climate is a key factor in the overall levels of hygiene and disease, as well as the prevalence of those annoying little insects....

Africa

NORTH AFRICA: The climate here varies widely from the warm and pleasant greenery of a Mediterranean climate in the coastal regions to the arid heat of the deep Sahara. Rains on the coast usually fall between September and May and are heavy but not prolonged. It can get cool enough for snow to settle in the mountainous areas, but temperatures will not usually fall below freezing, even in winter. In summer, temperatures are high (up to around 40°C) but bearable.

THE SAHARA, on the other hand, is extreme, with maximum summer temperatures of around 50°C and minimum winter temperatures of around 3°C. The temperature can fall extremely rapidly, with freezing nights following blisteringly hot days. What little, if any, rain there is can fall at any time of the year. The desert is also prone to strong winds and dust storms.

WEST AFRICA: At no time is the climate in West Africa likely to be comfortable, although some areas and times of the year are worse than others. The coastal areas are extremely wet and humid, with up to 2,500mm of rain falling in two rainy seasons (May and June and then again in October). In the north there is considerably less rain, with only one wet period between June and September. However, the humidity is still high, only lessened by the arrival of the *harmattan*, a hot, dry and dusty north-easterly wind which blows from the Sahara. Temperatures remain high and relatively even throughout the year.

EAST AFRICA: Although much of this area is on or near the equator, little of it has an 'equatorial' climate. The lowlands of Djibouti in the extreme east have a very low, uncertain rainfall, creating near-desert conditions plagued by severe droughts. Further down the coast, the high lowland temperatures are moderated by constant sea breezes. The temperatures inland are brought down by high-altitude plateaux and mountain ranges to about the level found in Britain at the height of summer. Temperatures are reasonably stable all year round, although the Kenyan highlands have a cooler, cloudy 'winter' from June to September. There are rainy seasons in most areas in April and May and, in some areas, for a couple of months between July and November, depending on the latitude.

SOUTH AFRICA: The whole area from Angola, Zambia and Malawi southwards tends to be fairly pleasant and healthy, although there are major variations from the Mediterranean climate of Cape Province, with its mild winters and warm, sunny summers, to the semi-desert sprawl of the Kalahari and the relatively wet areas of Swaziland, inland Mozambique and the Zimbabwe highlands to the east. In the more northerly areas, there is a definite summer rainy season, from December to March, when the temperatures are highest. On the south coast, there is usually some rain all year round. The west coast, with little rain, has cloud and fog due to the cold Benguela current, which also helps keep down the temperature. The best times of the year to visit are April, May and September, when the weather is fine but not too hot or humid.

The Americas

NORTH AMERICA: Almost half of Canada and most of Alaska in the north lies beyond the Arctic Circle and suffers from the desperately harsh weather associated with this latitude. In these areas, even in summer, the ice over the tundra rarely melts more than a metre or so, and even though summer temperatures are often surprisingly high, the season is short-lived. Snow and frost are possible at any time of the year, while the northern areas have permanent snow cover. The coast is ice-bound for most of the year.

The whole centre of the continent is prone to severe and very changeable weather, as the low-lying land of the Great Plains and the Canadian Prairies offers no resistance to sweeping winds that tear across the continent both from the Gulf and the Arctic. The east is fairly wet but the west has very little rain, resulting in desert and semi-desert country in the south.

Winter temperatures in the north can go as low as -40°C and can be very low even in the south, with strong winds and blizzards. In the north, winter is long-lived. Summers are sunny and often scorchingly hot.

In general, the coastal areas of North America are far kinder than the centre of the continent. The Pacific coast is blocked by the Rockies from the sweeping winds, and in the Vancouver area the climate is similar to that of the UK. Sea breezes keep it cool further south.

Seasons change fairly gradually on the east coast, but the northerly areas still suffer from the extremes of temperature that give New York its fabled humid heat waves in summer and frigid winter temperatures. New York, in spite of being far further north, is often much hotter than San Francisco. The

Newfoundland area has heavy fog and icebergs for shipping to contend with. Florida and the Gulf States to the south have a tropical climate, with warm weather all year round, and winter sun and summer thunderstorms. This is the area most likely to be affected by hurricanes and tornadoes, although cyclones are possible throughout the country.

MEXICO AND CENTRAL AMERICA: The best time to visit this area is during the dry season (winter) from November to April. However, the mountains and the plains facing the Caribbean have heavy rainfall throughout the year, which is usually at its worst from September to February. Mountains and plains facing the Pacific have negligible rainfall from December to April.

Central and northern Mexico tend to have a longer dry season, and the wet season is seldom troublesome to the traveller as it usually rains only between 4pm and 5pm. The temperature is affected by the altitude. The unpleasant combination of excessive heat and humidity at the height of the wet season should be avoided, if possible, at the lower altitudes.

SOUTH AMERICA: The climatic conditions of the South American continent are determined to a great extent by the trade winds, which, if they originate in high pressure areas, are not necessarily carriers of moisture. With a few regional exceptions, rain in South America is confined to the summer months, both north and south of the Equator. The exceptions are: southern Brazil and the eastern coast of Argentina and Uruguay, the southern Chilean coastal winter rainfall region, the coastal area of northeast Brazil.

The highest rainfall in South America is recorded in the Amazon basin, the coast lands of Guyana and Surinam, the coastlines of Colombia, Ecuador and southwest Chile. Altitude determines temperature, especially in the Andean countries near to the equator: hot—up to 1,000m; temperate—1,000 to 2,000m; cold—above 2,000m.

ARGENTINA: The winter months, June to October, are the best time for visiting Argentina. Buenos Aires can be oppressively hot and humid from mid-December to the end of February. Climate ranges from the sub-tropical north to sub-Antarctic in Tierra del Fuego.

BRAZIL: The dry season runs from May to October, apart from in the Amazon Basin and the Recife area, which have a tropical rainy season from April to July.

BOLIVIA: Heavy rainfall on the high western plateau from May to November. Rains in all seasons to the eastern part of the country.

CHILE: Just over the border from Bolivia, one of the driest deserts in the world faces the Pacific coast.

ECUADOR: Dry seasons from June to October. The coast is very hot and wet, especially during the December to May period. The mountain roads can be very dangerous during the wet season owing to landslides.

PARAGUAY: The best time for a visit is from May to October when it is relatively dry. The heaviest rainfall is from December to March, at which time it is most likely to be oppressively hot and humid.

PERU: During the colder months, June to November, there is little rainfall but it is damp on the coast, with high humidity and fog. From December to May, travel through the mountains can be hazardous owing to heavy rain, which may result in landslides, causing road blockage and long delays.

PARAGUAY: The best time for a visit is from May to October when it is relatively dry. The heaviest rainfall is from December to March, at which time it is most likely to be oppressively hot and humid.

Asia

HONG KONG: Subtropical climate; hot, humid and wet summer with a cool, but generally dry winter. Typhoon season is usually from July to August. The autumn, which lasts from late September to early December, is the best time for visiting as the temperature and humidity will have fallen and there are many clear, sunny days. Macao has a similar climate, but the summers are a little more bearable on account of the greater exposure to sea breezes. There is also an abundance of trees for shelter during the hot summer.

JAPAN: Japan lies in the northern temperate zone. Spring and autumn are the best times for a visit. With the exception of

Hokkaido, the large cities are extremely hot in summer. Hokkaido is very cold in winter. Seasonal vacation periods, especially school holidays, should be avoided if one is going to enjoy visiting temples, palaces and the like in relative comfort.

KOREA: Located in the northern temperate zone, with spring and autumn the best times for touring. The deep blue skies of late September/October and early November, along with the warm sunny days and cool evenings, are among Korea's most beautiful natural assets. Though it tends to be rather windy, spring is also a very pleasant time for a Korean visit. There is a short but pronounced wet season starting towards the end of June and lasting into early August. Over 50 per cent of the year's rain falls during this period and it is usually very hot and humid.

MALAYSIA: There are no marked wet or dry seasons in Malaysia. October to January is the wettest period on the east coast, October/November on the west coast. Sabah has an equable tropical climate, October and April/May are usually the best times for a visit. Sarawak is seldom uncomfortably hot but is apt to be extremely wet. Typhoons are almost unknown in East Malaysia.

THAILAND: Hot, tropical climate with high humidity. Best time for touring is from November to February. March to May is extremely hot and the wet season arrives with the southwest monsoon during June and lasts until October.

SINGAPORE: Like Malaysia, Singapore has no pronounced wet or dry season. The even, constant heat is mitigated by sea breezes. The frequent rain showers have a negligible cooling effect.

THE PHILIPPINES: The Philippines have a similar climate to Thailand. The best time to travel in the islands is during the dry season, November to March. March to May is usually dry and extremely hot. The southwest monsoon brings the rain from May to November. The islands north of Samar through Luzon are prone to be affected by typhoons during the period July to September. The Visayas Islands, Mindanao and Palawan, are affected to a lesser degree by the southwest monsoon and it is still possible to travel comfortably during the wet season south of

Samar Island—long sunny periods are usually interspersed with heavy rain showers.

Indian subcontinent

Sri Lanka: The southwest monsoon brings rain from May to August in Colombo and in the southwest generally, while the northeast monsoon determines the rainy season from November to February in the northeast. The most popular time for a visit is during the northern hemisphere's winter.

India: The climate of south India is similar to that of Southeast Asia: warm and humid. The southwest monsoon brings the rainy season to most parts of India, starting in the southwest and spreading north and east from mid-May through June. Assam has an extremely heavy rainfall during monsoon seasons. Generally speaking, the period from November to April is the best time to visit. From April until the start of the southwest monsoon, the northern Indian plains are extremely hot, though the northern hill stations provide a pleasant alternative until the start of the monsoon rains. These places usually have a severe winter.

Nepal: March is pleasant, as this is when all the rhododendrons are in bloom. The monsoon rains begin in April.

Middle East

A large proportion of this area is desert: flat, low-lying land with virtually no rain and some of the hottest temperatures on earth. Humidity is high along the coast and travellers should beware of heat exhaustion and even heat stroke. What little rain there is falls between November and March. To the north, in Iran and Iraq, the desert gives way to the great steppes, which are prone to extremes of heat and cold, with rain in winter and spring.

Melting snow from the surrounding mountains causes spectacular floods from March to May. The climate is considerably more pleasant in the Mediterranean areas, with long, hot, sunny summers and mild, wet winters. The coast is humid, but even this is tempered by steady sea breezes. The only really unpleasant aspect of the climate here is the hot, dry and dusty desert wind which blows at the beginning and end of summer.

Europe

Only in the far north and those areas a long way from the sea does the climate in Europe get to be extreme. In northern Scandinavia and some of the inland eastern countries such as Bulgaria, there are long, bitterly cold winters with heavy snow and, at times, arctic temperatures. In western Europe the snow tends to settle only for a few days at a time. In Britain, the Benelux countries and Germany, winter is characterised chiefly by continuous cloud cover, with rain or sleet. In the Alps, heavy snow showers tend to alternate with brilliant sunshine, offering ideal conditions for winter sports. There are four distinct seasons, and while good weather cannot be guaranteed during any of them, all are worth seeing. Summer is generally short, and the temperature varies widely from one year to the next, climbing at times to match that of the Mediterranean.

For sun worshippers, the Mediterranean is probably the ideal location, hot for much of the year but rarely too hot or humid to be unbearable. Rain falls in short, sharp bursts, unlike the continuous drizzle to be found further north. Winter is mild and snow rare.

Australasia

AUSTRALIA: For such a vast land mass, there are few variations in the weather here. A crescent-shaped rain belt follows the coast to provide a habitable stretch around the enormous semi-desert 'outback'. The Snowy Mountains in the east do, as their name suggests, have significant snowfalls, although even here it does not lie long. The east is the wettest part of the country, owing to trade winds that blow off the Pacific. The rainfall pattern varies throughout the country: the north and northeast have definite summer rains between November and April, the south and west have winter rains, while in the east and southeast the rains fall year-round. Tropical cyclones with high winds and torrential rain occur fairly frequently in the northeast and northwest. Tasmania, further south and more mountainous than the mainland, has a temperate climate similar to Britain's.

NEW ZEALAND: Although at a different latitude, the great expanse of water around New Zealand gives it a maritime climate similar to Britain's. The far north has a sub-tropical climate with mild winters and warm, humid summers. There are year-round snow fields in the south, and snow falls on most areas in winter. Although the weather is changeable, there is a surprising amount of sunshine, making this country ideal for most outdoor activities. The best time to visit is from December to March, at the height of summer.

PAPUA NEW GUINEA: The climate here is a fairly standard tropical one: hot and wet all year, although the time and amount of the rains are greatly influenced by the high mountains that run the length of the country. The rains are heavy, but not continuous. While the coast tends to be humid, the highlands are pleasant. ❧

VACCINATIONS
by Drs Nick Beeching and Sharon Welby

IMMUNISATIONS MAY BE NECESSARY to prevent illnesses that are common in many countries but which are rarely encountered in Western Europe, North America or Australasia. In the UK you can get most vaccinations through a general practitioner or a specialised vaccination centre (see *Directory*). Some will be free of charge, but the majority will have to be paid for privately. The exact requirements for a traveller will depend on his or her lifestyle, intended destinations and personal vaccination history, but should be considered at least two months before departure. However, even if you are travelling at short notice it is worth visiting your travel clinic or GP.

Modern immunisations are remarkably safe and well-tolerated. However, some vaccines contain traces of penicillin or neomycin and allergy to these antibiotics should be declared. Some vaccines are prepared in eggs and serious allergy to eggs will preclude some inoculations. Patients with chronic illness, particularly immune deficiency due to steroid treatment, cancer chemotherapy or HIV infection, should not receive most vaccines containing live organisms (such as oral polio or typhoid vaccines, oral typhoid, BCG and yellow fever vaccine), while pregnancy is also a contra-indication for several vaccines.

International regulations cover the minimum legal requirements for a few vaccinations, particularly yellow fever which has to be administered in a designated centre and recorded on a specific internationally recognised certificate. Some countries may have idiosyncratic certificate requirements—cholera vaccinations, for example—and the situation will change if an epidemic is in progress, hence the need for up-to-date information before you travel. If in doubt about the need for International Certificates for yellow fever, it may be wise to obtain one before travel rather than being forced to accept vaccination (using needles of dubious origin and sterility) on arrival at your destination.

It is equally important that the traveller has adequate protection against infections such as hepatitis A, polio and tetanus, even though proof of this will not be required by immigration officials at your destination. All travellers should have up-to-date tetanus immunisations, and travellers outside Europe, the Americas and Australasia should ensure that polio immunisation is adequate. Children should have received all their childhood immunisations, and children who are going to live in the tropics, or who will be staying for a month or more (especially if stopping with friends or relatives) should have early immunisation against tuberculosis (BCG), measles (MMR) and hepatitis B infection.

The following list summarises information on the most commonly required vaccinations. For a guideline of requirements for each country see the *Worldwide Vaccinations Guide* in the *Directory*. You can have as many vaccines as you like on one day, if you are feeling brave, but the live vaccines (poliomyelitis, yellow fever, BCG and MMR) should either be given on the same day or three weeks apart, otherwise the protection is reduced. The information below is in alphabetical order.

CHOLERA: A profuse diarrhoeal illness which poses little risk to the majority of travellers, and which is acquired from contaminated food or water. There have recently been large epidemics in much of South America and regions of Central Africa and the Indian subcontinent. The risk of travellers contracting cholera is very low and simple precautions such as sticking to safe water and food (especially avoiding raw or under cooked seafood) reduce that risk. Currently there is no cholera vaccine available in the UK. New oral vaccines available in Europe may become available in the UK in the near future particularly for the higher risk traveller. There are two new oral vaccines: Orochol from Switzerland (CVD103HgR) is a live attenuated vaccine which is given as a single dose, is well tolerated and gives good protection against several strains of cholera; a vaccine from Sweden, derived from sub-unit B of cholera toxin (rCTB-WC), consists of two doses and gives 85 per cent protection. However, none of these vaccines protects against the new strain of cholera emerging from the Indian subcontinent.

Some countries may still insist on a cholera vaccination certificate, even though this is no longer supposed to be a legal entry requirement. If we hear rumours that travellers have been asked to produce vaccination certificates, usually when trying to cross a remote border post during an epidemic of cholera, we can issue a cholera exclusion certificate.

DIPHTHERIA: A booster dose of diphtheria vaccine is recommended for all travellers to the Russian Federation, Ukraine and Tajikistan and for longer-term visitors (more than four weeks) to Africa, Asia, and South America if the last vaccine dose was more than ten years ago. Routine immunisation started on a national scale in 1940, and travellers who are travelling to high risk places and have never been immunised should have a primary course of diphtheria (three doses of vaccine given one month apart).

ENCEPHALITIS (JAPANESE): A rare virus infection causing severe encephalitis (inflammation of the brain) primarily in rural areas of Asia, especially during the rainy season. Two different effective vaccines are obtainable, usually through specialist vaccination clinics and are mainly recommended for those wandering off the beaten track for prolonged periods during the rainy seasons. Three injections of Je-VAX, spaced over one month, provide protection at the end of the month which lasts for two years. Two injections of the Korean Green Cross vaccine one or two weeks apart last for one year and a booster gives protection for two years. The vaccine is associated with a low incidence of serious but treatable side-effects and is not recommended for people who have a history of 'urticarial' rash ('hives'). The risk of allergic side-effects lasts for two weeks after each vaccination so it is advisable not to be travelling to remote areas during that time in case you run in to difficulties.

ENCEPHALITIS (TICK-BORNE): This is a viral infection transmitted by ticks in endemic forested areas in Europe, and causes an inflammation of the brain. There is another vaccine-sensitive form of tick-borne encephalitis (Russian spring-summer encephalitis) which occurs in the Eastern parts of Russia, China and Korea. The vaccine is safe but expensive. It is recommended for people spending prolonged periods of time walking and or camping in endemic areas. Two vaccine doses, a month apart, give protection for a year and a further booster dose at a year will extend the protection for three years. Travellers to these areas should follow anti-tick bite measures. If a tick bite occurs the tick should be removed and emergency immunoglobulin should be given within three days. This is usually available at airports and special clinics in the affected country.

HEPATITIS A: A water-borne virus infection that poses a significant health hazard for travellers to all parts of the tropics. The illness has an incubation period of three to six weeks and causes lethargy and jaundice for several weeks. The illness is often very mild in children aged less than five, and often goes completely unnoticed in this age group, so some adults will already have immunity even if they never had jaundice.

There are two options for protection. The old-fashioned immunisation with a gamma globulin injection just prior to travel provides reasonable protection for about three months. However, this is a blood-derived product and with the recent concerns that blood and blood-derived products may transmit the human form of 'mad cow disease' it is preferable to use the newer hepatitis A vaccines (e.g. Havrix or Avaxim). Gamma globulin should be reserved for adults travelling at short notice (within ten days) in whom the vaccine would not have time to become effective.

The actual risk of hepatitis A disease has to be balanced with any possible theoretical risk from the gamma globulin. Most travellers are recommended to have the hepatitis A vaccine, one dose of which at least ten days before travelling gives good protection for at least one year. A booster dose six to twelve months later gives protection for ten years. The vaccine is expensive and people who have lived in the tropics as a child and people over 50 years of age can ask for a blood test first to see if they are already immune to hepatitis A. Travellers particularly frightened of needles will be glad to know that there are now combination vaccines of hepatitis A and typhoid (e.g. Hepatyrix).

HEPATITIS B: A common infection in the tropics and countries bordering the Mediterranean, hepatitis B is caused by a virus that is transmitted by sex, by an infusion of contaminated blood or by sharing or reusing hypodermic needles. Hepatitis B can also be transmitted by acupuncture, body-piercing, tattoos and by sharing toothbrushes and razors. Hepatitis B causes similar symptoms to those of hepatitis A but sometimes is more severe and may lead to lasting liver damage. It is preventable with safe and highly effective injections given at three intervals, ideally with the second and third injections following at one and six month intervals after the first. More rapid protection can be provided by giving the third dose two months after the first, or an even faster regimen is now available giving the second injection a week later followed by the third at three or four weeks. Both these schedules have to be boosted by a fourth dose at one year if protection is to last for several years.

The vaccination is recommended for health workers and those working in refugee camps and similar environments, as well as for people planning to live in the tropics. It should also be considered by all adults who might have sexual contact with travellers (or anyone other than their regular partner), travellers playing contact sports, travellers who are more likely to come in to contact with the health services (e.g. travellers with pre-existing illnesses or travellers doing high risk activities such as climbing) and by all people who misuse intravenous drugs.

HEPATITIS A AND B COMBINED VACCINE: Combined vaccines (e.g. Twinrix) are now available which give protection against both hepatitis A and hepatitis B. This vaccine is particularly useful for the frequent business traveller and the back packer who have not been previously vaccinated, the advantage being the reduction in the number of vaccinations from five to three. Three injections are required, the second is given one month after the first and the third at six months. Protection is provided after the second injection and the booster dose will give further protection for five years. However, evidence is accumulating that Twinrix may be used in an accelerated schedule with three doses over a month, especially useful for the traveller who leaves it rather late to get immunised.

MALARIA: No vaccine available, see the section on *Malaria* in Chapter 3, for details about prevention.

MENINGOCOCCAL MENINGITIS: Epidemics recur in many parts of sub-Saharan Africa (mainly in the dry season) and an epidemic which began in Nepal moved to many other countries via the 1987 Haj pilgrimage to Mecca. The Saudi Arabian authorities now require Haj pilgrims to have certificates of vaccination against the infection, and a safe and effective vaccine against strains A and C of the organism has been available for several years. This vaccine does not protect against strain B of the meningococcus which is now the commonest strain found in the UK. In recent years we have seen more disease caused by strain C but this will decline as more people are routinely immunised with the new vaccine against the C strain alone, called meningitis conjugate C vaccine. This vaccine does not give protection to travellers to the tropics, where most epidemics are caused by the A strain. Meningococcal vaccine is not normally required by tourists unless travelling to an area with a current epidemic, or unless you plan to work in a region (especially in hospitals or schools) where the infection is common. One injection at least ten days before travel provides protection for three years. If you have to have the combined A & C vaccine for travel purposes, current advice is to wait for six months before having the new conjugate C vaccine which will probably then provide life-long protection against strain C.

POLIOMYELITIS (POLIO): Most adults have been immunised (immunisations started in 1958) but should receive a booster if this has not been given in the past ten years. Vaccination is usually given by mouth using a 'live' polio virus variant that provides protection but does not cause illness. Patients with immune suppression can receive injections of killed organisms instead (the 'Salk' vaccine).

RABIES: Vaccination before travel is safe but is usually only recommended for people working with animals or planning expeditions or employment in remote areas (see section on *Rabies* in Chapter 3). Three injections given subcutaneously over one month give protection for two years. The vaccine may also be given into the skin (intradermally); this smaller dose is an effective and cheaper alternative but is unlicensed. The intradermal route cannot be used if choloroquine is being taken concurrently for malaria prophylaxis. Further booster doses are needed if you have a possible exposure to a rabid animal. The emergency rabies immune serum is not then required (and is often not readily available in the tropics).

SMALLPOX: This vaccination is no longer required following the successful world-wide eradication of smallpox.

TETANUS: Vaccination effectively prevents this disease. A booster dose will be needed for adults who have not been immunised in the last ten years. Routine childhood immunisation did not begin in the UK until 1961 and older adults may need a full course of immunisation if they have missed out on this. However, if you have had a total of at least five tetanus vaccinations in your life, no further jabs are needed unless you have a tetanus-prone wound. In order to avoid unnecessary contact with health services in the tropics (and the risk of non-sterile needles), a booster dose of tetanus vaccine is often recommended prior to travel. Any contaminated wounds received while abroad should be cleaned and medical consultation sought concerning the need for antibiotics and additional vaccination.

TUBERCULOSIS: Although this bacterial infection is widespread in the tropics, it does not pose a major hazard for most travellers. Most British (but not North American) adults, and children aged over thirteen, will have already been immunised against TB (BCG vaccination). Those embarking on prolonged travel or employment abroad should consult their doctor about their TB immune status. Pre-employment medical examinations usually include this. Children who are travelling for more than a month abroad should have their BCG vaccine early.

TYPHOID: This bacterial infection is acquired from contaminated food, water or milk in any area of poor sanitation outside Europe, North America or Australasia. Typhoid vaccination is not necessary for most short-stay tourists, but should be considered by all planning prolonged or remote travel in areas of poor hygiene. The old-fashioned TAB (typhoid and paratyphoid A and B vaccine) and typhoid vaccines are no longer used, as there are now several alternatives. Injectable vaccines such as Typhim Vi and Typherix give moderate protection after one dose which lasts for about 3 years. The alternative is a course of capsules containing a live vaccine strain (e.g. Vivotif L or Typhoral L) taken by mouth over several days. This may appeal to those with a phobia of needles, but the course is expensive, must be taken strictly according to the manufacturer's instructions, and only provides immunity for one year after which it will need to be repeated. It cannot be taken at the same time as oral polio vaccine or any antibiotic, or within twelve hours after taking antimalarial drugs. As with other live vaccines, it is not recommended for pregnant women.

YELLOW FEVER: This virus infection, causing a lethal hepatitis, is transmitted by mosquitoes and is restricted to parts of Africa and South and Central America. It can be prevented by a highly effective and safe vaccine, the certificate for which is valid for ten years, starting ten days after vaccination. Vaccination and the International Certificate can only be given at World Health Organisation approved centres—in Britain this has now been extended to include many general practitioners. 🖎

THE ESSENTIAL MEDICAL KIT
by Drs Nick Beeching and Sharon Welby

INDIVIDUAL REQUIREMENTS VARY GREATLY and most travellers do not need to carry enormous bags of medical supplies. This section covers a few health items that the majority of travellers should consider. Those going to malarious areas should read the section on *Malaria* in Chapter 3, and those going to areas without ready access to medical care should read the *Medical Kit Checklist*, in the *Directory*.

First-aid training is appropriate for travellers to remote areas and those going on prolonged expeditions which might include a medical officer. As the medical needs of expeditions vary so much, an expedition kit bag list has not been included here. Expedition leaders should consult their own organisation or one of the specialist agencies for advice.

PAINKILLERS: We always carry soluble aspirin (in foil-sealed packs) which is an excellent painkiller and reduces inflammation associated with sunburn (just be careful about the water you dissolve it in). Aspirin should not be given to children aged less than twelve, and take paracetamol syrup for young children. Both paracetamol and aspirin reduce fever associated with infections. Adults who cannot tolerate aspirin because of ulcer problems, gastritis or asthma should instead take paracetamol (not paracetamol/codeine preparations). To avoid potential embarrassment or difficulty with customs officials, stronger painkillers should only be carried with evidence that they have been prescribed.

CUTS AND GRAZES: A small supply of waterproof dressings (e.g. Band-Aids) is useful and a tube of antiseptic cream such as Savlon—especially if travelling with children.

SUNBURN: British travellers frequently underestimate the dangers of sunburn and should take particular care that children do not get burnt. Protect exposed areas from the sun, remembering the back of the neck. Sunbathing exposure times should be gradually increased and use adequate sunblock creams (waterproof if swimming), particularly at high altitude where UV light exposure is higher. Sunburn should be treated with rest, plenty of non-alcoholic drinks and paracetamol or aspirin. Those who burn easily may wish to take a tube of hydrocortisone cream for excessively burnt areas. (See section *If You Can't Stand The Heat...* in Chapter 3.)

MOTION SICKNESS: If liable to travel sickness, try to sleep through as much of the journey as possible and avoid reading. Also avoid watching the horizon through the window and, if travelling by boat, remain on deck as much as possible.

Several types of medication give potential relief from motion sickness when taken before the start of a journey, and sufferers should experiment to find out which suits them best. Antihistamines (e.g. Phenergan) are popular, especially for children, but should not be taken with alcohol. Adults should not drive until all sedative effects of antihistamines have worn off. Other remedies include Kwells (hyoscine tablets), Dramamine (dimenhydrinate) and Stugeron (cinnarazine). Scopoderm patches, only available on prescription, release hyoscine through the skin for up to three days. Hyoscine taken by mouth or by skin patch causes a dry mouth and can cause sedation.

CONSTIPATION: The immobility of prolonged travel, body clock disruption, dehydration during heat acclimatisation and reluctance to use toilets of dubious cleanliness all contribute to constipation. Drink plenty of fluids and try to eat a high-fibre diet. Those who are already prone to constipation may wish to take additional laxatives or fibre substitutes (e.g. Fybogel).

DIARRHOEA: Although this is a common problem, it is usually self-limiting and most travellers do not need to carry anti-diarrhoea medication with them. (See the section *Diarrhoeal Illness* in Chapter 4.) Diarrhoea reduces absorption of the contraceptive pill and women may wish to carry supplies of alternative contraceptives in case of this.

FEMALE PROBLEMS: Women who suffer from recurrent cystitis or vaginal thrush should consult their doctor to obtain appropriate antibiotics to take with them. Tampons are often difficult to buy in many countries and should be bought before travelling. Periods are often irregular or may cease altogether during travel but this does not mean that you cannot become pregnant.

INSECT BITES: Insect bites are a nuisance in most parts of the world and also transmit a variety of infections, the most important of which is malaria. Personal insect repellents will be needed by most travellers and usually contain DEET (diethyltoluamide). Liquid formulations are the cheapest but are less convenient to carry. Lotions and cream are available and sprays are the easiest to apply but are bulky to carry. Sticks of repellent are easier to carry and last the longest. All these should be applied to the skin and to clothing adjacent to exposed areas of skin, but should not be applied around the eyes, nose and mouth (take care with children).

DEET dissolves plastics, including carrier bags, so beware. An alternative to DEET-containing repellents is Mosiguard Natural. Marketed by MASTA, this is made from a blend of eucalyptus oils and is as effective as repellents based on DEET. It is more suitable for people who are sensitive to DEET.

When abroad, try to reduce the amount of skin exposed to biting insects by wearing long sleeves, and long trousers or skirts. If a mosquito net is provided with your bed, use it. Permethrin-impregnated mosquito nets are effective and can be purchased before travel to malarious areas. 'Knock-down' insecticide sprays may be needed, and mosquito coils are easy to carry. Electric buzzers (that imitate male mosquito noises) are useless and candles and repellent strips (containing citronella) are not very effective. If bitten by insects, try to avoid scratching, which can introduce infection, particularly in the tropics. Eurax cream or calamine lotion can relieve local irritation, and antihistamine tablets may help those who have been bitten extensively. (See also sections on *Malaria* and *Medical Kit Check List*.)

Antihistamine creams should be used with caution as they can cause local reactions, and we prefer to use weak hydrocortisone cream on bites that are very irritating. Hydrocortisone cream should only be used if the skin is not obviously broken or infected. Increasing pain, redness, swelling or obvious pus suggest infection, and medical attention should be sought.

HIV PREVENTION: Most HIV infections are acquired sexually (see section *Sex Abroad* in Chapter 4). All adults should consider taking a supply of condoms. Travellers to countries with limited medical facilities should consider taking a supply of sterile needles and syringes so that injections required abroad are not given with re-usable needles of doubtful sterility.

Personal supplies of syringes and needles can make customs officials very suspicious, and condoms are not acceptable in some countries—particularly the Middle East. To avoid problems at the border, it is worth buying these items as part of a small HIV/AIDS prevention pack which is available from most of the medical equipment suppliers listed in the *Directory*. Larger 'HIV prevention packs' which include blood product substitutes are rarely worth carrying. ❧

MEDICAL INSURANCE
by Ian Irvine

No matter how carefully you read this book, sickness and accidents may occur whilst you are travelling, and the wise traveller needs to be aware of the best action to take to ensure that when the chips are down, he has the best possible care.

The most important step to attaining this is being aware that no one should travel without medical insurance. It is essential to make sure that the medical insurance is adequate (currently not less than one million pounds), includes repatriation cover, does not have unusual exclusions, covers all activities in which the traveller is likely to participate, and has an emergency service available at all times to provide assistance. If you have any doubts at all about insurance, you should consult a registered insurance broker, who will be happy to assist you without cost.

If you are suffering from any pre-existing medical condition, you must disclose full particulars to your medical insurers before arranging the insurance. Whilst you have a duty to do this, it does also give your insurers an opportunity to assess your condition and possibly offer advice. They will also notify you of any limitations which might apply to the medical insurance because of such a condition.

In general terms, medical claims for sickness and accident fall into two separate categories. There are those which are not serious, normally of short duration and the costs for which are comparatively minor. Most sensible travellers, with appropriate medical advice, can sort out such incidents without difficulty and whilst incurring expenditure, can normally pay for this themselves and recover their outlay under medical insurance on their return to the UK. More serious medical problems can cause difficulty, are normally of long duration and sometimes necessitate the cancellation of travel and the return home of the traveller. It is impossible to issue guidelines for every type of travel situation, but suffice it to say that medical opinion regarding any sickness or accident should be sought. Immediate action should also be taken to prevent any deterioration in health and urgent arrangements made for the appropriate medical treatment to be given.

In the event of a serious accident or illness, the emergency service provided by medical insurers should be contacted at the earliest opportunity and full details of the sickness or accident given. Very often treatment overseas is only available when it is known that payment is guaranteed, and most travellers are not in a position to do this. This facility is provided by the emergency service of the medical insurers, and once they have full details of the problem and have had an opportunity to discuss the course of action to be taken with local medical advisers, they are normally quite prepared to guarantee the cost of the treatment. This may relate to hospital charges, doctors', surgeons' or anaesthetists' fees, medication and transportation—all of which is quite normal and something the emergency service is experienced in handling.

Sometimes a traveller may suffer from an illness or accident in a remote location where there are inadequate medical facilities. In this situation, movement to a location which has better facilities may be necessary and this is something which the emergency service will organise and co-ordinate within the terms of the policy.

In the event of a very serious problem, it is sometimes impossible to arrange for treatment to UK standards to be provided locally. If such a situation should arise, it may become necessary to arrange repatriation to the UK or a nearer location where adequate medical facilities exist. Equally, if a traveller has suffered a serious illness or accident, has received some treatment and is making a recovery but is unwell enough to return to their country of residence without assistance, then repatriation may also be provided. The emergency services of the medical insurers are used to arranging repatriation and whether this necessitates a row of seats on an aircraft, or a special medical jet with a medical team on board, will be determined by the emergency service. Appropriate arrangements will be made and co-ordinated by them, to ensure the traveller's safe return home.

Reciprocal health agreements exist in certain foreign countries, although these normally only relate to direct costs incurred for medical treatment. They certainly do not provide for any repatriation or transportation costs and therefore do not mean that medical insurance should not be acquired.

The principal area of reciprocal health agreements is within the European Community, and to secure treatment the UK traveller must carry an E111 form, which can be obtained from any Department of Social Security office. This is a certificate which entitles the bearer to health benefits during a stay in a member country of the European Community. The regulations for each country in the European Community do differ, as does the level of benefit available, and details are currently available in the Department of Social Security leaflet N138.

British residents travelling to Australia are entitled to reciprocal health arrangements under the Medicare scheme. Whilst medical facilities in Australia are superb, no repatriation or transportation cover is provided—which, if necessary, could result in a heavy expenditure. For that reason, it is particularly important that travellers to Australia should arrange adequate medical insurance.

Elsewhere in the world, including North America, it is most

unlikely that any medical treatment will be available without either being paid for at the time, or guaranteed by the emergency service of medical insurers. Such being the case, it is a fool who travels without proper cover.

WEXAS Annual Traveller Insurance

Members of WEXAS (publishers of this book) can take advantage of a choice of two annual policies for multiple journeys:

1. The Holiday Traveller annual policy costs £59 a year for Europe and £75 a year worldwide. This policy provides cover for up to a maximum of 31 days' travel per trip and includes winter sports cover for up to 17 days a year.

2. The Global Traveller annual policy costs £99 a year and provides cover for both business and leisure travel up to a maximum of 92 days per trip. Winter sports cover for up to 21 days a year is also included. All WEXAS Traveller insurance policies provide an extensive medical cover of up to £10,000,000.

Conclusion

How often have we heard the old adage 'prevention is better than cure'? For travellers this is particularly relevant and the further afield you travel, and the more remote the location, the more relevant these words become. Notwithstanding this, it is inevitable that sickness and accidents do occur from time to time, and, if they are serious, even the most experienced traveller will need assistance. ❧

Chapter 2 : **Day-to-day health** ❧

GENERAL ISSUES
By Dr Nick Beeching

IT GOES WITHOUT SAYING that travellers should always seek qualified medical attention if any illness they are suffering from gets worse despite their own remedies, or, for that matter, any of those mentioned in this book! But finding and dealing with doctors in a foreign country can be a daunting task. This section will help you to locate a doctor and, with a bit of background knowledge, to get the best out of him or her once you have fallen ill. So far we have spoken only about prevention of disease and illness. This chapter is for those of you who are already ill or are in need of medication or qualified medical attention. We will also deal with more everyday problems such as food and water and coming to terms with culture shock.

Travellers should always seek qualified medical attention if any illness they are suffering gets worse despite their own remedies. Large hotels usually have access to doctors, typically a local family doctor or private clinic. In more remote areas, the nearest qualified help will be a rural dispensary or pharmacist, but seek advice from local expatriate groups, your consulate or embassy for details of local doctors. In large towns, university-affiliated hospitals should be used in preference to other hospitals. In remote areas, mission hospitals usually offer excellent care and often have English-speaking doctors. The International Association for Medical Assistance to Travellers (IAMAT) produces directories of English-speaking doctors (www.sentex.net/~iamat/ci.html) and some addresses are listed in the *Directory*.

If you feel that your medical condition is deteriorating despite (or because of) local medical attention, consider travelling home or to a city or country with more advanced medical expertise—sooner rather than later.

Medication

Medicines sold in tropical pharmacies may be sub-standard. Always check the expiry date and check that medications that should have been refrigerated are not being sold on open shelves. There is a growing market in counterfeit drugs, and locally-prepared substitutes are often of low potency. Stick to brand names manufactured by large international companies, even if these cost more. Insist on buying bottles that have unbroken seals and, wherever possible, purchase tablets or capsules that are individually sealed in foil or plastic wrappers. It is difficult to adulterate or substitute the contents of such packaging.

It is usually wise to avoid medications that include several active pharmacological ingredients, most of which will be ineffective and will push up the cost. Medication that is not clearly labelled with the pharmacological name as well as the brand name of ingredients is to be considered suspect (e.g. Nivaquine contains chloroquine).

Fevers

Fever may herald a number of exotic infections, especially when accompanied by a rash. Fever in a malarious area should be investigated by blood tests, even if you are taking antimalarials. A raised temperature is more commonly due to virus infections such as influenza, or localised bacterial infections that have obvious localising features such as middle ear infections or sinusitis (local pain), urinary tract infections (pain or blood passing water), skin infections (obvious) or chest infections including pneumonia (cough, chest pain or shortness of breath).

If medical attention is not available, the best antibiotic for amateurs is cotrimoxazole (Bactrim or Septrin) which contains a sulphur drug together with trimethoprim. This covers all the above bacterial infections as well as typhoid fever. Travellers who are allergic to sulphur drugs could use trimethoprim alone or coamoxyclav (Augmentin) which is a combined oral penicillin preparation.

Local infections

ATHLETE'S FOOT: Can become very florid in the tropics so treat this problem before departure. The newer antifungal creams, e.g. Canesten, are very effective and supersede antifungal dusting powders, but do not eliminate the need for sensible foot hygiene. In very moist conditions, e.g. in rain forests, on cave explorations or in small boats, lacerated feet can become a real and incapacitating problem. An adequate supply of silicon-based barrier cream is essential under these conditions.

BLISTERS: Burst with a sterile blade or needle (boiled for three minutes or held in a flame until red hot). Remove dead skin. Cover the raw area with zinc oxide plaster and leave in place for several days to allow new skin to form.

EARS: Keep dry with a light plug of cotton wool but don't poke matches or cotton-buds in. If there is discharge and pain, take an antibiotic.

EYES: If the eyes are pink and feel gritty, wear dark glasses and put in chloromycetin ointment or drugs. Seek medical attention if relief is not rapid or if a foreign body is present in the eye.

FEET: Feet take a hammering so boots must fit and be comfortable. Climbing boots are rarely necessary on the approach march to a mountain; trainers are useful. At the first sign of rubbing put on a plaster.

SINUSITIS: Gives a headache (feels worse on stooping), 'toothache' in the upper jaw, and often a thick, snotty discharge from the nose. Inhale steam or sniff a tea brew with a towel over your head to help drainage. Decongestant drops may clear the nose if it is mildly bunged up, but true sinusitis needs an antibiotic so seek advice.

SKIN INFECTIONS: In muddy or wet conditions, many travellers will get some skin sepsis or infections in small wounds. Without sensible hygiene these can be disabling, especially in jungle conditions. Cuts and grazes should be washed thoroughly with soap and water or an antiseptic solution. Large abrasions should be covered with a vaseline gauze, e.g. Jelonet or Sofratulle, then a dry gauze, and kept covered until a dry scab forms, after which they can be left exposed. Anchor dressings are useful for awkward places e.g. fingers or heels. If a cut is clean and gaping, bring the edges together with Steristrips in place of stitches.

TEETH: When it is difficult to brush your teeth, chew gum. If a filling comes out, a plug of cotton wool soaked in oil of cloves eases the pain; gutta-percha, softened in boiling water, is easily plastered into the hole as a temporary filling. Hot salt mouth-washes encourage pus to discharge from a dental abscess but an antibiotic will be needed.

THROAT: Cold dry air irritates the throat and makes it sore. Gargle with a couple of aspirins or table salt dissolved in warm water, or suck antiseptic lozenges.

Unconsciousness

The causes range from drowning to head injury, diabetes to epilepsy. Untrained laymen should merely attempt to place the victim in the coma position—lying on their side (preferably the left side) with the head lower than the chest to allow secretions, blood or vomit to drain away from the lungs. Hold the chin forward to prevent the tongue falling back and obstructing the airway. Don't try any fancy manoeuvres unless you are practised, as you may do more harm than good. *All unconscious patients, from any cause, but particularly after trauma, should be placed in the coma position until they recover. This takes priority over any other first aid manoeuvre.*

In cases of fainting, lay the unconscious person down and raise the legs to return extra blood to the brain.

Injury

Nature is a wonderful healer if given adequate encouragement.

BURNS: Superficial burns are simply skin wounds. Leave open to the air to form a dry crust under which healing goes on. If this is not possible, cover with Melolin dressings. Burn creams offer no magic. Deep burns must be kept scrupulously clean and treated urgently by a doctor. Give drinks freely to replace lost fluids.

SPRAINS: A sprained ankle ligament, usually on the outside of the joint, is a common and likely injury. With broad Elasto-plast 'stirrup strapping', walking may still be possible. Put two or three long lengths from mid-calf on the non-injured side, attach along the calf on the injured side. Follow this with circular strapping from toes to mid-calf overlapping by half on each turn. First Aid treatment of sprains and bruises is: immobilis-ation (I), cold e.g. cold compresses (C), and elevation (E);

remember 'ICE'. If painful movement and swelling persist, suspect a fracture.

FRACTURES: Immobilise the part by splinting to a rigid structure; the arm can be strapped to the chest, both legs can be tied together. Temporary splints can be made from a rolled newspaper, an ice-axe or a branch. Pain may be agonising and is due to movement of broken bone ends on each other; full doses of strong pain killers are needed.

The aim of splinting fractures is to reduce pain and bleeding at the fracture site and thereby reduce shock. Comfort is the best criterion by which to judge the efficiency of a splint, but remember that to immobilise a fracture when the victim is being carried, splints may need to be tighter than seems necessary for comfort when at rest, particularly over rough ground.

Wounds at a fracture site or visible bones must be covered immediately with sterile material or the cleanest material available, and if this happens, start antibiotic treatment at once. Pneumatic splints provide excellent support but may be inadequate when a victim with a broken leg has a difficult stretcher ride across rough ground. They are of no value for fractured femurs (thigh bones). If you decide to take them, get the Athletic Long Splint which fits over a climbing boot where the Standard Long Leg splint does not.

WOUNDS (DEEP WOUNDS): Firm pressure on a wound dressing will stop most bleeding. If blood seeps through, put more dressings on top, secured with absorbent crepe bandages and keep up the pressure. Elevate the injured part if possible.

On expeditions to remote spots, at least one member of the party should learn to put in simple sutures. This is not difficult—a friendly doctor or casualty sister can teach the essentials in ten minutes. People have practised on a piece of raw meat and on several occasions this has been put to good use. Pulling the wound edges together is all that is necessary, a neat cosmetic result is usually not important.

Swimming

(See also *Creatures That Bite* in Chapter 4.)

SAFE SWIMMING: Try to swim in pairs: a friend nearby in the

water is more likely to distinguish between waving and drowning and can also help to avoid panic.

WHEN TO SWIM: Drowning seems rather too obvious a risk to mention here but it is simultaneously the most common and the most serious risk of any water sport, and in many cases alcohol is involved. Don't swim drunk. Some authorities still maintain that swimming after meals runs a risk of stomach cramps, although this is now a minority view.

WHERE TO SWIM: Safe swimmers find local advice before taking to the water. Deserted beaches are often deserted for a reason, whether it be sharks, invisible jellyfish, or vicious rip tides. Beware of polluted water as it is almost impossible to avoid swallowing some. Never dive into water of unknown depth. Broken necks caused by careless diving are a far greater hazard to travellers than crocodiles.

FRESHWATER SWIMMING: Is not advisable when crocodiles or hippopotamuses are in the vicinity. Lakes, ponds, reservoirs, dams, slow streams and irrigation ditches may harbour bilharzia (schistosomiasis). This is a widespread infection in Africa, the Middle East and parts of the Far East and South America, and is a genuine hazard for swimmers. (See *Common Illnesses*, Chapter 3.)

STRONG CURRENTS: In the sea and rivers, watch out for tides and rips: even a current of one knot is usually enough to exhaust most swimmers quickly. Swimming directly against a strong current is especially exhausting, and, if possible, it is best to swim across the flow, and so gradually make your way to the shore.

SNORKELLING: Snorkelling is a great way to see the seabed, provided that a proper mask is used, enclosing the nose. Eye-goggles can cause bruising and eye damage from the pressure of water. A more serious risk is the practice of hyperventilating (taking several deep breaths) before diving, in the hope of extending a dive. This can kill. Normally, the lungs tell the body to surface for air when the carbon dioxide level is too high. Hyperventilation disrupts this mechanism, so the body can run out of oxygen before the lungs send out their danger signals. This can lead to underwater blackouts, and drowning.

Scuba diving: Scuba divers should be sure that local instruction and equipment is adequate and should always swim with a partner. Do not fly within three hours of diving, or within 24 hours of any dive that requires a decompression stop on the way back to the surface. Travellers who anticipate scuba diving in their travels are strongly advised to have proper training before setting out. 🏊

WATER PURIFICATION
by Julian McIntosh

POLLUTED WATER CAN AT BEST lead to discomfort and mild illness, at worst to death, so the travelling layman needs to know not only what methods and products are available for water purification, but also how to improvise a treatment system in an emergency.

Three points about advice on water treatment cause misunderstanding. Firstly, there is no need to kill or remove all the micro-organisms in water. Germs do not necessarily cause disease. Only those responsible for diseases transmitted by drinking water need be treated. And even some water-borne diseases are harmless when drunk. Legionnaires' disease, for example, is caught by breathing in droplets of water containing the bacteria, and not by drinking them.

Secondly, in theory, no normal treatment method will produce infinitely safe drinking water. There is always a chance, however small, that a germ might, by virtue of small size or resistance to chemicals or heat, survive and cause disease. But the more exacting your water treatment process, the smaller the risk—until such time as the risk is so tiny as to be discounted. The skill of the experts lies in assessing when water is, in practice, safe to drink. Unfortunately different experts set their standards at different levels.

Thirdly, beware the use of words like 'pure', 'disinfect' and 'protection', common claims in many manufacturers' carefully written prose. Read the descriptions critically and you will find that most are not offering absolutely safe water but only a relative improvement.

Suspended solids

If you put dirty water in a glass the suspended solids are the tiny particles that do not readily sink to the bottom. The resolution of the human eye is about one-hundredth of a millimetre, so a particle half that size (five microns) is totally invisible to the naked eye—and yet there can be over ten million such particles in a litre of water without any visible trace. Suspended solids are usually materials such as decaying vegetable matter or mud and clay. Normally mud and clay contamination is harmless, but extremely fine rock particles including mica or asbestos occasionally remain in glacier water or water running through some types of clay.

Microbiological contamination

EGGS, WORMS, FLUKES, ETC: These organisms, amongst others, lead to infections of roundworm (*Ascaris*), canine roundworm (*Toxocara canis*), guinea worm (*Dracunculus*) and bilharzia (schistosomiasis). They are relatively large, although still microscopic, and can be removed by even crude forms of filtration. The very tiny black things that you sometimes see wriggling in very still water are insect larvae, not germs, and are not harmful. Practically any form of pre-treatment will remove them.

PROTOZOA: In this group of small, single-celled animals, are the organisms that cause giardiasis (*Giardia lamblia*), an unpleasant form of chronic diarrhoea, and amoebic dysentery (*Entamoeba histolytica*). Both of these protozoa have a cyst stage in their life cycle, during which they are inert and resistant to some forms of chemical treatment. However, they quickly become active and develop when they encounter suitable conditions such as the human digestive tract. They are sufficiently large to be separable from the water by the careful use of some types of pre-filter. This is not always true for a common water borne protozoan called *Cryptosporidium parvum* that causes diarrhoea in all parts of the world and which may be lethal in immunocompromised people, e.g. those with advanced AIDS. The cysts are small enough to pass through many filters and are relatively resistant to chlorine. They are best destroyed by boiling the water.

BACTERIA: These very small, single-celled organisms are responsible for many illnesses from cholera, salmonella, typhoid and bacillary dysentery to the less serious forms of diarrhoea known to travellers as Montezuma's Revenge or Delhi Belly. A healthy person would need to drink thousands of a particular bacterium to catch a serious disease. Luckily, the harmful bacteria transmitted by drinking contaminated water are fairly 'soft' and succumb to chemical treatment—their minute size means only a very few filters can be relied upon to remove them all.

VIRUSES: These exceptionally small organisms live and multiply within host cells. Some viruses, such as hepatitis A, and a variety of intestinal infections, are transmitted through drinking water. Even the finest filters are too coarse to retain viruses. The polio and hepatitis viruses are about 50 times smaller than the pore size in even the finest ceramic filter.

Selection of a water supply

Whatever method of water treatment you use, it is essential to start with the best possible supply of water. Learning to assess the potential suitability of a water supply is one of the traveller's most useful skills.

GOOD SOURCES: Ground water, e.g. wells, boreholes, springs; water away from or upstream of human habitation; fast-running water; water above a sand or rock bed; clear, colourless and odourless water. Fast running water is a hostile environment for the snails that support bilharzia.

BAD SOURCES: Water close to sources of industrial, human or animal contamination; stagnant water; water containing decaying vegetation; water with odour or a scum on its surface; discoloured or muddy water.

Wells and boreholes can be contaminated by debris and excreta falling or being washed in from the surface, so the top should be protected. A narrow wall will stop debris. A broad wall is not so effective, as people will stand on it and dirt from their feet can fall in. Any wall is better than no wall at all.

Pre-treatment

If you are using water from a river, pool or lake, try to not to draw in extra dirt from the bottom or floating debris from the surface. If the source is surface water, such as a lake or river, and very poor, some benefit may even be gained by digging a hole adjacent to the source. As the water seeps through, a form of pre-filtration will take place, leaving behind at least the coarsest contamination.

Pouring the water through finely woven fabrics will also remove some of the larger contamination. If you have fine, clean sand available, perhaps taken from a stream or lake bed, an improvised sand filter can be made using a tin can or similar container with a hole in the bottom. Even a (clean) sock will do. Pour the water into the top, over the sand. Take care to disturb the surface of the sand as little as possible. Collect the water that has drained through the sand. The longer the filter is used, the better the quality of the water, so re-filter or discard the first water poured through. Discard the contaminated sand after use.

If you are able to store the water without disturbing it, you could also try sedimentation. Much of the dirt in water will settle out if left over a long enough period. Bilharzia flukes die after about 48 hours. The cleaner water can then be drawn off at the top. Very great care will be needed not to disturb the dirt at the bottom. Siphoning is the best method.

If the water you are using has an unpleasant taste or smell, an improvement can be achieved by using coarsely crushed wood charcoal wrapped in cloth. When the 'bag' of charcoal is placed in the water, or the water is run through the charcoal (like a sand filter), the organic chemicals responsible for practically all the unpleasant tastes and smells will be removed. Some colour improvement may also be noticed. The water will still not be safe to drink without further treatment, but you should notice some benefit.

Treatment of a water supply

BOILING: Boiling at 100°C kills all the harmful organisms found in water, except a few such as slow viruses and spores which are not dangerous if drunk. However, as your altitude above sea level increases, the weight of the atmosphere above you decreases, the air pressure drops, as does the temperature at which water boils. A rule of thumb for calculating this is that water boils at 1°C less for every 300 metres of altitude. Thus if you are on the summit of Kilimanjaro, at 5895 metres, the water will boil at only 80°C.

At temperatures below 100°C, most organisms can still be killed but it takes longer. At temperatures below 70°C, some of the harmful organisms can survive indefinitely and as the temperature continues to drop, so they will flourish.

There is one more important consideration. When water is boiling vigorously, there is a lot of turbulence and all the water is at the same temperature. While water is coming to the boil, even if bubbles are rising, there is not only a marked and important difference between the temperature of the water and the temperature at a full boil, but there can also be a substantial difference in temperature between water in different parts of the pan, with the result that harmful organisms may still survive.

To make water safe for drinking, you should bring water to a full boil for at least two minutes. Boil water for one minute extra for every 300 metres above sea level. Do not cool water down with untreated water.

FILTRATION: The key to understanding the usefulness of a filter is ensuring that you know the size of the particles that it will reliably separate, and the dirt-load the filter can tolerate before it clogs up. If the pores in the filter are too large, harmful particles can pass through. If small enough to stop harmful particles, the pores can block up quickly, preventing any more water from being filtered.

To reduce this problem, manufacturers employ ingenious means to increase the filter area, and filter in at progressively smaller stages. But even in one apparently clean litre of water there can be a hundred thousand million particles the same size or larger than bacteria. And to stop a bacterium, the filter has to take out all the other particles as well. If the filter is small (of the drinking-straw type for instance) or if the water is at all visibly dirty, the filter will block in next to no time.

There are three solutions: water can be filtered first through a coarse filter to remove most of the dirt, and then again through a fine filter to remove the harmful bacteria; a re-cleanable filter can be used; or finally, only apparently clean water could be used with the filter. The use of a coarser filter is called pre-filtration. Viruses are so small they cannot be filtered out of drinking water by normal means. However, because they are normally found with their host infected cells and these are large enough to be filtered, the finest filters are also able to reduce the risk of virus infection from drinking water.

A filter collects quite a lot of miscellaneous debris on its surface and, in order to prevent this providing a breeding ground for bacteria, the filter needs to be sterilised from time to time. Some are self-sterilising and need no action, but others should be boiled for 20 to 30 minutes at least once every two weeks. Where filters are described as combining a chemical treatment, this is for self-sterilisation. The chemical is in such small concentrations and in contact with water passing through the filter for such a short period that its use in improving the quality of the filtered water is negligible.

PRE-FILTRATION: Pre-filters should remove particles larger than five to ten microns in size and be very simple to maintain. They will be more resistant to clogging since they take out only the larger particles. They will remove larger microbiological contamination including protozoal cysts, flukes and larger debris that might form a refuge for bacteria and viruses. Pre-filtration is normally adequate for washing. Further treatment is essential for safe drinking supplies.

FINE FILTRATION: To remove all harmful bacteria from water, a filter must remove all particles larger than 0.5 microns (some harmless bacteria are as small as 0.2 microns). Filters using a disposable cartridge are generally more compact and have high initial flow rates, but they are more expensive to operate. Alternatively there are ceramic filters that use porous ceramic 'candles'. These have low flow rates and are fairly heavy. Some need special care in transport to ensure they do not get cracked or chipped thus enabling untreated water to get through. Ceramic filters can be cleaned easily and are very economic in use.

ACTIVATED CARBON/CHARCOAL FILTERS: These remove a very wide range of chemicals from water, including chlorine and iodine, and can greatly improve the quality and palatability of water. But they do not kill or remove germs, and may even provide an ideal breeding ground unless self-sterilising. Some filters combine carbon and other elements to improve the taste and this also removes harmful organisms.

Chemical treatment

Broadly speaking, there are three germicidal chemicals used for drinking-water treatment. For ease of use, efficiency and storage life, the active chemical is usually made up as a tablet suitable for a fixed volume of water, although the heavier the contamination, the larger the dose required. Germs can also be embedded in other matter and protected from the effects of a chemical, so where water is visibly dirty you must pre-filter first. Chlorine and iodine have no lasting germicidal effect so on no account should untreated water be added to water already treated.

SILVER: Completely harmless, taste-free and very long-lasting effect, protecting stored water for up to six months. The sterilisation process is quite slow and it is necessary to leave water for at least two hours before use. Silver compounds are not effective against cysts of *Amoeba* and *Giardia*, so use pre-filtration first if the water is of poor quality.

CHLORINE: Completely harmless, fast-acting and 100 per cent effective if used correctly. A minimum of ten minutes is required before water can be used. The cysts of *Amoeba* and *Giardia* are about ten times more resistant to chlorine than bacteria, but both are killed if treatment time and dose are adequate. If in doubt, we recommend that the period before use be extended to at least 20 and preferably 30 minutes. If heavy contamination is suspected, double the dosage. Alternatively, pre-filter. Some people find the taste of chlorine unpleasant particularly if larger doses are being used. The concentration of chlorine drops quickly over several hours and more so in warm temperatures so there is very little lasting effect. Excess chlorine may be removed using sodium thiosulphate or carbon filters.

IODINE: Fast acting and very effective, normally taking ten minutes before water is safe to use. It has a quicker action against cysts than chlorine. Double dosage and extended treatment times or pre-filtration are still very strongly recommended if heavy contamination is suspected. Iodine is more volatile than chlorine and the lasting effect is negligible. Excess iodine may be removed by sodium thiosulphate or a carbon filter.

Iodine can have serious, lasting physiological side effects and should not be used over an extended period. Groups particularly at risk are those with thyroid problems and the unborn foetuses of pregnant women. Thyroid problems may only become apparent when the gland is faced with excess iodine, so in the event of the use of iodine compounds being unavoidable, ask your doctor to arrange for a thyroid test beforehand—or use a good carbon filter to remove excess iodine from the water.

Rules for treatment

ORDER OF TREATMENT: If chemical treatment and filtration are being combined, filter first. Filtration removes organic matter which would absorb the chemical and make it less effective. If of a carbon type, the filter would also absorb the chemical leaving none for residual treatment. In some cases, the filter may also be a source of contamination. If water is being stored prior to treatment then it is worthwhile treating chemically as soon as the water is collected and again after filtration. The first chemical dose prevents algae growing in the stored water.

STORAGE OF WATER: Use separate containers for treated and untreated water, mark them accordingly and don't mix them up. If you are unable to use separate containers take particular care to sterilise the area round the filler and cap before treated water is stored or at the time treatment takes place. In any case, containers for untreated water should be sterilised every two to three weeks. Treated water should never be contaminated with any untreated water. Treated water should never be stored in an open container. Treated water left uncovered and not used straight away should be regarded as suspect and re-treated. ❧

FOOD ON THE MOVE
by Ingrid Cranfield

L IVING A REGULAR LIFE, in one place most of the time, people
get to know what foods they like and dislike, and they base
a balanced diet on this rather than on textbook nutrition. The
problem is, how do you ensure you will have good food on the
move? When travelling, you are constantly faced with new foods
and it can be easy to lose track of how you are eating, simply because your rule-of-thumb menu-planning breaks down. This
can lead to fatigue, a lack of energy and even poor health.

Eating nutritiously

Essentially there are two ways of coping. You can either pick up
local food as you travel, or you can take with you all your needs
for the duration. Eating local food may give you a feeling of
being closer to a country's way of life, but could also make you
severely ill. Taking your own supplies is safe and very necessary
if you are going into the wilds, but how do you stop your palate
becoming jaded with endless supplies of dried food?

It is sensible to be able to recognise the constitution of all
foods and to know what is necessary to keep you well fed. A balanced diet breaks down into six main areas: sugars, carbohydrates, fats, proteins, minerals/vitamins/salts and water—all are
necessary, some in greater quantities than others.

SUGARS: Technically called simple sugars, these are the sim-
plest form of energy-stored-as-food. Because they are simple,
the body finds them easy to absorb into the bloodstream—
hence the term blood sugar. From here sugars are either turned
directly to energy, or are stored as glycogen. The brain is very
partial to using sugars for energy and if it is forced to run on
other forms of food energy it complains by making you feel
tired, headachy, and a bit wobbly-kneed.

Though it is important to have some sugars in your diet, try
not to depend on them too much. Weight for weight they give
you fewer calories than other food types. Also, if you take in lots

of sugars at once, the body will react by over-producing insulin because your blood sugar is too high, so that in the end your blood sugar is taken down to a lower level than before. If you feel a desperate need for instant energy, try to take sugars with other food types to prevent this happening. While travelling, it is simple enough to recognise foods with lots of sugars—they are sweet. In less developed areas, sugar is still something of a luxury, so there will be less temptation!

CARBOHYDRATES: Basically, carbohydrates are complex structures of simple sugars. Plants generally store energy as carbohydrate while animals store food energy as fat or glycogen. Carbohydrates have to be broken down into simple sugars by the body before they can be used as energy, so it takes longer to benefit from them after eating. Weight for weight, however, you will get three or four times more calories from carbohydrates than from sugars.

Carbohydrates are stodgy, starchy and very filling: breads in the Western world, mealies in Africa, rice in the East, etc. The majority of food energy comes from carbohydrates, so, when travelling, find the local equivalent and base a diet around it.

FATS: Next to carbohydrates, most of our energy comes from fats. Our bodies store energy as fat, because it is the most efficient way to do so. Weight for weight, fats give you nearly three times the energy of carbohydrates, so they are an extremely efficient way of carrying food energy.

Fats, of course, are fatty, oily, creamy and sometimes congeal. Foods high in fat include butter, dairy foods, etc., although there are other high-fat foods that are less well known, such as egg yolk or nut kernels. Fats are necessary now and again because one reclusive vitamin is generated from a fat and, more obviously, because without these concentrated doses of energy it would take a lot longer to eat all the food you need, as with cows or elephants.

PROTEINS: One of the most misunderstood types of food in the West is protein. Traditionally thought of as something essential, and the more the better, the truth is that for adults very little is needed each day, and bodies in the West work very hard to convert unnecessary protein into urea so that it can be flushed away. Protein is used to build and repair bodies, so children need plenty of it, as do adults recovering from injury. Otherwise, the amount of protein needed each day is small—maybe a small egg's worth.

Other than that, protein cannot be readily used for energy, and the body does not bother converting it unless it is heading for a state of starvation. Those people on a red meat diet are using very little of the protein it contains, relying on the fat content which can be up to 45 per cent. When you are wondering where protein appears in your food, bear in mind that protein is for growth, so young mammals have protein-packed milk, un-hatched chicks have their own supply inside an egg, and to help trees off to a good start there is a healthy package of protein in nuts.

MINERALS, VITAMINS AND SALTS: All of these are essential for all-round health and fitness. Most of them cannot be stored by the body and so they should be taken regularly, preferably daily. Ten days' shortage of Vitamin C, for instance, and you feel run-down, tired and lethargic—perhaps without knowing why.

In the normal diet, most of your minerals and vitamins come from fresh fruit and vegetables. If you feel that you may not get enough fresh food, take a course of multivitamin tablets with you for the duration of your travels. They do not weigh very much and can save you lots of trouble.

If you are getting your vitamins and minerals from fresh foods, remember that they are usually tucked away just under the skin, if not in the skin itself. Polished and refined foodstuffs have lost a lot, if not all, of their vitamins, minerals and dietary fibre.

As regards salts, there is little cause for concern. It is easier to take too much than too little, and if you do err on the low side your body tells you by craving salty foods. Do not take salt tablets, you could upset your stomach lining.

How much to eat?

Nutritionists have a term for the amount of food energy needed to keep a body ticking over—the basal metabolic rate. Take a man and put him in a room at ideal temperature, humidity, etc., and make sure he does no work at all except stay alive, and he will use about 600 kCal in a day. This is identified as his basal metabolic rate.

Those of us who do not lie stock still in a room all day need energy over and above that basic amount, to work and to keep warm. For living and working in average conditions, our daily energy requirement rises to about 2500 kCal. If you are going to be physically active (backpacking, say) in a temperate climate, your energy use will go up to around 3500 kCal per day. If we do the same hard work in an extremely cold climate, our energy rate could go up to 5000 kCal. To require more than this, we would need to do an immense amount of work or have an incredibly fast metabolism. Sadly for women, they do not burn up nearly as much energy doing the same work as men.

A little experience will tell you whether you need a little more or a little less than the average. With this knowledge, you are ready to plan just how much food you need to take for the number of days you are travelling. When you come to work out amounts of various foodstuffs that make up your calorie intake for the day, books for slimmers or the health conscious are invaluable. They list not only calories, but often protein and other nutritional breakdown. Nutritional information is also given on the packet of most foodstuffs.

Eating safely

Before handling food of any kind, always wash your hands in water that has been chlorinated or otherwise purified. This is especially important in developing countries when you may have been in contact with unhygienic materials.

Eating in developed countries is not entirely hazard-free. You should remember that Delhi Belly is no respecter of language and is just as likely to strike in Spain as in India. The rules for avoiding tummy trouble are: stick to foods that are simple and hygienically prepared, and as close as possible to those you know and love—at least until your digestive system slowly adapts to change.

Always look for food that is as fresh as possible. If you can watch livestock being killed and cooked or any other food being prepared before you eat it, so much the better. Do not be deceived by plush surroundings and glib assurances. Often the large restaurant with its questionable standard of hygiene and practice of cooking food ahead of time is a less safe bet than the wayside vendor from whom you can take food cooked on an open fire, without giving flies or another person the chance to contaminate it.

When buying foodstuffs, bear these rules in mind:

■ Rice and other grains and pulses will probably have preservatives added to them. These will need to be removed by thorough washing as they are indigestible.

■ In developing countries, canned, powdered and dried foods are usually safe to eat, provided they are made up with purified water. Staple ingredients such as flour and cooking oils are nearly always safe.

■ Meat, poultry, fish and shellfish should look and smell fresh and be thoroughly cooked, though not over-cooked, as soon as possible after purchasing. They should be eaten while still hot or kept continuously refrigerated after preparation. Protect freshly bought meat from flies and insects with a muslin cover. Eggs are safe enough if reasonably fresh and thoroughly cooked.

■ It is wise to avoid steak tartare and other forms of raw meat in the tropics, as there is a risk of tapeworm. Meat that is just 'on the turn' can sometimes be saved by washing it in strong salty water. If this removes the glistening appearance and sickly sweet smell, the meat is probably safe to eat.

■ Cold or half-warmed foods may have been left standing and are therefore a risk. Boil such meats and poultry for at least ten minutes to destroy bacteria before serving. Remember that hot spices and chillies do not sterilise meat.

■ Milk may harbour disease-producing organisms (tuberculosis, brucellosis). The 'pasteurised' label in underdeveloped countries should not be depended upon. For safety, if not ideal taste, boil the milk before drinking. (Canned or powdered milk made up with purified water may generally be used without boiling for drinking or in cooking.)

■ Butter and margarine are safe unless obviously rancid. Margarine's keeping qualities are better than those of butter.

Cheeses, especially hard and semi-hard varieties, are normally quite safe; soft cheeses are not so reliable.

■ Vegetables for cooking are safe if boiled for a short time. Do check, though, that on fruit or vegetables the skin or peel is intact. Wash them thoroughly and peel them yourself if you plan to eat them raw.

■ Moist or cream pastries should not be eaten unless they have been continuously refrigerated. Dry baked goods, such as bread and cakes, are usually safe even without refrigeration.

■ Ice-cream is to be avoided in all developing countries.

■ Fruit juice is safe if pressed in front of you.

In restaurants, the same rules apply for which foods are safe to eat. Restaurants buy their food from shops, just as you would.

Off the beaten track

There is no right menu for a camping trip, because we all have slightly different tastes in food and there is an almost endless number of menu possibilities. So, what should you pack? Here are a few points you will want to consider when choosing the right foods: weight, bulk, cost per kg.

Obviously, water-weighted, tinned foods are out. So are most perishables—especially if you are going to be lugging your pantry on your back. You will want only lightweight, long-lasting, compact food. Some of the lightest, of course, are the freeze-drieds. You can buy complete freeze-dried meals that are very easily prepared: just add boiling water and wait five minutes. They have their drawbacks, however. First, they are very expensive. Second, even if you like these pre-packaged offerings, and many people do not, you can get tired of them very quickly.

A much more exciting and economical method is to buy dehydrated foods at the supermarket and combine them to create your own imaginative dinners. Dried beans, cereals, instant potato, meat bars, crackers, dry soup mixes, cocoa, pudding, gingerbread and instant cheesecake mixes are just a few of the possibilities. But do not forget to pack a few spices to make your creations possible.

Most people tend to work up a big appetite outdoors: about 0.9kg to 1.2kg of food per person per day is average. How much of which foods will make up that weight is up to you. You can guess pretty accurately about how much macaroni or cheese or how many pudding mixes you are likely to need.

Last, but not least, what do you like? If you do not care for instant butterscotch pudding or freeze-dried stew at home, you will probably like it even less after two days on the trail. And if you have never tried something before, don't take the chance. Do your experimenting first. Do not shock your digestive system with a lot of strange or different new foods. Stick as closely as possible to what you are used to in order to avoid stomach upsets and indigestion. And make sure you pack a wide enough variety of foods to ensure you will not be subjected to five oatmeal breakfasts in a row or be locked into an inflexible plan.

After purchasing your food, the next step is to re-package it. Except for freeze-dried meals or other specially sealed foods, it is a good idea to store supplies and spices in small freezer bags. Just pour in your pudding powder, salt or gingerbread mix, drop an identifying label in, to take all the guesswork (and fun) out of it, and tie a loose knot. Taking plastic into the wilderness may offend one's sensibilities but it works well. Out in the wilds, you learn just how handy these lightweight, flexible, recyclable, moisture-proof bags really are.

Although cooking over an open fire is great fun, many areas do not allow and cannot support campfires, so don't head off without a stove. When choosing a stove, remember that the further off the beaten track you go, the more important size, weight and reliability become. Aside from a stove, you will also need a collapsible water container, means of water purification, and a heavy bag in which to store your soot-bottomed pans. You will need individual eating utensils: spoon, cup and bowl will do. Also take a few recipes with you, or learn them before you leave. You can even have such luxuries as freshly baked bread, if you are prepared to make the effort. Here are some tips about camp cooking, learned the hard way.

1. Cook on a low heat to avoid scorching.
2. Taste before salting (the bouillon cubes and powdered bases often added to camp casseroles are very salty: don't overdo it by adding more).

3. Add rice, pasta, etc., to boiling water to avoid sticky or slimy textures and add a knob of butter or margarine to stop the pan from boiling over.
4. Add freeze-dried or dehydrated foods early on in your recipes to allow time for rehydration.
5. Add powdered milk, eggs, cheese and thickeners to recipes last when heating.
6. When melting snow for water, do not let the bottom of the pan go dry or it will scorch (keep packing the snow down to the bottom).
7. Add extra water at high altitudes when boiling (water evaporates more rapidly as you gain altitude) and allow longer cooking times—twenty minutes at 1,000m, for example, as against ten minutes at sea level.

CLEANING UP: soap residue can make you sick. Most seasoned campers, after one experience with 'soap sickness of the stomach', recommend using only a scouring pad and water. Boiling water can be used to sterilise and, if you have ignored the above advice, is good for removing the remains of your glued-on pasta or cheese dinners. Soak and then scrub.

Use those recyclable plastic bags to store leftovers and to carry away any litter. Leave the wilderness kitchen clean—and ready for your next feat of mealtime magic! ✖

TRAVEL STRESS
by Hilary Bradt

THE SCENE IS FAMILIAR: a crowded bus station in some Third World country; passengers push and shove excitedly; an angry and discordant voice rings out, 'But I've got a reserved seat! Look, it says number 18, but there's someone sitting there!' The foreigner may or may not win this battle, but ultimately he will lose the war between 'what should be' (his expectations) and 'what is' (their culture)—and he becomes yet another victim of stress.

It is ironic that this complaint, so fashionable among businessmen, should be such a problem for many travellers who believe they are escaping such pressures when they leave home. But, by travelling rough, they are immediately immersing themselves in a different culture and thus subjecting themselves to a new set of psychological stresses.

The physical deprivations that are inherent in budget travel are not usually a problem. Most travellers adjust well enough to having a shower every two months, eating beans and rice every day and sleeping in dirty, lumpy beds in company with the local wildlife. These are part of the certainties of this mode of travel. It is the uncertainties that wear people down: the buses that double-book their seats, usually leaving an hour late but occasionally slipping away early; the landslide that blocks the road to the coast on the one day of the month that a boat leaves for Paradise Island; the inevitable *mañana* response; the struggle with a foreign language and foreign attitudes.

Culture shock

It is this 'foreignness' that often comes as an unexpected shock. The people are different, their customs are different—and so are their basic values and moralities. Irritatingly, these differences are most frequently exhibited by those who amble down the Third World Corridors of Power that control the fate of travellers. But ordinary people are different, too, and believers in Universal Brotherhood often find this hard to accept—as do women travelling alone. Many travellers escape back to their own culture periodically by mixing with the upper classes of the countries in which they are travelling—people who were educated in Europe or America and are westernised in their outlook. Come to think of it, maybe this is why hitchhikers show so few signs of travel stress: they meet wealthier car owners and can often lapse into a childlike dependence on their hosts.

Fear and anxiety

At least hitchhikers can alternate between blissful relaxation and sheer terror, as can other adventurous travellers. Fear, in small doses, never did anyone any harm. It seems to be a necessary ingredient of everyday life; consciously or unconsciously, most people seek out danger. If they don't rock climb or parachute jump, they drive too fast, refuse to give up smoking or resign from their safe jobs to travel the world. The stab of fear that travellers experience as they traverse a glacier, eye a gun-toting soldier or approach a 'difficult' border is followed by a feeling of exhilaration once the perceived danger has passed.

A rush of adrenaline is OK. The hazard is the prolonged state of tension or stress, to which the body reacts in a variety of ways: irritability, headaches, inability to sleep at night and a continuous feeling of anxiety. The budget traveller is particularly at risk because money shortages provoke so many additional anxieties to the cultural stresses mentioned earlier. The day-to-day worry of running out of money is an obvious one, but there is also the fear of being robbed (no money to replace stolen items) and of becoming ill. Many travellers worry about their health anyway, but those who cannot afford a doctor, let alone a stay in hospital, can become quite obsessional. Yet these are the people who travel in a manner most likely to jeopardise their health. Since their plan is often 'to travel until the money runs out', those diseases with a long incubation period, such as hepatitis, will manifest themselves during the trip. Chronic illnesses such as amoebic dysentery undermine the health and well-being of many budget travellers, leaving them far more susceptible to psychological pressures. Even the open-endedness of their journey may cause anxiety.

Easing the situation

Now I've convinced you that half the world's travellers are heading for a nervous breakdown rather than the nearest beach, let's see what can be done to ease the situation (apart from bringing more money). There are tranquillisers. This is how most doctors treat the symptoms of stress since they assume that the problems causing the anxiety are an unavoidable part of everyday life. Travellers should not rule tranquillisers out (I've met people who consume Valium until they scarcely know who they are), but since they have chosen to be in their situation it should be possible to eliminate some of the causes of stress.

They can begin by asking themselves why they decided to travel in the first place. If the answer is that it was 'to get away from it all', journeying for long distances seems a bit pointless— better to hole up in a small village or island and begin the lotus-eating life. If the motive for travel is a keen interest in natural history, archaeology or people, then the problems inherent in getting to the destination are usually overridden in the excitement of arriving. However, those who find the lets and hindrances that stand between them and their goal too nerve-racking (and the more enthusiastic they are, the more frustrated they will become) should consider relaxing their budget in favour of spending more money on transportation, etc., even if it does mean a shorter trip.

The average overlander, however, considers the journey to be the object and will probably find that time on the road will gradually eliminate his anxieties (like a young man I met in Ecuador: he was forever thinking about his money, but when I met him again in Bolivia he was a changed man, relaxed and happy. 'Well,' he said, in answer to my question, 'You remember I was always worrying about running out of money? Now I have, so I have nothing to worry about!').

If a traveller can learn the language and appreciate the differences between the countries he visits and his own, he will come a long way towards understanding and finally accepting them. His tensions and frustrations will then finally disappear.

But travellers should not expect too much of themselves. You are what you are, and a few months of travel are not going to undo the conditioning of your formative years. Know yourself, your strengths and weaknesses, and plan your trip accordingly. And if you don't know yourself at the start of a long journey, you will by the end. 🍂

CULTURE SHOCK
by Adrian Furnham

NEARLY EVERY TRAVELLER must have experienced culture shock at some time or other. Like jet lag, it is an aspect of travel that is both negative and difficult to define. But what precisely is it? When and why does it occur? And, more importantly, how can we prevent it—or at least cope with it?

Although the experience of culture shock has no doubt been around for centuries, it was only 25 years ago that an anthropologist called Oberg coined the term. Others have attempted to improve upon and extend the concept and have come up with alternative jargon, such as 'culture fatigue', 'role shock' and 'pervasive ambiguity'.

Strain

From the writings of travellers and interviews with tourists, foreign students, migrants and refugees, psychologists have attempted to specify the exact nature of this unpleasant experience. It seems that the syndrome has six facets. Firstly, there is strain caused by the effort of making necessary psychological adaptations—speaking another language, coping with the currency, driving on the other side of the road, etc. Secondly, there is often a sense of loss and a feeling of deprivation with regard to friends, possessions and status. If you are in a place where nobody knows, loves, respects and confides in you, you may feel anonymous and deprived of your status and role in society, as well as bereft of familiar and useful objects. Thirdly, there is often a feeling of rejection—your rejection of the natives and their rejection of you. Travellers stand out by virtue of their skin, clothes and language. Depending on the experience of the natives, they may be seen as unwanted intruders, an easy rip-off or friends.

A fourth symptom of culture shock is confusion. Travellers can become unsure about their roles, their values, their feelings and sometimes about who they are. When a people lives by a different moral and social code from your own, interaction for even a comparatively short period can be very confusing. Once one becomes more aware of cultural differences, typical reactions of surprise, anxiety, even disgust and indignation occur. The way foreigners treat their animals, eat food, worship their god or perform their toilettes often cause amazement and horror to naive travellers. Finally, culture shock often involves feelings of impotence, due to an inability to cope with the new environment.

Little England

Observers of sojourners and long-term travellers have noted that there are usually two extreme reactions to culture shock: those who act as if they 'never left home' and those who immediately 'go native'. The former chauvinists create 'little Englands' in foreign fields, refusing to compromise their diet or dress and, like the proverbial mad dogs, insisting on going out in the midday sun. The latter reject all aspects of their own culture and enthusiastically do in Rome as the Romans do.

Most travellers, however, experience less dramatic but equally uncomfortable reactions to culture shock. These may include excessive concern over drinking water, food, dishes and bedding; fits of anger over delays and other minor frustrations; excessive fear of being cheated, robbed or injured; great concern over minor pains and interruptions; and a longing to be back at the idealised home, 'where you can get a good cup of tea and talk to sensible people'.

But, as any seasoned traveller will know, often one begins to get used to, and even learns to like, the new culture. In fact writers have suggested that people go through a number of phases when living in a new culture. Oberg, in his original writings, listed five stages: the 'honeymoon', which is characterised by enchantment, fascination, enthusiasm and admiration for the new culture, as well as the formation of cordial (but superficial) relationships. In this stage, people are generally intrigued and euphoric. Many tourists never stay long enough to move out of the honeymoon period. The second phase heralds crisis and disintegration. It is now that the traveller feels loss, isolation, loneliness and inadequacy, and tends to become depressed and withdrawn. This happens most often after two to six months of living in the new culture.

The third phase is the most problematic and involves reintegration. At this point people tend to reject the host culture, becoming opinionated and negative, partly as a means of showing their self-assertion and growing self-esteem. The fourth stage of 'autonomy' finds the traveller assured, relaxed, warm and empathic because he or she is socially and linguistically capable of negotiating most new and different social situations in the culture.

And finally the 'independent' phase is achieved—characterised by trust, humour and the acceptance and enjoyment of social, psychological and cultural differences.

U-curve

For obvious reasons, this independent phase is called the 'U-curve' hypothesis. If you plot satisfaction and adaptation (x axis) over time (y axis), you see a high point at the beginning, followed by a steep decline, a period at the bottom, but then a steady climb back up. More interestingly, some researchers have shown evidence not of a U-curve but a 'W-curve', i.e. once travellers return to their home country, they often undergo a similar re-acculturation, again in the shape of a U. Hence a 'double-U-' or W-curve.

Other research has shown similar intriguing findings. Imagine, for instance, that you are going to Morocco for the first time. You are asked to describe or rate both the average Briton and the average Moroccan in terms of their humour, wealth, trustworthiness, etc., both before you go and after you return. Frequently, it has been found that people change their opinions of their own countrymen and women more than that of the foreigners. In other words, travel makes you look much more critically at yourself and your culture than most people think. And this self-criticism may itself be rather unhelpful.

The trouble with these stage theories is that not everyone goes through the stages. Not everyone feels like Nancy Mitford did when she wrote: 'I loathe abroad, nothing would induce me to live there… and, as for foreigners, they are all the same and make me sick.' But I suspect that Robert Morley was not far from the truth when he remarked: 'The British tourist is always happy abroad, so long as the natives are waiters.'

Then there is also the shock of being visited. Anyone who lives in a popular tourist town soon becomes aware that it is not only the tourist but also the native who experiences culture shock. Of course, the amount and type of shock that tourists can impart to local people is an indication of a number of things, such as the relative proportion of tourists to natives, the duration of their stay, the comparative wealth and development of the two groups and the racial and ethnic prejudices of both.

Of course not everybody will experience culture shock. Older, better-educated, confident and skilful adults (particularly those who speak the language) tend to adapt best. Yet there is considerable evidence that sojourners, such as foreign students, voluntary workers, businessmen, diplomats and even military people, become so confused and depressed that they have to be sent home at great expense. That is why many organisations attempt to lessen culture shock by a number of training techniques. The Foreign Office, the British Council and many multinational companies do this for good reason, having learned from bitter experience.

Training

For a number of reasons, information and advice in the form of lectures and pamphlets, etc., is very popular but not always very useful. The 'facts' that are given are often too general to have any clear, specific application in particular circumstances. Facts emphasise the exotic and ignore the mundane (how to hail a taxi, for example). This technique also gives the impression that the culture can be easily understood; and even if facts are retained, they do not necessarily lead to accommodating behaviour.

A second technique is 'isomorphic training'. This is based on the theory that a major cause of cross-cultural communication problems comes from the fact that most people tend to offer different explanations for each other's behaviour. This technique introduces various episodes that end in embarrassment, misunderstanding or hostility between people from two different cultures. The trainee is then presented with four or five alternative explanations of what went wrong, all of which correspond to different attributions of the observed behaviour. Only one is correct from the perspective of the culture being learned. This is an interesting and useful technique, but depends for much of its success on the relevance of the various episodes chosen.

Perhaps the most successful method is 'skills training'. It has been pointed out that socially inadequate or inept individuals have not mastered the social conventions of their own society. Either they are unaware of the rules and processes of everyday behaviour or, if aware of the rules, they are unable or unwilling to abide by them. They are therefore like strangers in their own land. People newly arrived in an alien culture will be in a similar position and may benefit from simple skills training.

This involves analysing everyday encounters such as buying and selling, introductions and refusal of requests. You will also observe successful culture models engaging in these acts and will practice yourself, helped in the learning process by a video tape of your efforts. This may all sound very clinical, but can be great fun and very informative.

Practical advice

Many travellers, unless on business and with considerable company resources behind them, do not have the time or money to go on courses that prevent or minimise culture shock. They have to leap in at the deep end and hope that they can swim. But there are some simple things they can do that may well prevent the shock and improve communications.

Before departure it is important to learn as much as possible about the society you are visiting. Areas of great importance include:

■ LANGUAGE: Not only vocabulary but polite usage, when to use higher and lower forms, and particularly how to say 'yes' and 'no'.

■ NON-VERBAL CUES: Gestures, body contact and eye gaze patterns differ significantly from one country to another and carry very important meanings. Cues of this sort for greeting, parting and eating are most important, and are relatively easily learnt.

■ **SOCIAL RULES:** Every society develops a framework of rules that regulate behaviour so that social goals can be attained and needs satisfied. Some of the most important rules concern gifts, buying and selling, eating and drinking, timekeeping and bribery and nepotism.

■ **SOCIAL RELATIONSHIPS:** Family relationships, classes and castes, and working relationships often differ from culture to culture. The different social roles of the two sexes is perhaps the most dramatic difference between societies, and travellers should pay special attention to this.

■ **MOTIVATION:** Being assertive, extrovert and achievement oriented may be desirable in America and Western Europe but this is not necessarily the case elsewhere. How to present oneself, maintain face, etc., is well worth knowing.

Once you have arrived, there are a few simple steps that you can take to help reduce perplexity and understand the natives:

■ **CHOOSE LOCALS FOR FRIENDS:** Avoid mixing only with your compatriots or other foreigners. Get to know the natives, who can introduce you to the subtleties and nuances of the culture.

■ **PRACTICAL SOCIAL ACTIVITIES:** Do not be put off more complex social encounters but ask for information on appropriate etiquette. People are frequently happy to help and teach genuinely interested and courteous foreigners.

■ **AVOID 'GOOD/BAD' OR 'US/THEM' COMPARISONS:** Try to establish how and why people perceive and explain the same act differently, have different expectations, etc. Social behaviour has resulted from different historical and economic conditions and may be looked at from various perspectives.

■ **ATTEMPT MEDIATION:** Rather than reject your or their cultural tradition, attempt to select, combine and synthesise the appropriate features of different social systems, whether it is in dress, food or behaviour.

When you return home, the benefits of foreign travel and the prevention of the 'W-curve' may be helped by the following:

■ **BECOME MORE SELF-OBSERVANT:** Returning home makes one realise the comparative and normative nature of one's own behaviour, which was previously taken for granted. This in turn may alert one to behaviour that is culturally at odds (and, perhaps, why)—in itself helpful for all future travel.

■ **HELPING THE FOREIGNER:** There is no better teaching aid than personal experience. That is why many foreign language schools send their teachers abroad not only to improve their language but to experience the difficulties their students have. Remembering this, we should perhaps be in a better position to help the hapless traveller who comes to our country. Travel does broaden the mind (and frequently the behind), but requires some effort. Preparation, it is said, prevents a pretty poor performance, and travelling in different social environments is no exception. But this preparation may require social, as well as geographic, maps. ❧

JET LAG
by Jack Barker

JET LAG AFFECTS EVERY AIR TRAVELLER to some degree. A major survey by FARSA, New Zealand's flight crew union, found in 1994 that 96 per cent of flight attendants arriving in New Zealand, one of the world's longest-haul destinations, complained of jet lag symptoms that included tiredness, loss of energy, broken sleep and impaired motivation. Even those who claim they are immune often give themselves away by revealing slips of bad temper, and sometimes deny the symptoms in an attempt to override their body's natural reaction to international air travel.

The symptoms of jet lag include disorientation and confusion, as well as irritability and irrational anger. The most obvious symptom is tiredness, with many travellers feeling drained for days, as well as finding that they lack concentration and motivation. This can affect business skills as well as impair the enjoyment of a holiday. Unfortunately, another symptom is that travellers wake in the middle of the night and want to fall asleep during the day, which makes recovery from tiredness more difficult. These symptoms can last for some time: the US space agency NASA estimates you need one day for every time-zone crossed to recover normal rhythm and energy patterns.

The situation is further complicated by some very obvious factors which ensure that air travel is a physically stressful experience. Dehydration caused by the aircraft's compression can cause headaches, dry skin, and nasal irritation, which make travellers more susceptible to the common and exotic viruses and bacteria given off by their fellow passengers and recirculated by the confined airflow system. The World Health Organisation links jet lag with the high incidence of digestive disorders abroad. Estimating that about 50 per cent of long distance travellers suffer from digestive problems, their report suggests that, 'travel fatigue and jet lag may aggravate the problem by reducing travellers' resistance and making them more susceptible'.

The decompression and forced inactivity can also cause the swelling of limbs and feet which sometimes prevents travellers from wearing their normal shoes for up to 24 hours on arrival. This is dangerous because swollen legs can cause blood clots which, when they break free, can lodge in the lungs and cause a pulmonary embolism. A 1988 report in *The Lancet* estimated that, over three years at Heathrow Airport, 18 per cent of the 61 sudden deaths of long-distance passengers were caused by clots on the lungs, a figure far higher than the incidence in the general population.

The main cause of jet lag is crossing time zones. This has the effect of putting the body's Circadian Rhythms, which dictate what time you go to sleep, wake up and have meals, out of phase with the timescale of your new destination. Circadian Rhythms are maintained by minute releases of hormones and seratonins in the blood to dictate appetite and sleep patterns. As these chemical triggers were developed when we were living in caves, it is perhaps understandable that they have trouble adapting to travel by supersonic plane and it takes them some time to settle down to a new routine in a different time zone. Travellers flying east generally report worse symptoms, but lesser symptoms are also displayed going west and even those flying north or south or vice versa are not immune. Many travellers feel that day flights incur less severe jet lag, but this might be partly because they miss less sleep while travelling.

There are a number of simple steps that travellers can take to minimise the worst effects of jet lag:

1. **ADJUST.** As soon as you are settled on the plane, adjust your watch to match the new time zone and start to try to think on the daily schedule of your destination.

2. **SLEEP.** By far the best way to get through the minor stresses and discomforts of a long flight is to get plenty of rest. Blindfold masks, neck rests and earplugs can all help. Kick off your shoes — although if your feet are likely to swell, make sure your shoes are a type you can fit back on at the end of the flight. Although sleeping is good, resist the temptation to take sleeping pills to make certain of rest. This causes near-comatose immobility, and little or no movement increases the chance of blood clots.

3. **DRINK WATER.** Coffee dehydrates, and tea also contains tannin, especially when poured from a cool airline teapot. Orange squash is also an abrasive drink, especially for people not accustomed to it. Alcohol has an increased effect in the rarefied atmosphere of a pressurised plane and aggravates both dehydration and the swelling of limbs and feet. A good hangover might mask the effects of jet lag but without making it in any sense better. The water in the toilets is not usually treated, but there is usually a dispenser just outside the toilet door: asking the stewards to bring water to your seat usually results in a small plastic beaker that contains a bit of water with a lot of ice. They seem to be strangely reluctant to bring a litre bottle of mineral water and leave it for you to drink at will, but this is the answer. Insist upon it.

4. **EXERCISE.** When not otherwise engaged by being asleep or drinking water, take exercise. Walk about, stretch, wriggle your toes. Get off the plane at stopovers and take a walk. Seize the chance of a shower if available during stopovers, or if available in First Class. A shower is not only refreshing but it also improves circulation.

5. **ORIENTATE.** When flying west, you are lengthening your day, so it is best to avoid sleeping on the plane; this will increase your chances of a decent night's sleep once you arrive. The opposite applies when flying east, especially overnight, so eat as little as possible and try to get as much sleep as possible.

Taking medication to fight jet lag is a controversial issue. Conventional sleeping tablets are not recommended while travelling for the reasons shown above, but they can help restore sleep patterns on arrival.

Homeopathy and aromatherapy

Various homeopathic remedies are recommended for jet lag's various symptoms. Arnica is recommended for sleeplessness, restlessness, mental strain and shock. Bellis Perennis, extracted from the common daisy, is suggested to alleviate venous congestion due to mechanical causes and waking mid-sleep. Chamomilla is prescribed to alleviate emotional and mental stress, sleeplessness, impatience, intolerance and disorientation while Ipecacuanha is thought to help minimise the effects of dehydration.

Leading aromatherapist Valerie Ann Worwood suggests two treatments for swollen feet and ankles but they do need preparing in advance. Damp a small piece of cotton with water and add five drops of lavender essential oil: place in a plastic bag and apply this as a compress, as well as massaging your feet in an upwards motion during and after the journey. Alternatively, massage with an oil made from lavender or eucalyptus essential oil and massage oil, mixed in a proportion of five drops to one teaspoon. On arrival, restore your body's time-clock by using peppermint and eucalyptus essential oils in morning baths, and lavender and geranium in the evenings, either in the bath or applied with a face cloth. To revitalise after a long flight, she suggests a long soak in a hot bath tanged with the aroma of grapefruit oil.

Personally, I always use Melatonin, which is the seratonin that tells the body's Circadian Rhythm that it's time for bed. A 3 mg tablet taken on the plane makes it much easier to go to sleep, and Melatonin, which influences the body's hormones, can be used in the same way as a sleeping pill to reset sleep patterns to a new time zone without the residual doziness. Note that Melatonin does not work for everyone, especially if carbohydrate is consumed after taking the tablet. Until recently, Melatonin was available over the counter in the UK and can still be easily bought in America or mail-order over the internet: most doctors are quite aware of Melatonin and are generally prepared to write a private prescription. ❧

FLYING IN COMFORT

by Ian Wilson

FLYING IS PHYSICALLY A LOT MORE STRESSFUL than many people realise. And there is more to the problem than time zones. Modern jet aircraft are artificially pressurised at an altitude pressure of around 1,500 to 2,000 metres. That means that when you are flying at an altitude of, say, 12,000 metres in a Boeing 747, the cabin pressure inside is what it would be if you were outside at a height of 1,500 to 2,000 metres above sea level. Most people live a lot closer to sea level than this, and to be rocketed almost instantly to a height of 2,000 metres (so far as their body is concerned) takes a considerable amount of adjustment. Fortunately, the human body is a remarkably adaptable organism, and for most individuals the experience is stressful, but not fatal.

Although it might seem more practical to pressurise the cabin to sea level pressure, this is currently impossible. A modern jet with sea level cabin pressure would have to have extremely strong (and therefore heavy) outside walls to prevent the difference between inside and outside walls causing the aircraft walls to rupture in mid-flight. At present, there is no economically viable lightweight material that is strong enough to do the job. Another problem is that if there were a rupture at, say,

14,000 metres, with an interior pressure equal to that at sea level, there would be no chance for the oxygen masks to drop in the huge sucking process that would result from the air inside the cabin emptying through the hole in the aircraft. A 2,000 metres equivalent pressure at least gives passengers and oxygen masks a chance if this occurs.

Inside the cabin, humidifiers and fragrance disguise all the odours of large numbers of people in a confined space. On a long flight you are breathing polluted air.

What can you do to help your body survive the onslaught? First, you can loosen your clothing. The body swells in the thinner air of the cabin, so take off your shoes (wear loose shoes anyway, it can be agony putting tight ones back on at the end of the flight), undo your belt, tilt your seat right back, put a couple of pillows in the lumbar region of your back and one behind your neck, and whether you are trying to sleep or simply rest, cover your eyes with a pair of air travel blinkers (ask the stewardess for a pair if you have not brought any with you).

Temperatures rise and fall notoriously inside an aircraft, so have a blanket ready over your knees in case you nod off and later find that you are freezing. When I look at all the space wasted over passengers' heads in a Boeing 747, and all those half-empty hand baggage lockers, I often wonder why aircraft manufacturers do not arrange things so that comfortable hammocks can be slung over our heads for those who want to sleep—or better still, small couchettes in tiers like those found in modern submarines. Personally, I would prefer such comfort, whatever it might do to the tidiness of the cabin interior. However, if you can pay and do not mind doing so, you can actually lie down in a bed in some airlines' First Class sections. BA will even tuck you up in a 'comfort suit', with hot chocolate and biscuits to complete the experience.

On a long flight it is tempting to feel you are not getting your money's worth if you do not eat and drink everything that is going. Resist the temptation—even if you are travelling in First Class and all that food and drink seems to be what most of the extra cost is about. Most people find it best to eat lightly before leaving home and little or nothing during the flights. Foods that are too rich or spicy, and foods that you are unaccustomed to, will do little to make you feel good in flight. Neither will alcohol. Some people claim that they travel better if they drink fizzy drinks in flight, although if inclined to indigestion, the gas can cause discomfort as it is affected by the lower pressure in the cabin. Tea and coffee are diuretics (increase urine output) and so have the undesirable effect of further dehydrating the drinker, who is already in the very dry atmosphere of the cabin. Fruit juices and plain water are best.

Smoking raises the level of carbon monoxide in the blood (and, incidentally, in the atmosphere, so that non-smokers can also suffer the ill-effects if seated close to smokers) and reduces the smoker's tolerance to altitude. A smoker is already effectively at 1,500 to 2,000 metres before leaving the ground.

Walk up and down as frequently as possible during a flight to keep your circulation in shape, and do not resist the urge to go to the loo (avoid the queues by going before meals). The time will pass more quickly, and you will feel better for it, if you get well into an unputdownable novel before leaving home and try to finish it during the flight. This trick always works better than flicking half-heartedly through an in-flight magazine.

It may be worth trying to find out how full a plane is before you book, or, given the circumstances, choosing to fly in the low season to increase your chance of getting empty seats to stretch out on for a good sleep. If you have got a choice of seats on a plane, remember there is usually more leg room by the emergency exit over the wings. On the other hand, stewardesses tend to gather at the tail end of the plane on most airlines, so they try not to give seats there away unless asked. That means you may have more chance of ending up with empty seats next to you if you go for the two back rows (also statistically the safest place in a crash). Seats in the middle compartment over the forward part of the wing are said to give the smoothest ride; the front area of the plane is, however, the quietest.

If possible, take your own pillow, which will be a useful supplement to the postage-stamp sized pillows supplied by most airlines.

Finally, if you plan to sleep during the flight, put a 'Do Not

Disturb' notice by your seat and pass up the chance of another free drink or face towel every time your friendly neighbourhood stewardess comes round. You probably will not arrive at the other end raring to go, but if you have planned wisely to arrive just before nightfall, and if you take a brisk walk before going to bed, you might just get lucky and go straight to sleep without waking up on home-time two hours later. 🍃

COMING HOME
by Colonel John Blashford-Snell

UNTIL RULA LENSKA JOINED US on a quest in Nepal I had no idea that actors and expeditioners suffer from the same problem at the end of the show. Both tend to get 'post-project depression' (PPD) or 'after-expedition blues'.

When a play ends or the filming of a series finishes, Rula explained, the cast is suddenly split up, left to find new jobs or return home for a well-earned rest. The friendships and working relationships break up, the team disappears and a different lifestyle starts overnight. So it is with expeditioners and, I imagine, ocean voyagers.

Dr John Davies, one of Britain's leading exploration medics, once started a lecture at the Scientific Exploration Society with the statement: 'Expeditions may endanger your health.' He went on to point out that, for the novice, the experience can be an introduction to the negative aspects of one's personality that are easily suppressed in normal daily life. However, with appropriate counselling and support, this can be a journey of self-discovery leading to increased confidence and a more enlightened to others.

Seasoned adventurers, like experienced actors, recognise post-expedition blues, the symptoms of which are similar to bereavement. This is triggered by the loss of one's new-found 'family' of expedition friends in a widely different culture and suddenly being cut off from the excitement on return home.

"I just can't face going back to nine to five in the Tax Office," groaned an Inland Revenue Officer who had spent three months in the Gobi. A routine and mundane lifestyle aggravates the condition and, for many, it is cured only by involvement in another challenge. Returning explorers also face isolation from family and colleagues, who have no concept of their recent intense experience. They are often perplexed by the indifferent response to their stories and may end up silent and withdrawn. The envy and resentment of the uninitiated, who imagine that one has been on a jolly picnic or at best some self-inflicted masochism, is also common.

"Don't know what you've done to my mother," complained a son after his mum had returned from one of the Discovery Expeditions in South America. "She's awfully quiet." But meeting the lady in question at a reunion a few months later I found her in great spirits, reliving the experience with her old pals.

John Davies, with whom I have been on many trips, advises 'returnees', especially the older ones, to spend several days enquiring about the day-to-day problems that have occurred in their absence before slowly beginning to recount their experiences. So, on being met by my wife as I stepped off a comfortable British Airways flight from Delhi recently, I asked: "How are those new trees in the garden coming on?"—"Have you gone mad?" replied Judith, well used to a dozen tales of high adventure before we reached the car park. But perhaps I'm beyond hope!

However, there may be medical problems after returning, as I discovered a year after a Sandhurst expedition in Ethiopia, when my right leg started shaking uncontrollably while I was lecturing. 'How strange,' I thought, trying not to notice the offending limb. Two weeks later, lying racked with a fever in hospital, it was found that I had malaria, by which time I also had blurred vision and had lost nine kilos in weight. But, once diagnosed, malaria is usually fairly easily cured, and the doctors knew I'd been to the tropics.

Sadly not all ailments are so quickly dealt with, as I realised after 12 months of visits to the St Pancras Hospital for Tropical Diseases. Strange hot flushes, violent stabbing pains in my stomach, aches and itches in awkward places were making life extremely uncomfortable. "There's nothing wrong with you," boomed one of the world's leading specialists in tropical diseases after exhaustive tests proved negative. "You young fellows imagine you've caught everything under the sun if you spend six weeks in the jungle. When I was in Burma…" he droned on. My morale at was rock bottom and it took great courage to return to the hospital a few weeks later, after the symptoms had become almost unbearable.

As luck would have it, a charming and much more sympathetic Asian doctor was on duty and, in no time, he had me facedown on a trolley with a flexible viewing device inserted up my rear end and my shirt over my head. "Keep him still," he beseeched as two strapping Fijian nurses pinned me down. "Oh, my goodness," exclaimed the physician. "What a fine example. Excuse me, sir, but you have a splendid parasite. It is quite unusual to see one so well developed. Would you mind if we allowed a class of medical students to see it?"

Before I could even protest, I was wheeled in to a theatre full of students, many of them, I noted, looking between my legs, were extremely attractive young women. One by one they came forward, without even a titter, to peer intently up my bottom. At last I was taken away and the awful tube removed. "What now?" I asked.—"Oh, just swallow these pills and you'll be as right as rain," smiled the doctor.

So it is my advice that if you feel ill after an overseas visit, go straight to your GP and say where you have been. Mark you, they might diagnose jet lag, which can affect one more than most care to admit.

This handbook contains useful tips on surviving the onslaught and reducing its effects to the minimum, so I'll not dwell on it. Suffice to say that when I get home I keep going until nightfall, doing simple, uncomplicated things such as unpacking or weeding, then I take a very mild sleeping pill and totter off to bed. With luck I can usually sleep for six hours. The important thing is to avoid stressful situations and don't make any important decisions until after your body has readjusted. In my case this usually takes 24 hours. Indeed, even weeding may not be a good idea. Having stepped off a long flight from Mongolia, I pulled up all my wife's carefully planted ground cover instead of the weeds.

If I am still feeling low, I concentrate on writing my thank-you letters (if not done on the plane) and amending my packing list while memory of all the things I forgot to take and all unnecessary items that went with me is still fresh. Then it's down to sorting out photos, slides, videos and writing reports and articles. Next come repairs to kit, getting cameras serviced and preparing lectures.

If you start to feel sorry for yourself, you are not really bringing the benefits of your experiences to your life at home. Indeed I expect you will discover that you have changed but the world has not.

The whole point is to keep active and look forward to the next challenge. If you can't afford another trip, why not use your vigour and energy to help others in your area, sick children, old people or anyone who could use some voluntary assistance?

For the adventurous there is the opportunity of supporting organisations such as the Duke of Edinburgh's Award or Riding for the Disabled and there are dozens of environmental groups needing help.

The great cry is, if you want to avoid PPD, keep busy. ❧

Chapter 3 : **Common illnesses** ✨

TRAVELLERS' DISEASES
by Dr Nick Beeching

IN READING THIS CHAPTER, one might be forgiven for thinking that going abroad is the quickest way of signing your life away, or your admission form for the nearest available hospital, as you are certain to pick up some exotic disease or another. So far we have dealt with the prevention of disease and those niggling everyday health concerns. Here, however, we tackle some bigger problems, the diseases that keep you awake at night in a cold sweat at the mere thought of contracting them.

The aim here, though, is to allay your fears by equipping you with the knowledge to deal with these problems in the unlikely event that they do actually arise. Though the chances of you having diarrhoeal symptoms may be as much as 50 per cent, the chances of you catching malaria whilst abroad are between two and three per cent (see *The Relative Risks* in the *Directory*).

So let us begin with the bane of all tropical travellers: malaria.

MALARIA
by Drs Sharon Welby and Nick Beeching

MALARIA REMAINS RIFE throughout much of the tropics, and causes a huge burden in terms of illness and death for the indigenous population. It poses a significant and difficult problem for the traveller. The ever-changing pattern of drug resistance, along with concerns about side-effects of anti-malarial drugs, result in confusion regarding the selection of anti-malarial drugs. Awareness of the very real hazard of malaria and the importance of gaining accurate pre-travel advice is vital for travellers to the tropics.

Malaria is a parasitic blood infection transmitted by the bite of the female anopheline mosquito. There are four types of malaria: *Plasmodium falciparum*, *Plasmodium ovale*, *Plasmodium vivax* and *Plasmodium malariae*. *P. falciparum*, also known as malignant malaria, is the most serious: more than two million people living in endemic areas die as a result of it each year.

In spite of persisting efforts, adequate control of malaria has not yet been achieved and there is a significant risk for travellers to most parts of the Indian subcontinent and the Far East, sub-Saharan Africa and parts of Central and South America. The risks in North Africa and countries in the eastern Mediterranean littoral and the Middle East are more variable.

The illness

The incubation period after a mosquito bite varies, from a minimum of eight to ten days, up to several years. Most people who are infected by *falciparum* malaria develop symptoms within a couple of months, but the longest symptom-free period we have seen was over a year. The earliest symptoms are non-specific and are often wrongly diagnosed as 'flu or gastroenteritis. Most people develop symptoms of fever, headache and generalised aches and pains, and about a quarter of people have pronounced vomiting and diarrhoea.

It is therefore essential that travellers have an immediate blood test for malaria if they develop a fever more than a week after arriving in a malarious area or within a year or two of their return. If left untreated, patients (especially expatriates who have not been exposed to malaria before) can rapidly develop high fevers or lapse into a coma and die. Between five and 15 people die of malaria infection in the UK each year, and many of these are due to delay in seeking medical advice.

The other three forms of malaria are rarely life-threatening but can have a more prolonged incubation period of up to two years. They cannot be distinguished from life-threatening *falciparum* malaria unless a blood film is examined. The *ovale* and *vivax* forms of malaria sometimes relapse after effective treatment of the first illness, so further drug treatment is usually required for these using a different drug called primaquine.

Prevention

Personal protection for the traveller focuses on two main aspects, the first is to prevent being bitten by mosquitoes and the second relies on taking antimalarial drugs regularly.

When a malaria-carrying mosquito bites a person, the malaria parasites travel to the liver via the blood stream and develop there without causing any signs of illness. Once the parasite is ready, it leaves the liver and attacks the red blood cells. This is the stage at which anti-malarial drugs act, by preventing the parasite from infecting blood cells and thereby preventing the symptoms of malaria from developing. It is important to keep taking anti-malarials regularly while abroad, so that drug levels in the blood are sufficient to prevent disease, and to continue taking the drugs for four weeks after leaving the malarious area, so that the incubation period after any potential bites is covered by the drugs.

The malaria-carrying mosquitoes bite from dusk to dawn and bites can be prevented by using a combination of methods:

CLOTHING: Wear shirts and trousers after dusk. Clothing can also be soaked in repellent, 30 millilitres of repellent dissolved in 250 millilitres of water is an effective mixture, or sprayed with 100 per cent DEET (use only on cotton not synthetic clothes).

BARRIERS: Sleep in an air-conditioned or a screened room, or under a bednet (preferably one impregnated with permethrin: 0.2 grams of permethrin per metre of material).

REPELLENTS: Repel or kill any mosquitoes which have entered the bedroom with pyrethrum sprays, mosquito coils or electrical insecticide dispensers. Electronic buzzers are not effective.Using repellents containing diethyltoluamide (DEET) 50 per cent DEET is more effective, and recommended for malarious areas. Children, pregnant women and travellers with skin conditions may prefer to use eucalyptus-based repellent Mosiguard Natural. (See also *The Essential Medical Kit* page 33.)

Anti-malarial drugs

Anti-malarial drug therapy is an area fraught with difficulty. The changing pattern of drug resistance, together with possible side-effects of the drugs, have made it increasingly difficult to choose the correct regimens. With this in mind, it is advisable for all travellers to obtain specialist advice prior to their trip.

In Britain there are currently four main anti-malarial drugs in use: chloroquine, proguanil, mefloquine and doxycycline.

CHLOROQUINE AND PROGUANIL (PALUDRINE): these are the oldest and most widely used. They are safe to take long-term (however, annual eye check-ups are recommended after three years of chloroquine use). The wealth of experience suggests that they are safe to use during pregnancy (it is recommended that folic acid 5 mgs daily is added to the regimen during pregnancy when proguanil is taken). Unfortunately, there is now widespread resistance to these drugs, rendering them much less effective in some parts of the world.

Depending on the area to be visited, they are either taken alone or together. Travellers should start anti-malarials at least a week before travel, mainly to make sure that they do not react to the medication, continue whilst there and for at least four weeks after leaving a malarious area. The usual adult dose is chloroquine two tablets once a week together with proguanil two tablets daily (a total of sixteen tablets per week).

The main side-effects of the chloroquine/proguanil combination (apart from an unpleasant taste) are nausea, stomach upsets and mouth ulcers. Chloroquine should not be taken by people who are currently suffering from epilepsy or have had epilepsy in the past, or by people who suffer from psoriasis, a common skin disorder.

MEFLOQUINE (LARIAM): There has been a lot of controversy surrounding the use of mefloquine for malaria prophylaxis. Publicity in the media and conflicting medical advice have led to confusion, and subsequently some travellers are not taking any drug prophylaxis at all for countries where it is recommended. This could lead to potentially life-threatening malaria infection. Every traveller needs to consider the pros and cons of mefloquine and decide if the drug is suitable for them.

All drugs have side effects: studies have shown that mefloquine can cause problems such as dizziness, headache, insomnia, vivid dreams and depression in a few people, and that these problems seem to affect women more than men. A recent study showed that around a quarter of those people taking mefloquine and an eighth taking chloroquine and proguanil experienced problems. Some studies have shown that, in about one in ten people, the side-effects interfered with planned activities and in one in 10,000 people a severe side-effect occurred. Some of the side effects experienced with mefloquine (especially headaches and vivid dreams) may be helped by taking half a tablet twice a week. The majority of side-effects with mefloquine start within three weeks of starting the drug and stop within three weeks of stopping. It is recommended that you start mefloquine at least two weeks before travelling so that if any side-effects occur you can change to an alternative drug.

Studies from Africa show that mefloquine is more effective at preventing malaria infection then a combination of chloroquine and proguanil (90 per cent compared to 60-70 per cent). Mefloquine is also convenient to take as it is a weekly dose, and it is now licensed to be used for up to one year. However, it is relatively expensive. If travellers are tolerating mefloquine and remain at high risk of malaria infection, we now advise people to continue for 2-3 years. Mefloquine has now been used by over 6,000 Peace Corps workers for 2-3 years without evidence of serious adverse reaction.

Mefloquine is first choice for areas where there is widespread chloroquine resistance, such as sub-Saharan Africa, the Amazon basin and parts of South-East Asia. Mefloquine is not suitable for everyone and it is not recommended for:

■ Women in the first 12 weeks of pregnancy, women who are breast-feeding or women who might become pregnant within three months of taking the last tablet. However, evidence is accumulating that women who have taken mefloquine in the early stages of pregnancy, or just prior to becoming pregnant, do not appear to have an increased risk of having a child with congenital problems compared to the background risk.

■ People with a history of epilepsy or a strong family history of epilepsy.

■ People who have any mental health problems, e.g. depression, anxiety attacks or mood disturbances.

■ People who have cardiac rhythm problems.

■ People whose jobs depend on a high degree of co-ordination, such as airline pilots or professional divers.

■ It is not suitable for young children under 5 kg . For children between 5-13 kg it is difficult to break up the tablets to get the correct dose, which is 5 mg/kg, since the tablet contains 250 mg of mefloquine, and therefore less than a quarter of a tablet is required. As yet there are no paediatric formulations available.

■ People with liver problems or severe kidney disease.

DOXYCYCLINE: The third alternative is an antibiotic called doxycycline (a form of tetracycline). This is particularly popular with Australian travellers, but British authorities mainly recommend it for travellers to the border areas of Thailand/Myanmar (Burma) and Thailand/Cambodia, as well as the western province of Cambodia, where *falciparum* malaria is often resistant to both chloroquine and mefloquine. Studies show that doxycycline gives around 85 per cent protection against malaria infection, though this effectiveness quickly falls if compliance is poor. Doxycycline is increasingly being used by the higher risk traveller to sub-Saharan Africa if mefloquine is contra-indicated or if there is a reluctance to take it.

Doxycycline is recommended for short term prophylaxis (for 3-4 months) and concern about possible side effects restricts its use for longer. Balancing these side effects, doxycycline provides good anti-malarial protection and also reduces the incidence and duration of travellers' diarrhoea.

Doxycycline should not be taken by pregnant women or children under the age of ten (American recommendations allow its use in children aged eight or over). It should be taken with liberal quantities of fluid to prevent ulceration and discomfort in the oesophagus (gullet). The main side-effect is that some people become very sensitive to the sun and become sunburnt easily (a good sun tan cream is recommended—factor 15+). Doxycycline interferes with the contraceptive pill and it is recommended that women also use barrier methods of contraception in the first 2 weeks of starting doxycycline. Women taking regular doxycycline may be prone to recurrent vaginal thrush.

MALARONE: Malarone (a combination of atovaquone and proguanil) is a new drug combination which has recently been licensed for the treatment of malaria. In a small number of studies in Africa the drug is looking very promising, effective and well tolerated. Large-scale trials of Malarone for chemoprophylaxis in travellers are still being carried out. One of the big advantages of Malarone is that it can be stopped one week after leaving a malaria endemic area, while the main disadvantage is that it is very expensive.

Current British guidelines

The current British guidelines balance the risk of malaria infection with the possible side-effects of anti-malarial drugs. The guidelines continue to support the use of mefloquine by people who have no contraindications to the drug and who are visiting regions where the risk of malaria is high. However, the guidelines state that an alternative to mefloquine for people on package tours of two weeks or less to the East African coast (and who are not planning to stay in rural areas or go on safari) is the less protective chloroquine and proguanil regimen. This minimises the risk of side-effects but means that the need to take precautions against mosquito bites is even greater. The guidelines for the Gambia suggest that chloroquine and proguanil will give reasonable protection from January to May, whereas mefloquine is the drug of choice for the rest of the year.

Children and pregnant women

Pregnant women and infants are prone to severe malaria attacks and should be advised not to travel to areas with a significant malaria risk—especially sub-Saharan Africa—unless it is unavoidable, when they must take malaria prophylaxis. It is recommended that pregnant women also take folic acid (a vitamin) at the same time as proguanil.

Children require lower doses of anti-malarials, depending on their age and weight. They soon learn to dislike both chloroquine and proguanil. Although chloroquine syrup is available, proguanil is only available as tablets. The tablets can be ground up and hidden in treats (jam, sandwiches, chocolates etc.) to persuade children to take them.

Expatriates

Long-term expatriates are more difficult to advise. Many adopt a 'macho' attitude to malaria and discontinue any malaria prophylaxis in the mistaken belief that they have developed protective immunity. Due to the rapid emergence of drug-resistant malaria, we believe that this is an unwise option and we continue to see such people evacuated for emergency medical treatment for life-threatening malaria (those that make it back). The best advice will be given on a personal level by your GP or travel clinic because all these cases will be different.

Stand-by treatment

The more adventurous traveller going to places where rapid access to medical advice is not available may wish to carry a course of anti-malarial 'stand-by' treatment. This should be taken if symptoms of possible malaria develop, but it is not a substitute for medical care, and it is important to seek medical advice and a blood film. There are malaria diagnostic kits available which enable travellers to do a blood test on themselves to decide if their illness is due to malaria or not. However, studies have shown that travellers have difficulties performing and interpreting these tests when they are shivering with fever! We think it is safer to treat presumptively and seek medical advice than to try to do a test which may not be interpreted correctly and which may then delay taking life-saving malaria treatment.

The stand-by regime will depend on the drug resistance in the area which you are visiting and on which anti-malarial drugs are being taken. It is advisable to seek specialist advice. Some examples of stand-by medications are:

■ FANSIDAR: three tablets taken at the same time is the most convenient, but this is not suitable for people who are allergic to sulphur drugs.

■ MEFLOQUINE: two tablets taken together followed by two tablets 12 hours later. The main problem with this dose of mefloquine is severe nausea and vomiting and the increased risk of neuropsychiatric side-effects.

■ HALOFANTRINE: until recently a third option, halofantrine (Halfan) was very popular for self-treatment, particularly in

East Africa, but side-effects of this drug affecting the heart have now been identified and we recommend that it should not be used.

■ **QUININE:** (adult dose: two tablets, three times a day for three days) and tetracycline (adult dose: one tablet, four times a day for seven days) are recommended as stand-by medication in areas with a lot of drug resistance.

■ **MALORONE:** in the future Malarone may be recommended as a stand-by treatment. The adult dose is four tablets daily for three days.

Summary

The risk of malaria infection poses a real and significant problem for the traveller. It is essential that pre-travel advice is sought and that each traveller takes anti-mosquito bite measures and decides which anti-malarial drug regimen is suitable for them. It is important to remember that no anti-malarial drug is 100 per cent effective and any illness, especially if there is fever, must lead to a blood test to exclude malaria infection. It is also important to inform the doctor that you have been to a malarious area within the preceding two years. If this advice is ignored, the diagnosis of malaria will not be considered until too late, and tragic and preventable deaths will continue to occur.

Key Points

1. Take measures to prevent mosquito bites: repellents, impregnated bed nets, suitable clothing, sleep in a screened room with knock-down insecticides, coils or electronic vapourisers.
2. Take appropriate anti-malarial drugs regularly and complete the course.
3. Remember that no prophylaxis is 100 per cent effective and, in the event of any illness, especially if there is fever, seek immediate diagnosis (with a blood film) and treatment.
4. Consider carrying a 'stand-by treatment'. 🍂

IF YOU CAN'T STAND THE HEAT…
by Sarah Thorowgood

AFTER A PARTICULARLY LONG NIGHT DRIVE, I once found myself on a beach in the Algarve at nine o'clock in the morning, tired and exhausted after driving all the way from Granada in Spain in one go. I promptly fell asleep on the already warm sand until about four in the afternoon. When I awoke, apart from feeling a little groggy, nothing appeared to be amiss. It was only a couple of hours later that the effects of soaking up half the sun's UV rays for an entire day really began to take its toll. Quite apart from feeling that I could probably radiate enough heat for an entire Mediterranean holiday season, it became quite exceptionally difficult and painful to sit down. Then the blisters came, followed by great lumps of skin that fell off my back for the next two weeks.

Sunburn

I was lucky not to suffer more severely from sun stroke, but who knows what untold damage lurks beneath the surface in terms of skin cancer? Some doctors contend that one bad dose of sunburn is all it can take to trigger skin cancer in later life. With the thinning of the ozone layer and greater awareness of the damage that the sun can do to your skin, not to mention an increase annually in the number of people taking summer holidays in hot, sunny locations, people are crying out for guidelines as to what is a safe amount of sun and what is not.

Here are a few ways to minimise the risk of sunburn, or anything more sinister:

■ The longer-term effects of sun on the skin are the signs of ageing and possible skin cancer. Many of the so-called signs of ageing are now thought to be caused directly by sun exposure: just look at the difference in skin texture between the inner and outer parts of your arm.

■ Try always to avoid the very strong sun between 11 am and 3 pm, especially if you are in the tropics.

■ Gradually build up your exposure to the sun. A tan gives you a natural protection equivalent to sun protection factor 3.

■ Use sun-screens. These undoubtedly help to protect you from the worst excesses of sunburn, but only up to a limited amount of exposure. There are two different types of sun-screen—absorbent and reflective. Absorbent creams only absorb UVB rays. Reflective creams are the type you see Australian cricketers wearing: they have colour in them to reflect every kind of light thrown at them and will protect you from both UVA and UVB rays.

■ Sun Protection Factors (SPFs) are merely guides which tell you how long you can stay in the sun without burning. They are a multiple number of the time you could stay in the sun without burning if you were not wearing any protective cream. For example, if it took you 15 minutes to burn in the midday sun without protection, it would take you 4 x 15 minutes to burn in the midday sun if you were wearing SPF 4 (i.e. one hour). After this, reapplication of the same strength cream will not give you any more protection. High protection factor creams may allow you to stay out in the sun longer without burning, but if they are absorbent creams, they can be dangerous, because they will only protect you from UVB rays and will encourage greater exposure to the sun. Children, in particular, are vulnerable, and prolonged exposure to the sun, even if high SPF cream is used, can lead to problems in later life from skin cancer caused by the UVA rays.

Treatment of sunburn

There are a few ways to relieve the pain of sunburn, but really once you have got to this stage the damage has already been done and you will have to put up with painful and peeling skin for a few days. Cooling lotion such as Calamine is very soothing and aspirin is useful for its anti-inflammatory properties.

For current medical wisdom on blisters, see page 41. If they puncture, the skin should be peeled away using tweezers sterilised with a flame. Beware of oily creams if your skin is burnt because they will keep the heat trapped inside.

Hydrocortisone cream can be useful for very badly burnt

areas. Remember that burns have a dehydrating effect, so drink lots of water to replace fluids.

Heat illness

In hot, dry climates, protection from the heat is relatively simple: stay in the shade and drink lots of water. Heat exhaustion and heat stroke are much more likely in tropical, humid environments because it is much harder for the body to cool itself when the sweat it produces does not evaporate (a process which causes cooling). Heat exhaustion is a problem that will affect people who try to do too much too soon after arriving in the tropics, especially if they are overweight. Give your body a chance to readjust to the environment before taking exercise.

The symptoms of heat exhaustion

■ Excessive sweating—this is the body's attempt to cool down, but it also can cause dehydration and a pounding headache, weakness, muscle cramps, a rapid pulse and vomiting.
■ The body also tries to cool down by bringing the blood nearer to the surface of the skin. In temperate conditions this helps to cool the body rapidly, but in the tropics the process will take longer, which means that the brain is getting less blood than normal and fainting may occur.
■ The sufferer may have a temperature of up to 104°F.

Treatment of heat illness

It is important to act quickly if someone is displaying these symptoms. The first thing to do is to move the person into the coolest place you can find, an air-conditioned room, or just into the shade if there is no other option. Remove the patient's clothes and sponge the body with cool, but not freezing, water. Fan the patient to promote evaporation and give paracetamol to reduce the temperature and help relieve any headache or muscle cramps.

If possible, make the person drink lots of water: dehydration is almost certain to have occurred and as much as two or three litres may need to be given in the first hour. Continue to cool the patient until his temperature has dropped to below 100°F.

The symptoms of heat stroke

This is not as common as heat exhaustion but carries a high mortality if not treated promptly. The symptoms of heat exhaustion may be displayed but they will also be accompanied by:

■ A very high temperature, above 104°F.
■ Malco-ordination, delirium and irrational behaviour.
■ A high pulse and respiratory rate.
■ Possible convulsions followed by unconsciousness.

Treatment of heat stroke

If the patient falls into unconsciousness, then hospitalisation is needed urgently, because if not treated quickly, this can lead to permanent disability or death. Treat the patient as you would for symptoms of heat exhaustion, whilst arranging for transfer to hospital. It is important to keep a close eye on the person's temperature, because excessive cooling may even lead to hypothermia. After cooling the patient, cover them up to prevent this from happening. ❧

DIARRHOEAL ILLNESS
by Dr Nick Beeching

THE WORLD-WIDE DISTRIBUTION of traveller's diarrhoea is reflected in its many geographical synonyms—Delhi belly, the Aztec two-step, Turista, Malta dog, Rangoon runs, to name a few. Typically, the illness starts a few days after arrival at your destination and consists of diarrhoea without blood, nausea with some vomiting and perhaps a mild fever. The mainstay of treatment is adequate rehydration and rest, and the illness is usually self-limiting within a few days. Antibiotics to treat or prevent this common illness are not usually prescribed in anticipation of an infection. Exceptions to this rule are business travellers or others embarking on short trips (less than two to three weeks) for whom even a short period of illness would be disastrous, e.g. athletes attending international meetings.

The most important aspect of the treatment of diarrhoea is the replacement of fluids and salts that have been lost from the body. For most adults, non-carbonated, non-alcoholic drinks that do not contain large amounts of sugar are quite adequate. For adults with prolonged diarrhoea and for children, it is more important to use balanced weak salt solutions which contain a small amount of sugar that promotes absorption of the salts. These can be obtained in pre-packaged sachets of powder (e.g. Dioralyte, Rehidrat) that are convenient to carry and are dissolved in a fixed amount of sterile water.

Dioralyte can also be bought in the UK as effervescent tablets, or as Dioralyte Relief sachets which contain pre-cooked rice powder. This has the advantage of returning the watery stools to normal more rapidly, as well as replacing the salts which have been lost in the diarrhoea. If pre-packaged mixtures are not available, a simple rehydration solution can be prepared by adding eight level teaspoonfuls of sugar or honey and half a teaspoon of salt to one litre of water (with flavouring to tempt small children).

Nausea, which frequently accompanies diarrhoea, can usually be overcome by taking small amounts of fluid as often as possible. For small children it may be necessary to give spoonfuls of fluid every few minutes for prolonged periods. If you or your child have severe vomiting which prevents any fluids being taken, medical attention must be sought immediately.

Anti-diarrhoeal drugs are not usually recommended and should rarely be given to children. Kaopectate is safe for children aged over two years but not very effective (Kaolin and morphine should not be carried). For adults, codeine phosphate, loperamide (Imodium or Arret) or diphenoxylate (Lomotil) are sometimes useful. These drugs should never be given to children and should not be used for bloody or prolonged diarrhoea. They are best reserved for occasional use to prevent accidents while travelling—for example before a prolonged rural bus trip. Prolonged use of these medications may prevent your body from eliminating the diarrhoea—causing organisms and toxins which may lead to constipation.

Preparations containing clioquinol are still widely available outside the UK, where it was previously sold under the trade name Enterovioform. These preparations are useless and should not be taken (they have been linked with severe side effects in some parts of the world). Other than rehydration solutions or the specific medications discussed here, I do not recommend purchasing medicines for diarrhoea from pharmacies or chemists.

Prevention

Travellers who wish to prevent diarrhoea should consult their medical adviser about preventative medication (a controversial issue within the profession) before travel. Liquid bismuth preparations (not an antibiotic) are effective but huge volumes need to be carried in luggage (very messy if broken), and bismuth tablets are difficult to obtain in the UK. Various groups of antibiotics may be used, including tetracyclines (e.g. doxycycline), sulphur containing antibiotics (e.g. Steptrotriad or cotrimoxazole, Septrin or Bactrim) and quinolone agents (e.g. ciprofloxacin, norfloxacin).

Prophylactic antibiotics are not recommended for the majority of travellers because of the limited duration of effectiveness and the possibility of side effects, including, paradoxically, diarrhoea. Vaccines are currently being developed to help prevent traveller's diarrhoea. The most promising vaccine is currently undergoing field trials in travellers and is looking safe and effective. This may be a good option for the future.

Self-treatment

Self-treatment with antibiotics for established diarrhoeal illness is usually inappropriate unless qualified medical attention is impossible to obtain. Travellers to remote areas may wish to carry a course of antibiotics for this eventuality.

■ Bloody diarrhoea with abdominal pain and fever may be due to bacillary dysentery (shigella organisms) or a variety of other organisms such as campylobacter or salmonella. The most appropriate antibiotic would be a quinolone such as cipro-floxacin, or a sulphur drug such as cotrimoxazole.

■ Prolonged bloody diarrhoea with mucus (jelly), especially without much fever, may be due to amoebic dysentery which is treated with metronidazole (Flagyl) or tinidazole (Fasigyn).

■ Prolonged, explosive diarrhoea with pale creamy motions may be due to giardia, a common hazard for overlanders travelling through the Indian subcontinent. This responds to metronidazole or tinidazole. These two antibiotics should not be taken at the same time as alcohol because of severe reactions between them.

If you have to treat yourself, obtain qualified medical investigation and help at the earliest opportunity. This is essential if symptoms do not settle after medication. Diarrhoea may be caused by other, more severe illnesses, including typhoid and malaria, and these would need specific treatment

Travellers who anticipate the need for self-treatment should take Richard Dawood's book *Travellers Health: How to Stay Healthy Abroad* (OUP). ❧

SEX ABROAD
by Drs Nick Beeching and Sharon Welby

MANY TRAVELLERS ENJOY HOLIDAY ROMANCES, but few take the necessary precautions, behaving differently from how they would at home.

HIV/AIDS

HIV infection resulting from sex abroad is the single most frequent cause of lethal infection in travellers.

The commonest route for the spread of HIV infection worldwide is through heterosexual intercourse, despite the emphasis in the western press on 'high risk groups' such as homosexual men and intravenous drug-users. By 1998, there were more new heterosexual infections with HIV diagnosed in England and Wales than there were due to homosexual contact. Most of the heterosexual HIV was acquired as a result of sex overseas, particularly in countries in Africa but also in other regions of the world where the risk is increasing rapidly.

In Britain, an anonymous study of travellers attending the Hospital for Tropical Diseases for tropical disease screening found that the HIV rate in heterosexual male travellers was 1.2 per cent.

This is probably just the tip of the iceberg. Many HIV infections go undiagnosed in the UK, because travellers do not realise the increased dangers of having sex with a new partner in a high HIV-prevalence country and therefore do not present themselves for HIV screening.

The HIV/AIDS epidemic is rampant in Africa, which has 90 per cent of the reported HIV/AIDS cases. In some areas of the world, up to 90 per cent of commercial sex workers of both sexes are HIV-positive, and as many as one in three of the adult population are infected. HIV rates are rapidly increasing in India, in countries around Asia's Golden Triangle, in many other parts of the tropics and in the former USSR.

In reality it is not possible to construct a world map showing global distribution of risk, as a lot of under-reporting goes on for a variety of social, cultural and economic reasons. While some places certainly have a higher incidence of sexually transmitted diseases than others, it is important to bear in mind that the risk depends on behaviour as well as geography—easy sex is the greatest risk factor.

A Swedish study of nearly 1,000 women showed that 28 per cent had had casual travel sex, more than 85 per cent of their partners had originated from Europe, 76 per cent of them were drunk during casual sex—and only 9 per cent used a condom.

The risk of becoming infected with HIV from a single sexual encounter is 0.01-1 per cent and is passed on more frequently from male to female. (This risk is increased in the presence of ulcerative genital disease.) The risk of HIV infection may be reduced by using condoms, especially condoms with spermicide.

Buy condoms before travelling (look for the British standards kitemark) and use them.

HIV eventually causes AIDS in the majority of people who have been infected. The interval between infection and the development of AIDS, however, may be more than ten years. At present there is no vaccine against HIV infection and there is no cure, although medical management of HIV-positive individuals is improving dramatically. The majority of HIV-positive individuals are unaware that they have been infected and cannot be distinguished from non-infected people.

HIV is not transmitted by hugging or social kissing, or using the same toilet seat, swimming pool or cup as a HIV infected person. There is no evidence that it is transmitted by mosquitoes or other insects.

Hepatitis B

Hepatitis B is spread by the same means as HIV but is 100 times more infectious than HIV and may also be spread by bed bugs.

It is another virus infection that is widespread in the tropics, and local people are usually infected at birth or in early childhood. A minority will continue to carry the virus but will have no obvious signs of infection. This minority is large—up to 20 per cent of young adults in the Far East and 5 to 15 per cent of young adults in Africa, the Middle East and South and Central America. There is an effective vaccine available for hepatitis B, (see *Vaccinations* in Chapter 1).

Other sexually transmitted diseases (STDs)

It has been estimated that each year, 1 in 20 adolescents worldwide contracts a sexually transmitted disease. The most serious are HIV and hepatitis B, but the classical venereal diseases such as syphilis and gonorrhoea are extremely common.

The incidence of syphilis has been increasing in the former states of the USSR, and in some of the eastern European countries that have taken over from the more traditional 'sex tourism' countries. There is worldwide concern about the spread of multi-resistant gonorrhoea, which means that if this disease is acquired abroad it may be harder to treat. A new sexual encounter anywhere in the world can pass on the usual infections such as lice, NSU (non-specific urethritis), herpes and genital warts, but travel to the tropics can lead to an occasional exotic infection such as chancroid which causes a genital ulcerative condition.

Self-medication should not be attempted and any sexual encounter with a new partner while travelling should be followed by a detailed check-up on return home, even if no symptoms are apparent. The Swedish study showed that one in four of the women who considered themselves healthy had an STD or a vaginal condition called bacterial vaginosis on screening. &

HIGH ALTITUDE, COLD FEET?
by Dr Saye Khoo

THE WORLD'S HIGH PLACES, long beloved by mountaineers, are increasingly visited by other travellers. The rewards may be great but the risks increase with isolation, likelihood of accidents and altitude-related sickness. The risk of altitude sickness can be minimised with advance preparation, preventative medicine and early treatment, so it is vitally important for any prospective trekker to be aware of the possible effects of altitude, to recognise the symptoms and to know how best to combat it when the need arises.

Altitude-related illness rarely occurs below 2,500 metres (8,200 feet) but becomes more frequent after 3,000 metres (9,850 feet), the risk increasing with higher ascent. The main areas of the world where this is likely to happen are: the Himalayas (India, Nepal); Karakorams (Pakistan, China); Tibet; the Andes (Chile, Peru, Ecuador, Columbia); Mts. Kenya and Kilimanjaro; the European Alps; the Rocky Mountains (North America); and, more rarely, peaks in Borneo, Irian Jaya, New Zealand, Japan and Hawaii.

Before you go

Ensure that you have insurance cover for altitude sickness as well as helicopter search-and-rescue in remoter regions. Check with commercial high-altitude trekking agencies what arrangements and equipment they will be providing in case of illness. Appropriate warm clothing, sleeping bags and equipment are essential, as well as a first aid kit, sunglasses (100 per cent UV protection) and suncream. If you have any pre-existing illness (diabetes, asthma, etc.), you should check with your doctor before travelling.

Minimising risk of Acute Mountain Sickness (AMS)

Ascent can only be made safe by allowing time to acclimatise and the risk of developing AMS is minimised by keeping two golden rules when above 3,000 metres:

■ Ascend slowly: no more than 300 metres per day, with one rest day every three days or 1,000 metres. Rate of ascent is critical; a faster ascent is more likely to cause AMS. Trekkers who are competitive in ascent are also more likely to develop AMS.

■ Climb high, sleep low: the height at which you sleep is all important—climbing higher during the day may help acclimatisation as long as the night is spent within the recommended altitude. Plan to cross a high mountain pass early in the day rather than getting stranded at the top as the sun sets. Allow rest days to acclimatise, especially if flying directly to a high destination (e.g. Leh, Lukla, Quito, La Paz, Cusco) or travelling in large groups (not everyone acclimatises at the same rate).

Anybody with symptoms of AMS (see below) should not ascend until further acclimatisation has taken place.

Many people use acetazolamide (Diamox) to prevent AMS, in a dosage of 250 mg twice a day, starting at least 24 hours before ascent. While this does reduce symptoms of AMS, side-effects are not uncommon (including frequent urination—a nuisance on a cold night—tingling and numbness of fingers, toes and around the mouth, and altered taste), and there is no evidence that more serious complications are prevented. Recommendations for safe ascent should not be ignored. Diamox must not be used to enable quicker ascent.

Altitude-related illnesses

ACUTE MOUNTAIN SICKNESS (AMS): Upon ascent, nearly all lowlanders will experience some symptoms. These include a throbbing headache, lethargy, nausea and loss of appetite. Sometimes the headache may be severe and associated with vomiting. These are common symptoms and signal that further time to acclimatise is required. The treatment is rest and aspirin or paracetamol: the symptoms will usually resolve with time at this stage. Do not ascend any further as there is a risk of developing serious complications such as HAPE or HACE (see below). Use of acetazolamide (Diamox) in a dose of 250 mg three times a day, and dexamethasone in a dose of 4 mg three times a day reduce symptoms, but if severe (e.g. persistent vomiting, headache not relieved by treatment) immediate descent should be considered.

HIGH ALTITUDE PULMONARY EDEMA (HAPE) AND HIGH ALTITUDE CEREBRAL EDEMA (HACE): HAPE is caused by fluid in the lung, leading to severe breathlessness and cough with frothy sputum, sometimes pink. The lips may become blue. HACE (fluid in the brain) produces severe headache with unsteadiness, confusion, drowsiness and in severe cases convulsions and malco-ordination leading to coma. Both are life-threatening complications. *Descend immediately* and seek urgent medical advice. Give oxygen if available. Drug treatment for HAPE is nifedipine (20 mg four times a day) and for HACE is dexamethasone (large initial dose (10-15 mg) followed by 8 mg three times a day). In both cases hyperbaric treatment is useful. Diamox and dexamethasone are given if AMS is also suspected; antibiotics are sometimes given in HAPE. If in doubt, it is always prudent to descend.

Portable hyperbaric chambers
(Gamow or Certec Bags, or their equivalent)

These are bags into which patients with HAPE or HACE are inserted and air is then pumped in to mimic the effects of descent. They are carried on many commercial treks and can be life-saving.

These chambers should not be used instead of, or to delay

descent and if at all possible, always choose descent. Use of the bag buys time rather than cures altitude sickness. People with chest injuries should not be treated (as there is the likelihood of a ruptured lung) and the patient should be able to lie flat and equalise pressure across the ears.

The bag has a zip, a pump fitting an air inlet, two relief valves that trigger at a preset pressure and a clear perspex window. Lie the patient in the bag (preferably on a mat) and zip it shut. Pump rapidly until the wall of the chamber is filled out, then much more slowly, checking every half minute that equalisation is taking place. Once the valves trigger (emitting a hissing sound), continuous pumping is required to cycle fresh air. This is around 8 to 12 pumps per minute (1 every 7 seconds) for the Certec and 12 pumps per minute (1 every 5 to 7 seconds) for the Gamow and Certec bags. Arrange a means of communication (walkie-talkie, writing pad or international diving signals) to include 'I'm OK', 'Stop', 'Deflate', etc. Bladder emptying beforehand is essential! Pumping is hard work so recruit volunteers.

Recommended treatment times are one to two hours and should be repeated if the patient remains unwell and descent is still not possible.

Other related conditions

INFECTIONS: Boil drinking water for longer (two minutes at sealevel, one minute extra for every 300 metres above this) or use a portable water filter or iodine to kill germs. There is anecdotal evidence that skin and respiratory infections are more frequent (especially over 4,000 metres) with reduced oxygen. Consider descending if infections linger.

COLD EXPOSURE: Cold injury affects the fingers, toes, nose, ears and other areas (e.g. buttocks, cheeks). Prevention with warm gloves (including a dry spare pair) and frequent checking of susceptible areas is essential. Frostnip (white discoloured skin) is characterised by pain followed by a loss of sensation with tingling upon rewarming, but full recovery is usual. Frostbite occurs when skin and tissues freeze then swell and mottle purple on rewarming, leading to blisters and black, dead tissue. It is seldom as bad as it looks. Keep the affected part warm (refreezing causes more damage), dry and most importantly, free of infection (bathe in antiseptic). Surgery should be avoided as far as possible. Seek specialist advice.

HYPOTHERMIA is also preventable with good equipment and planning of routes. If it develops, however, stop walking and seek shelter. Replace wet clothing, and use a sleeping bag and head covering to prevent heat loss. Rewarm slowly with warm water bottles or sandwiched between other people using sleeping bags zipped together. Dehydration and low blood sugar may be contributing factors, so warm, sweet fluids should be given (but never alcohol). Seek help.

SNOW BLINDNESS (watery, painful eyes with blurred vision): this is caused by UV light and is preventable using sunglasses with 100 per cent UVB protection. Protect from further damage with sunglasses and rest away from the sun. Take aspirin/paracetamol for pain. Eye drops containing steroids (hydrocortisone, Predsol, etc.) or cyclopentolate one per cent will help, and antibiotic drops/ointment will treat infection introduced by eye rubbing.

Children, pregnant women and contraception

Children are no less prone to altitude illness. Indeed, there is anecdotal evidence that those under five years are more at risk of AMS, HAPE and HACE. In addition, they are less likely to complain of specific symptoms and more likely to suffer from cold and dehydration (due to a relatively larger surface area for their size).

Little is known about pregnancy and altitude, but a lowlander should probably avoid going high (above 2,000 metres) because of reduced oxygen to the developing foetus. Although data are scant, both oral contraceptives and high altitude itself are associated with a slightly increased risk of thrombosis, and the use of alternative forms of contraception is preferable. ❧

RABIES
by Jack Barker

A DOG STAGGERS DOWN THE ROAD, stumbling and growling, foaming at the mouth. Frozen with fear you stay still, hoping it won't see you. Its head swings round, and you look into its bloodshot eyes. It lurches towards you. You scramble on a chair, on a table, but it just keeps coming. And then you wake up.

In the UK there is no rabies—for now—so scenes such as that are purely for nightmares. On the Continent the situation is better since the strategic dropping of bait laced with genetically-engineered vaccine, but in many areas of the world it can be a different matter.

Since 1975, 7,000 people in the UK have been treated for suspect bites. Between 1969 and 1989 there were 12 imported cases of human hydrophobia in people who had not sought treatment in time. All were fatal.

For a start, it's not just mad dogs that can transmit the disease. Insect-eating bats, cats and any other mammal can pass it on. Even wild animals pose a risk, made worse by the fact that one of the early symptoms of the illness, before full-blown hydrophobia sets in, can be an uncharacteristic docility. Beware of the rat who comes up to beg for sandwiches!

A headache is an early symptom, but things get worse quickly after that. Fever and spreading paralysis degenerate into episodes of confusion, aggression and hallucination, and by the time the illness has reached this stage it is too late for treatment.

The distinctive feature that gives the disease its name is the fear of water—hydrophobia. Attempts to drink produce powerful contractions of the muscles of the neck and the muscles involved in swallowing and breathing, associated with an extreme terror that would be more appropriate to a horror film. The patient dies after a few days of horrific delirium.

In India alone there are 50,000 deaths from rabies every year. So far only one person who started to display symptoms before being treated has lived to tell the tale.

The disease is widespread in parts of South America, the Indian subcontinent, Thailand, and the Philippines. Only a few countries are thought to be completely free of rabies: currently these are; Britain, Ireland, Norway, Sweden, Iceland, Malaysia, New Guinea, Borneo, Taiwan, Japan, Antarctica, Australia, and New Zealand.

Humans can catch rabies from any infected animal, whether domestic or wild, but the most common cause of infection is a bite from a dog. British statistics compiled in 1975 found that 74 per cent of bites reported in returning travellers were inflicted by dogs, 16 per cent by cats, and 12 per cent by wild animals. Surprisingly, the remaining eight per cent were inflicted by monkeys or chimpanzees, which were at the time popular as photo props in Spain.

In areas where the disease has become established it tends to circulate within a few specific species. In America, for example, vaccination programmes have largely eliminated canine rabies, but a bite from a North American skunk would present a very real threat of infection. Indian monkeys, African jackals, Central American vampire bats, insectivorous bats in Europe or the States, Arctic foxes, Indian rats and domestic cats are all quite capable of infecting humans.

Transmission occurs when the infected animal's saliva penetrates the victim's skin through a bite or scratch. However, infection can sometimes take place without broken skin: the virus can get through the membranes in the eye as well as those in the mouth or nose, which explains why the habit some dogs have of licking people's faces is even less popular abroad than it is in the UK. Cases have even occurred where infection has taken place as a result of inhaling the virus—from bat-infested caves or in laboratory accidents—with fatal results.

The incubation period for rabies is usually two to three months, but symptoms can start within a few days, or have been known to lie dormant for several years. Once symptoms show it is too late for treatment. The virus quickly enters the nerve endings in the muscles and spreads along the nerves to the brain and spinal cord.

It is easiest to catch and kill at the site of infection to prevent it reaching this stage. Any animal bite or lick should be cleaned immediately and thoroughly. This should be done even if there is no risk of rabies, as all animal teeth and saliva are contaminated with a variety of bacteria, viruses, and fungi which are potentially hazardous. The wound should be washed with soap and water, cleaned of broken teeth and debris, and rinsed in liberal amounts of water (the government advises scrubbing a wound for five minutes under a running tap). Then apply a dilute iodine solution or alcohol (gin or whisky will do in an emergency although stronger drink will work better). Mercurochrome, hydrogen peroxide, and the brightly-coloured ammonium antiseptics are not recommended, as they are not good at killing viruses. Deep or dirty wounds should be treated with a broadspectrum antibiotic, and an injection against tetanus should also be considered.

Treatment

The treatment for rabies is not simple, and it is essential to use a doctor who is fully conversant with the procedures. Although alternative medicine can be useful for some illnesses, there are no 'alternative' treatments for rabies that have yet been proved to be effective, so do not use herbalists, acupuncturists, gurus, or aromatherapists.

Go immediately to a qualified western-trained doctor at the nearest major health facility. There is no recommended minimum for the time that should elapse between possible exposure and the beginning of treatment: all authorities agree that treatment should be started as soon as possible. This is still necessary even if the victim has had a preventative immunisation against the disease.

Be suspicious if only offered a simple treatment: no-one should allow themselves to be sent away 'cured' after just one injection or tablet. It takes more than that to protect against rabies. There have been cases where bite victims have been charged handsomely for a single injection, sent away 'cured', and have died later.

UK doctors are recommended to give an immediate injection to boost the immune system, as well as a dose of human diploid cell vaccine. Booster injections should then be given 3, 7, 14 and 30 days later.

In the first rush of panic, don't lose your common sense. It would be unwise to accept an injection with a dirty needle from some bush-clinic in Congo, or to put much faith in a vaccine that has been stored in the hot tropical sun rather than the refrigerated conditions recommended by the manufacturer. In some parts of the world, the only vaccine on offer might be the old-fashioned painful stomach-injected type. In this situation, it is generally better to organise transportation to somewhere with better medical facilities, even if this means going all the way home.

Because the treatment can be drawn out and expensive, it is well worth keeping track of the animal that inflicted the bite if this is possible. If it stays healthy for 14 days, the doctor may decide that it is safe to stop the post-exposure vaccination course.

The new diploid vaccine makes immunisation prior to possible exposure to rabies acceptable for the first time. The old treatment for the illness, though effective, was so unpleasant that it would only be used when absolutely necessary. It involved such a weak vaccine that it needed to be injected in large quantities straight into the stomach. The new diploid vaccine is more effective, but also more expensive: most commercial clinics only administer a tiny dose as a prophylactic.

This was never intended to offer more than a partial protection. Although pre-immunisation is thought to extend the length of time that can be allowed to elapse between infection and proper medical treatment, by how much is still unknown. The medical advice is still to see a doctor without delay, so pre-vaccination is only really appropriate for those who will be travelling well off the beaten trail, or handling wild animals. (See also *Vaccinations* in Chapter 1.) ❧

BILHARZIA (schistosomiasis)
by Drs Sharon Welby and Nick Beeching

IN MANY AREAS OF AFRICA, the Middle East and some parts of South America and the Far East, the freshwater lakes and rivers are infested with a parasite which causes schistosomiasis (commonly known as bilharzia). The World Health Organisation estimates that at present 200 million people are infected with schistosomiasis in 76 countries in the tropics and the subtropics.

Places to avoid

You may become infected with this parasite if you wade or swim through fresh water lakes, rivers, ponds, reservoirs, dams, irrigation ditches or even temporary bodies of water, in endemic areas. Even deep water far off a lake shore cannot be regarded as safe from schistosomiasis. Swimming pools and showers which are supplied by untreated stream water can also be a source of infection.

However, if the swimming pool is adequately treated with chlorine it is usually safe, and any water which is left to stand for three days is safe (as long as it is stored in a snail-free environment) because the infective larvae form only survives for 48 hours in water. Neglected swimming pools and dams can become rapidly colonised with snails (which are involved in the schistosome life-cycle) which would make them unsafe for swimming in.

Human schistosomiasis cannot be acquired by swimming and wading in salt water.

Travellers are commonly misinformed by the locals (and tour operators) about the presence of schistosomiasis in lakes or rivers and, since there is no practical way to distinguish infested from non-infested water and no protective vaccine is available, fresh water swimming in endemic areas should be avoided. Water sports are particularly dangerous because they may involve exposure over a large area of surface water.

Life cycle

Infected snails release large numbers of minute free-swimming larvae (called cercariae) into the water. When humans come in contact with infested fresh water, the cercariae are capable of penetrating the unbroken skin. After penetration, the larva spends a period of time travelling around the body before it develops into an adult blood fluke. The adult then finds a partner and settles down in the blood vessels around the bladder or around the liver (depending on the species) to produce eggs at the rate of 300-1,500 per day. These eggs then pass out in the urine or faeces to the outside world and find their way into water, where they hatch to produce the larvae form that infects a snail. And so the cycle continues.

The time from the cercariae penetrating the skin to the adults producing eggs is usually four to 12 weeks. The flukes do not multiply within humans so the number of flukes is related to the initial exposure and, in general, severe illness only occurs after a heavy exposure over a long period of time.

The symptoms

Usually there are no symptoms with schistosomiasis infection, but occasionally people notice a generalised weakness and feeling of ill health. There may be an initial tingling of the skin, an itch or occasionally a rash, a few hours after contact with infested water, but this is usually short-lived and is due to the larvae penetrating the skin.

Sometimes people notice a few chest symptoms (wheezing) three to ten days after infection, but this is self-limiting. The eggs of the flukes can be detected on laboratory screening of the urine or faeces or even semen, and there is a blood test that looks for antibodies (which are protective proteins that fight against the parasite).

A few people develop an acute allergic response to the eggs, which usually occurs about two to three weeks or more after infection. This consists of fever, lack of appetite, weight loss, headaches, generalised aches and pains, diarrhoea, cough with or without wheezing and sometimes an itchy rash like 'hives'. An increased number of white blood cells (called eosinophils) in blood tests give a clue that invasive worms are around. This illness is called 'Katayama fever'.

Once the infection becomes established, abdominal pain and blood in the urine and/or stool can occur. Men sometimes notice change in colour or consistency of their semen. The harmful effects are due to the eggs: they cause bleeding, ulceration, and the formation of small growths as they penetrate the wall of the intestine and bladder.

Long-term effects are serious and include severe liver damage due to fibrosis, kidney failure and bladder cancer. On very rare occasions, especially with heavy infections, the eggs can find their way to different parts of the body and cause pressure effects. This can result in neurological problems such as weakness in the legs or convulsions.

Prevention and treatment

If contact with fresh water is unavoidable, try to cross upstream of any villages, cover exposed skin and wear boots. Rubber boots and wetsuits are protective but they must be dried quickly in the sun after use. The larvae die quickly when removed from water and cannot survive drying, so vigorous rubbing with a towel after possible exposure may reduce the chance of infection. If you have had possible exposure to schistosomiasis, ask your doctor for schistosomiasis screening tests three months after your last contact with freshwater. There is an effective treatment available, which is a single dose of a drug called praziquantel. This is usually well tolerated with only occasional gastro-intestinal side-effects. ❧

Chapter 4 : **Extreme situations** ❧

CREATURES THAT BITE: 1 MAMMALS
by Dr Nick Beeching

ALL MAMMALIAN BITES (including human ones) are likely to become infected, and medical advice should be obtained about appropriate antibiotics and tetanus immunisation. First aid measures start with immediate washing of the wound in running water for at least five minutes, scrubbing with soap or detergent, and removal of any embedded foreign material. Wiping with topical iodine, an alcohol injection swab or neat alcohol (gin or whisky will do) helps to sterilise the area. Colourful topical agents such as mercurochrome are useless. At the hospital or dispensary, the wound should be further cleaned and dressed as necessary, but do not allow the wound to be sutured.

Rabies is a serious hazard throughout most of the world, including continental Europe and the USA. See the separate section on *Rabies* in chapter 3. Domestic or wild animal contact should be avoided at all times, particularly if a normally wild animal is unusually docile or vice versa. Rabies affects a wide variety of mammals, particularly carnivores and bats. Wild dogs are a common nuisance in the tropics and should be given a wide berth.

Snakes

Snakes only attack humans if provoked, and snakebite is a rare hazard for most travellers. Never handle a snake, even if it appears to be dead, and try not to corner or threaten live snakes. If you encounter a snake on the path, keep absolutely still until it moves away. Always look for snakes on paths ahead, using a torch at night. If hiking on overgrown paths, through undergrowth or sand, wear adequate boots, socks and long trousers. Snakes are often found in wood piles, crevices or under rocks and these should not be handled. Integral groundsheets and tightly closed tent flaps help to keep snakes out of tents, and make it less likely that you will roll over on a snake in your sleep (generally viewed as threatening behaviour by the snake).

Not all snakes are venomous and only a minority of bites by venomous species are accompanied by a successful injection of venom. The most important first aid for a victim is to keep calm and provide reassurance that envenomation is unlikely. Immobilise the bitten limb by splinting and rest the victim. Do not offer alcohol. Even if venom has been injected, severe effects take several hours to develop and there should be adequate time to carry the patient to a dispensary or hospital for trained help. It is best to apply a tight pressure dressing over the bite or crepe bandaging on the affected limb (which should be immobilised). Tourniquets should be avoided and 'Boys' Own' remedies, such as incision of the wound to suck out the venom, are harmful and should not be employed. Local sprays, cold packs, topical antiseptics and even electric shocks are equally useless.

If the snake has already been killed, place it in a bag or box and take it for identification by medical staff attending the victim. Amateur attempts to capture a snake that has been provoked may result in further bites, and a good description of the snake by an unbitten comrade is obviously preferable. Depending on the type of snake, venom may reduce the clotting activity of the blood, causing bleeding, typically from the gums, or induce paralysis—first manifested by an inability to open the eyes properly, followed by breathing problems. Shock and kidney failure are possibilities, and some venoms cause extensive damage to tissue around the bitten area. Immediate pain relief should never include aspirin, which impairs the ability of blood to clot. All bites, with or without envenomation, carry a risk of infection.

Antivenom should never be used unless there are definite signs of envenomation, and then only with adequate medical support. Travellers should not routinely carry antivenom. Expatriates working in high-risk remote areas or expedition organisers may wish to carry a small stock of antivenom. British travellers who wish to carry antivenom should obtain specialist advice from the WHO Centre at the Liverpool School of Tropical Medicine several months before they intend to travel. Package inserts with multi-purpose antivenoms and even local advice are often incorrect.

Scorpions

Scorpion stings are far more likely than snake bites to be a problem for travellers, and are always very painful. Scorpions are widespread, particularly in hot, dry areas. If travelling in such areas wear strong footwear and always shake out your clothes and shoes before putting them on. The pain of stings requires medical attention, which may include strong, injected pain-killers. Many species are capable of inflicting fatal stings, particularly in children, and antivenoms should be available in areas where these species are present.

Other beasts

A myriad of other stinging and biting beasts threaten the traveller. Some spider bites can cause rapid paralysis and should be treated with a local pressure dressing or tight tourniquet until medical help is obtained. Leeches can be encouraged to drop off by applying salt, alcohol or vinegar or a lighted cigarette end. Do not pull them off, as infection may follow if parts of the mouth remain in the wound. Leeches inject an anticoagulant into the wound and local pressure may be required to reduce bleeding. If travelling in damp jungle areas through water with leeches, inspect all exposed areas regularly for leeches.

CREATURES THAT BITE: 2 MARINE LIFE
by Jack Barker

THE TEMPTATION TO EXPLORE below the surface of a blue tropical sea can be irresistible. But be warned: it's an environment designed for fish, and it's a survival game even for them. Behind the postcard image of a coral reef is a festering soup of malevolent life. With sea-urchins snapping around heels, stonefish lurking in the shallows, coral waiting to inflict highly infective scrapes and sharks and jellyfish patrolling the deep, it is quite surprising that the most common after-effect of subaquatic exploration is an ear infection, which can strike even from the smallest paddling pool. On this and other matters, medical advice is divided.

Ear infections

Ear infections are caused by the residue of water that hangs around in the outer canal of the ear, waiting to cause what the doctors casually refer to as an 'indolent infection', either fungal or bacterial.

Indolent it may be, but it certainly hurts, and can take months to shift. The Medical Advisory Service for Travellers Abroad (MASTA) recommends drying ears with a cotton bud, gently pulling the lobe of the ear back and inserting a the bud to soak up remaining water. They caution not to twist the bud, and to take care not to poke it through the eardrum (causing pain and irreparable deafness).

Surgeon Lieutenant Commander Simon Ridout, who looks after navy divers, disagrees. He says the only safe way to get water out of the ear is by shaking your head like a dog. In practice I find this makes my brain feel as if it is coming loose, but it is easy to see that it avoids the risk of inducing infection thought to be caused by microscopic cotton fragments left by even a sterile cotton bud. He also warns that diving or swimming with a cold or sore throat increases the risks of such infections.

Sea urchins

Sea urchins are vicious little balls of spines that spend their days in rock crevices waiting for an unwary foot. Nocturnal skinny-dippers should be warned that at night they also travel across open sand. Swimming shoes should be worn where sea urchins are found. Spines should be methodically removed after softening the skin in a two per cent salycilic solution. Be careful not to leave any remnants of spine in the wound.

Jellyfish

Jellyfish trail tentacles armed with stinging capsules. And to make matters worse, many species are invisible. MASTA suggest washing the wound with vinegar or dilute acetic acid, which neutralises the venom in the tentacles which are probably still wrapped around the victim. The Surf Lifesaving Association of Australia no longer recommends this treatment, however, and now suggest washing in plenty of ice and cold water. Once the jellyfish has been removed, all fragments of tentacle should be picked off the surface of the patient's skin. An itchy or painful rash is the usual result of a jellyfish sting, but some species are venomous enough to kill and allergic reactions can also complicate matters. If the patient becomes short of breath, starts to sweat, or shows signs of inflammation spreading from the sting, they should be taken to hospital and given cardiac massage and mouth-to-mouth respiration on the way if necessary.

Fish

Fish can cause a certain amount of havoc: stingrays, weeverfish, and scorpionfish are all equipped to kill humans. Most stings occur when the fish has been surprised, so shuffle along the seabed to warn the unsuspecting of your presence. If stung by any of the above, the sting should be removed, the wound bound tightly, the limb immobilised and the patient taken to hospital. Cardiac massage and artificial respiration should be used if the patient stops breathing. If removing the sting is not convenient (or possible) the poison from these fish can be destroyed by heat, so the excruciating pain and some of the worst toxic effects can be relieved by immersing the bite in hot, but not scalding, water (about 50°C).

Sharks

Sharks present less of a risk than is generally thought. There are about 100 recorded attacks each year, which is dwarfed by the drowning figures. Conventional wisdom states that the best policy is to sit on the seabed quietly until any prowling shark goes away, although this would clearly be difficult without breathing apparatus. As with all sea risks, it is best to take local advice. In high-risk areas such as Sydney, popular beaches are netted, although it has been suggested that sharks caught inside the nets are more, not less, likely to resort to crunching humans for food.

Coral

Coral does not have to be venomous to cause medical problems. Even minor coral scrapes can develop into tropical ulcers and take months to heal, and should be disinfected immediately. In Belize, my boatman treated cuts with a spray of an aerosol window-cleaner containing ammonia, which seemed to work perfectly, but the conventional advice is to use a zinc medication or a powder such as Cicatrin. ଏ

INJECTIONS AND BLOOD TRANSFUSIONS
by Drs Sharon Welby and Nick Beeching

MANY DISEASES ARE SPREAD BY BLOOD, blood products or instruments which may be contaminated with blood. When travelling in developing countries, it is vitally important to be aware of the potential risks associated with having injections or blood transfusions.

In some countries the health care facilities are under tremendous financial strain. Equipment may be reused without proper sterilisation and there may be no formal programme for screening donated blood for antibodies to HIV or hepatitis B or C. It is, therefore, always a wise precaution to take a commercially prepared HIV prevention kit when travelling to tropical and sub-tropical destinations.

The HIV prevention kit usually contains syringes, needles, intravenous cannulae and sometimes a dental needle and suture kit. They are available from most large chemists, camping shops and travel clinics, and the advantage of a commercial kit is that all the items are clearly labelled and you are unlikely to run into problems at customs. It is wise to keep these kits on you at all times because they will do you little good if left behind in your hotel. Bigger packs containing plasma expander solutions are of limited use, are inconvenient to carry, and are probably not necessary unless travelling as part of an expedition where medical help is available.

The risk associated with unscreened blood transfusions is significant given the high prevalence of HIV and hepatitis B infection in tropical countries. Blood transfusions can also transmit other viruses (hepatitis C, D and cytomegalovirus); bacteria (syphilis, typhoid and meliodosis); and parasites (including filariasis/'elephantiasis', visceral leishmaniasis, trypanosomiasis—sleeping sickness in Africa and Chagas' disease in the Americas—and malaria).

If you are in the unfortunate position of needing a blood transfusion, ask the attending doctors whether the transfusion is absolutely necessary to save life (in which case there is little choice). If transfusion is essential but can be deferred for a short period, members of your own party, local expatriates, or donors who know their own HIV and hepatitis B status may be able to donate blood for you. The embassy or consulate staff can often help with information about local donors. Establishing your blood group before travelling is a sensible precaution and there is a charitable organisation which guarantees to supply screened blood within 24 hours to members. Enquiries can be made to the Blood Care Foundation, PO Box 7, Sevenoaks, Kent, TN13 2SZ, Tel: 01293 425485, email: BCFGB@compuserve.com (fees start from £8.50 per month).

As with everything, prevention is better than cure when it comes to blood transfusions. The majority of transfusions are the result of accidents, road accidents in particular, so be aware that the risk of road accidents can be reduced by taking simple precautions: not travelling at night, not getting on overcrowded vehicles, avoiding motorcycles and not drinking and driving.

The risk of diseases spread by injections can be prevented by avoiding unnecessary injections and needles, for example, acupuncture, body or ear piercing and tattoos. It is also advisable not to share razors, so don't be tempted to have your face shaved in the street. Hepatitis B and C may also be transmitted by sharing toothbrushes, nail scissors and other items which can cause bleeding, and individuals should only use their own toiletry items.

If you do become unwell and the health care professional intends to give you an injection, question if it is really necessary and if there is an alternative treatment. Sometimes the injection or infusion is seen as a modern and more effective treatment, when in reality a tablet will be as effective. If the injection is absolutely essential, make sure a disposable needle pack is opened in front of you.

Drug users who share needles, syringes and other drug-injecting paraphernalia also share a large number of infections, including hepatitis B, HIV, malaria and some exotic diseases such as Chagas' disease found in South America. The risk of acquiring hepatitis or HIV is substantially increased if your partner is an injecting drug user. Intravenous drug users, who are not deterred by the serious legal consequences of their habit, should not share 'works' or 'mixing spoons' under any circumstances. To share is to invite disaster. 🙠

SURVIVING THE JUNGLE
by Robin Hanbury-Tenison

THE KEY TO SURVIVAL IN THE TROPICS is comfort. If your boots fit, your clothes don't itch, your wounds don't fester, you have enough to eat and you have the comforting presence of a local who is at home in the environment, then you are not likely to go far wrong.

Of course, jungle warfare is something else. The British, Americans and, for all I know, several other armies, have produced detailed manuals on how to survive under the most arduous conditions imaginable and with the minimum of resources. But most of us are extremely unlikely ever to find ourselves in such a situation. Even if you are unlucky enough to be caught in a guerrilla war or survive an air crash in the jungle, I believe that the following advice will be as useful as trying to remember sophisticated techniques that probably require equipment you do not have to hand anyway.

A positive will to survive is essential. The knowledge that others have travelled long distances and lived for days and even months without help or special knowledge gives confidence, while a calm appraisal of the circumstances can make them seem far less intimidating. The jungle need not be an uncomfortable place, although unfamiliarity may make it seem so. Morale is as important as ever, and comfort, both physical and mental, a vital ingredient.

Clothing and footwear

To start with, it is usually warm, but when you are wet, especially at night, you can become very cold very quickly. It is therefore important to be prepared and always try to keep a sleeping bag and a change of clothes dry. Excellent strong, lightweight plastic bags are now available in which these items should always be packed with the top folded over and tied. These can then be placed inside your rucksack or bag so that if dropped in a river or soaked by a sudden tropical downpour—and the effect is much the same—they, at least, will be dry. I usually have three such bags, one with dry clothes, one with camera equipment, notebooks, etc., and one with food. Wet clothes should be worn. This is unpleasant for the first 10 minutes in the morning, but they will soon be soaking wet with sweat and dripping in any case, and wearing them means you need carry only one change for the evening and sleeping in. It is well worth taking the time to rinse them out whenever you are in sunshine by a river so that you can dry them on hot rocks in half an hour or so. They can also be hung over the fire at night, which makes them more pleasant to put on in the morning, but also tends to make them stink of wood smoke.

Always wear loose clothes in the tropics. They may not be very becoming but constant wetting and drying will tend to shrink them and rubbing makes itches and scratches far worse. Cotton is excellent but should be of good quality so that the clothes do not rot and tear too easily. There are now many excellent specialist manufacturers of tropical clothing. Some are expensive, but it is worth investing in good quality for comfort and durability. One of the best suppliers is Nomad Camping at 3 Turnpike Lane, London, N8 (tel: 020 8889 7014).

For footwear, baseball boots or plimsolls are usually adequate, but for long distances good leather boots will protect your feet much better from bruising and blisters. In leech country, a shapeless cotton stocking worn between sock and shoe tied with a drawstring below the knee, outside long trousers, gives virtually complete protection. As far as I know, no one manufactures these yet, so they have to be made up specially, but they are well worth it.

Upsets and dangers

Hygiene is important in the tropics. Small cuts can turn nasty very quickly and sometimes will not heal for a long time. The best protection is to make an effort to wash all over at least once a day if possible, at the same time looking out for any sore places, cleaning and treating them at once. On the other hand, where food and drink are concerned, it is usually not practical or polite to attempt to maintain perfectionist standards. Almost no traveller in the tropics can avoid receiving hospitality and few would wish to do so. It is often best therefore to accept that a mild stomach upset is likely—and be prepared. There is an excellent medical section in this book (Chapter 3) with the best up-to-date advice on prevention and cure of all the illnesses to which travellers in the tropics are likely to be exposed and they should read it carefully. However, constant use of prophylactics and antibiotics can produce side-effects. Many of us now use homeopathic remedies, including malaria pills, while carrying conventional cures as well. Ainsworths of 36 New Cavendish Street, London, W1M 7LH (tel: 020 7935 5330/fax: 020 7486 4313/ email: enquiries@ainsworths.com; internet: www.ainsworths. com) has a good travel kit.

In real life and death conditions, there are only two essentials for survival, a knife or machete and a compass (provided you are not injured, when, if possible, the best thing to do is to crawl to water and wait for help). Other important items, I would put in order of priority as follows:

1) A map. 2) A waterproof cover, cape or large bag. 3) Means of making fire, lifeboat matches or a lighter with spare flints, gas or petrol. 4) A billycan. 5) Tea or coffee, sugar and dried milk.

There are few tropical terrains that cannot be crossed with these, given time and determination. Man can survive a long time without food, so try to keep your food supplies simple, basic and light. Water is less of a problem in the jungle, except in limestone mountains, but a metal or lightweight plastic water container should be carried and filled whenever possible. Rivers, streams and even puddles are unlikely to be dangerously contaminated, while rattans and lianas often contain water, as do some other plants whose leaves may form catchments, such as pitcher plants. It is easy to drink from these, though best instead to filter the liquid through cloth and avoid the 'gunge' at the bottom.

Hunting and trapping are unlikely to be worth the effort to the inexperienced, although it is surprising how much can be found in streams and caught with hands. Prawns, turtles, frogs and even fish can be captured with patience and almost all are edible—and even tasty if you're hungry enough. Fruits, even those that are ripe and being eaten by other animals, are less safe, while some edible-looking plants and fungi can be very poisonous and should be avoided. Don't try for the honey of wild bees unless you know what you are doing as stings can be dangerous and those of hornets even fatal.

As regards shelter, there is a clear distinction between South America and the rest of the tropical world. In the South American interior, almost everyone uses a hammock. Excellent waterproof hammocks are supplied to the Brazilian and US armies and are obtainable commercially. Otherwise, a waterproof sheet may be stretched across a line tied between the same two trees from which the hammock is slung.

Elsewhere, however, hammocks are rarely used and will tend to be a nuisance under normal conditions. Lightweight canvas stretchers through which poles may be inserted before being tied apart on a raised platform make excellent beds and, once again, a waterproof sheet provides shelter. Plenty of nylon cord is always useful.

Fight it or like it

The jungle can be a frightening place at first. Loud noises, quantities of unfamiliar creepy-crawlies, flying biting things and the sometimes oppressive heat can all conspire to get you down. But it can also be a very pleasant place if you decide to like it rather than fight it—and it is very seldom dangerous. Snakebite, for example is extremely rare. During the 15 months of the Royal Geographical Society's Mulu expedition, in Borneo, no one was bitten, although we saw and avoided or caught and photographed many snakes and even ate some! Most things, such as thorns, ants and sandflies, are more irritating than painful (taking care to treat rather than scratch usually prevents trouble).

Above all, the jungle is a fascinating place—the richest environment on earth. The best help for morale is to be interested in what is going on around you and the best guide is usually a local resident who is as at home there as most of us are in cities. Fortunately, in most parts of the world where jungles survive, there are still such people. By accepting their advice, recognising their expertise and asking them to travel with you, you may help to reinforce their self-respect in the face of often overwhelming forces that try to make them adopt a so-called 'modern' way of life. At the same time, you will appreciate the jungle far more yourself—and have a far better chance of surviving in it. ❧

SURVIVING THE DESERT
by Jack Jackson

THE MOST IMPORTANT THING about desert survival is to avoid the need for it in the first place! Be aware of your vehicle's capabilities and do not overload it, and know how to maintain and repair it. Carry adequate spares and tools. Be fit yourselves and get sufficient sleep. Start your journey with 25 per cent more fuel and water than you calculated would be needed to cover extra problems, such as bad terrain, leaking containers and extra time spent over repairs or sitting out a sandstorm.

Know accurately where your next supplies of fuel and water are. Carry plastic sheets to make desert stills and take space blankets with you. Pack more than one compass and know how to navigate properly. When using magnetic compasses, keep them well away from vehicles and cameras. Do not rely exclusively on electronic Global Positioning Systems (GPS) or the batteries that power them, and do not leave the piste unless you really do know what you are doing. Travel only during the local winter months. Know how correct your odometer is in relation to the wheels and tyres fitted to the vehicle. Make notes of distances, compass bearings and obvious landmarks as you go along so that you can retrace your route easily if you have to. Observe correct check-in and -out procedures with local authorities. If possible, travel in a convoy with other vehicles. When lost, do not continue. Stop, think and, if necessary, retrace your route.

Back-up plans

If you are travelling in a large party, you should arrange a search-and-rescue plan before you start out. This would include the use and recognition of radio beacons or flares for aircraft search. Many countries do not allow you to use radio communications, but if you can use them, carry modern portable satellite communications systems.

Should the worst happen, remember that, for most people, an air search is highly unlikely and high-flying commercial passenger aircraft passing overhead are unlikely to notice you, whatever you do. A search, if it does come, will be along the piste or markers. Most often this will consist of other vehicles travelling through the area, whose drivers have been asked by the local authorities to look out for you because you have failed to check in at a pre-appointed time and place.

Local drivers will not understand or appreciate coloured flares, so your best signal for local outside help is fire. If you hear a vehicle at night, cardboard boxes or wood are quickly and easily lit, but during the day you need lots of thick black smoke. The best fuel for this is a tyre. Bury most of a tyre in the sand to control the speed at which it burns (keep it well away from and downwind of the vehicles and fuel) and start the exposed part burning with a rag soaked in either petrol or diesel fuel. As the exposed part of the tyre burns away, you can uncover more from the sand to keep it going, or cover all of it with sand if you wish to put out the fire. Avoid inhaling the sulphurous fumes. While the battery still carries a charge, headlights switched on and off at night can also be used to draw attention to your plight. Should you be lucky enough to see low-flying aircraft overhead, it's worth remembering that the international ground/air code for a request to be picked up by such a plane is to stand up with your arms held aloft in an obvious 'V' shape.

A need to survive

Once you are in a 'need-to-survive' situation, the important things are morale and water. Concentrate on getting your vehicles moving again. This will keep you occupied and help to keep up morale. To minimise water loss, avoid manual work during the day and, instead, work at night or in the early morning. Build shade and stay under it as much as possible, keeping well covered with loose cotton clothing. 'Space blankets', with the reflective side facing out, make the coolest shade. Keep warm and out of the wind at night. In really hot climates, replacing lost potassium with Slow K can make a big difference to your general alertness.

Unless you are well off the piste with no chance of a search, you should stay with your vehicle. If someone must walk out, pick one or two of the strongest and most determined people to go. They must carry with them a compass and a GPS receiver, if available; a torch; salt; anti-diarrhoea medicine; loose, all-enveloping clothes; tough footwear; good sunglasses and as much water as they can sensibly carry. In soft sand, a jerrycan of water can easily be hauled along on a rope tied to the waist. On mixed ground, tie the jerrycan to a sand ladder, one end of which is padded and tied to the waist.

Those who walk out should follow the desert nomad pattern of walking in the evening until about 11pm, sleeping until 4am, walking again until 10 am, then digging a shallow hollow in the sand and lying in it under a space blanket, reflective side out, until the sun has lost its heat. If it's a full moon they can walk all night. In this way, fit men would make 60 to 70km on 10 litres of water—less in soft sand.

Water

In a 'sit-it-out-and-survive' situation, with all manual labour kept to a minimum, food is unimportant and dehydration staves off hunger, but water is vital. The average consumption of water in a hot, dry climate should be eight litres per person per day. This can be lowered to four litres a day in a real emergency. Diarrhoea increases dehydration, so should be controlled by medicine where necessary. Salt intake should be kept up—in the worst scenario, licking your bare arms will replace some lost salt.

Water supply should be improved by making as many desert stills as possible. To make one, dig a hole about one-third of a metre deep and one metre in circumference, place a clean saucepan or billycan in the centre of the hole, and cover it with a two-metre-square plastic sheet weighted down at the edges with stones, jerrycans or tools. Put a stone or another heavy object in the centre to weigh it down directly over the billy. Overnight, water vapour from the sand will evaporate and then condense on the underside of the plastic sheet. In the morning, running a finger down from the edge of the sheet to the centre will cause the condensation to run down and drip into the pan. The water so collected should be boiled or sterilised before drinking.

If you have antifreeze in your radiator, don't try to drink it as it is highly poisonous. Even if you have not put antifreeze in the radiator yourselves, there is still likely to be some left in it from previous use or from the factory at the time that the vehicle was first manufactured. Radiator water should be put into the desert still in the same way as the urine and the resulting condensate should be boiled or sterilised before drinking. Water from bad or brackish wells can be made drinkable in the same way. Note, however, that solar stills can take a lot of energy to create and will yield little water in return. Until the situation is really desperate, they are probably not worth considering as a viable means of collecting water.

The minimum amount of water per day required to maintain the body's water balance at rest in the shade is as follows: if the mean daily temperature is 35°C, you will need 5.3 litres per 24 hours. If it is 30°C, then 2.4 litres; if 25°C you need 1.2 litres; and at temperatures of 20°C and below, one litre will suffice. It must be stressed that this is the bare minimum necessary for survival. If such an intake is prolonged, there will be a gradual kidney malfunction and possibly urinary tract infection, with women more at risk than men.

The will to live is essential. Once you give up, you will be finished. If you find people in such a situation and do not have a doctor to handle them, feed them water to which rehydration salts have been added, a teaspoonful at a time, every few minutes for a couple of hours. If you do not have sachets of rehydration salts, you can make your own by adding one level teaspoon of salt and two tablespoons of sugar per litre of water. If the person is unconscious, the dissolved rehydration salts can be administered anally. It is essential to try to stabilise someone in this way before trying to take them on a long, tough drive to hospital. ❧

SURVIVING THE COLD: PART 1
by Dr Mike Stroud

'THE WIND WAS BLOWING BRISKLY as I stepped out of the tent, but the sun was shining and it didn't feel too bad. When I had been out earlier, briefly, answering nature's call, the air had been still, and despite it being −40°C it had seemed quite warm in the sunshine. I had decided to wear only a cotton windproof over underwear and fleece salopettes. It was amazing how little one needed to keep warm as long as you kept on working hard.

Ran and I took down the tent and packed up our sledges. The south pole was only 30 km away and, with luck, we would reach it within two days. It helped to have it so close. We had been going 12 hours a day for more than two months, and the effort had taken a terrible toll. It had been both mental and physical hell. It was not long after we set off that I realised my mistake. As well as only putting on a single jacket, I was wearing only thin contact gloves inside outer mitts and, after an hour, with the wind rising even more, my hands were suffering badly and not warming up despite moving. They became so bad that Ran had to help me put on the extra mittens from my sledge, my fingers were too useless to get them on. When we set off again, I was getting generally chilled. After the long stop fighting with the gloves, I found that I could barely pull the sledge with my cold muscles. I was in trouble, and I realised I would have to stop and put my fleece jacket on as well, but to do this meant removing my outer jacket completely and once again my fingers were useless and I was unable to do up the zips. Ran was there to help again, but I had entered a vicious circle. My thinking was beginning to fade, and although I kept walking for another half-hour or so, I was never with-it. It is only through Ran's description that I know what happened next.

I had apparently begun to move very slowly and to wander from side to side. When Ran asked if I was OK, I had been unintelligible, and he had realised immediately that I must be hypothermic. He then tried to get me to help with the tent, but I just stood around doing nothing. So he put it up alone and pushed me inside. Eventually he got me in my sleeping bag and forced me to take some hot drinks. After an hour or so I recovered, but it had been another close call. Obviously we were getting vulnerable and we discussed pulling out at the pole....'

The above is an excerpt from my book, *Shadows on the Wasteland*, about my crossing of Antarctica with Sir Ranulph Fiennes. Under the circumstances, it was perhaps not surprising that I became hypothermic, for cold easily creates casualties and can even kill. Yet, with the correct preparation, man can operate successfully even in the harshest of climates. The secret is to match the body's heat production—chiefly dictated by activity—with its heat losses—chiefly governed by clothing and shelter. You should aim to neither overheat nor cool down. Both can have unwelcome consequences.

An inactive adult produces about a light bulb's-worth of heat (100 watts), which is not really much to keep the whole body warm in the face of the cold, wind and rain. It is, therefore, generally wise to keep moving for the most of the time in cold conditions, until you have either reached or created proper shelter. However, many reasons, such as getting lost or injured, may force you to halt or lie up under adverse circumstances, and you are then going to need to reduce your heat losses to less than the 100 watts that you will be producing. This may be an impossibility if ill equipped or conditions are really harsh. If you can't reduce heat losses enough, your body will cool and you will start to shiver. This can increase your resting heat production to as much as 500 watts, but even this may be inadequate and the shivering itself is uncomfortable and tiring for the muscles. If cooling still continues, you will become hypothermic and can be in great danger. It is definitely best to carry enough protection to deal with getting stuck out in the worst possible conditions you may meet.

When you are active, things are quite different. Working hard leads the body to produce as much as a good room heater—2,000 watts or even more. It is therefore more common to get too hot rather than too cold, even in the worst conditions. Initially, getting too hot may not be important, but it does lead to sweating, which can ruin the insulation of your clothing by wetting it from the inside and later, when you have decreased your activity or the conditions have worsened, this wet clothing will have lost its ability to protect you properly. Sweating may also lead to dehydration, which in turn will make you vulnerable to fatigue, and it is with the onset of tiredness and the ensuing slow-down in activity that heat production will start to fall and you will cool rapidly to become at risk from the 'exhaustion/ hypothermia' syndrome. Even the most experienced of people have become victims under such circumstances.

In order to match heat losses to heat production, clothing must have the flexibility to be both cool and warm. It must also be able to provide windproofing and waterproofing. Such flexibility can only be achieved by the use of layers, which must be easy to put on and take off and comfortable to wear together. In all but the very coldest regions—where rain or melting snow won't occur—I would favour the use of modern synthetics in the insulation layers as they tend not to degrade very much when wetted by sweat or the environment, and they also dry spectacularly quickly. If affordable, waterproofs/windproofs should be moisture vapour permeable (MVP) since these will limit the accumulation of sweat and condensation in inner garments and will allow the evaporation of some sweat, which will help to keep you cool if overheating. However, it needs to be remembered that even MVP garments are only partially vapour permeable (especially in the cold, when water vapour will condense or even freeze on the inner surface of the garment and will then be trapped by its waterproof qualities), and so it is always better to remove the waterproof if it is not actually raining and activity is making you too hot.

Additional flexibility when trying to maintain a comfortable body temperature can be granted by changing your head covering. In the cold, when wearing good clothing, as much as 90 per cent of your heat losses can come from your head, so by putting on or taking off a warm hat or balaclava and by adjusting a windproof hood, you can make enormous changes to your heat losses much more easily than by adjusting other garments. It is often said that if you get cold hands you should put on a hat.

Eating is also an important factor in keeping warm. Even at rest a meal will rev up your metabolism and make that 100-watt bulb glow brighter, while during exercise it will considerably increase your heat output for any given level of activity. More importantly, food also helps to sustain the supply of fuels to the muscles, and this will allow you to continue working, or for that matter shivering, for longer. In addition, it will make it much less likely that you will develop a low blood sugar—a factor now thought to be important in the onset of some cases of exposure/exhaustion. Almost any food will help, but it is probably best for it to contain a fair amount of carbohydrate. Grain-based snack bars are as good as anything, but snacks based on chocolate are also excellent, even if there is a greater fat content.

When hypothermia does begin to occur in an individual, a number of changes are seen that make the diagnosis pretty easy as long as the possibility is carefully considered. Unfortunately, the person suffering from the cold is often unable to consider things properly, since he or she may not realise what is happening and often, after feeling cold, shivery and miserable initially, they may feel quite happy and even warm. It therefore goes without saying that a problem may only become evident when things have already become quite bad, and that if a victim is alone or everybody in a party becomes hypothermic simultaneously, things are very serious.

The signs to watch out for are quite similar to those seen when a person becomes increasingly drunk. At first the victim may slur speech and begin to be unnaturally happy with the situation. This normally corresponds to a core temperature of around 35°C, compared to the normal 37°C, although the actual temperature varies from individual to individual and some people feel quite unwell at 36°C. Then, as cooling continues, the victim may begin to stumble or stagger and may go on to become aggressive or confused. This often correlates with a core temperature of around 33° to 34°C.

Eventually, at a core temperature of around 32°C, they will collapse and become unconscious, and they can go on cooling to stop breathing at around 27°C. However, their heart may not stop until core temperature is as low as 22°C, and so it is vital to remember that, however bad things seem, attempting rewarming and resuscitation may still work.

When someone first starts getting cold, act quickly by increasing clothing insulation, increasing activity or by seeking shelter. However, if choosing to shelter, remember that it may entail lying up in bad conditions and the loss of activity will cut heat production right down. This may have devastating results, and so the decision to go on or to seek emergency protection requires great judgement. Generally, I would recommend that if the victim is only just beginning to cool, push on if proper warm conditions are likely to be reached reasonably quickly. Hot drinks and food are also of great value, but will only be helpful while the victim is conscious and cooperative. Once again, however, remember that sitting around preparing them may have adverse effects.

If the victim is worse and is actually showing signs of staggering or confusion, the situation is becoming dangerous. Obviously additional clothing, hot drinks or seeking a course out of the wind remain of paramount importance, but the question of carrying on becomes more difficult since now it is probably better to stop if reasonable shelter is available. When going out in cold environments, you should always plan to carry some sort of windproof and waterproof bivouac protection—noting that, although tempting weight-wise, lightweight silvered survival blankets have been shown to be no more effective than a plastic sheet and definitely worse than a plastic or more rugged waterproof bag. You may, of course, be planning on camping anyway, in which case you need only ensure that your tent is adequate and that you have practised pitching it when the wind is up. It is no good finding out that it cannot be done with your model when you need it in emergency. Ideally, you should also be carrying a sleeping bag, even if you had no plans to get trapped outside, for there is no doubt that putting a victim in a good bag, and if necessary getting in it with them, is the best course of action if you are forced to stop.

Obviously, shelter can be sought as well as carried. In an emergency, it is a nice warm building that is best, but this is not normally an option. The priority then becomes getting out of the wind and wet, and any natural feature that you can get under or into the lee of is of great value. Also remember that effective shelter may often be found close in on the windward side of an object, particularly if it has a vertical side that will generate back pressure and a 'dead spot' immediately in front of it. Much to many people's surprise, the shelter there may even be better than to leeward since swirling vortices of snow do not come curling round and drifting over you. In conditions with decent snow cover, compacted snow or ice can be used to create a whole range of possible shelters, ranging from simple snowholes to multiple-roomed camps, but really you need to have been taught how to make them and be carrying a suitable snow shovel. Reading about building such shelters cannot replace experience, and before going out in really severe conditions one should have practised in safe conditions. Ideally, you should have attended a proper course on winter survival such as those run by the British Mountaineering Council in Scotland or North Wales.

If a victim has cooled so much that they are unconscious, they need medical attention urgently. However, while this is sought or awaited, every measure mentioned above should be made to protect them from further cooling. As a general rule, never give up trying to protect and warm them, even if they appear to be dead. People have been successfully resuscitated many hours after they have apparently stopped breathing, and you cannot rely upon being able to feel a pulse or hear their heart. It is said that hypothermia victims are 'not dead until they are warm and dead' and so, generally speaking, it is impossible to be sure while you are still out in the field.

I would reiterate that, with the correct preparation, you can operate safely and relatively comfortably in terrible conditions, but doing so is an art. That art needs to be learned and it is a mixture of education, preparation and forethought. Remember that hypothermia could happen to you or one or your party even in a temperate climate and indeed, it is more likely to happen in milder, wetter conditions than in the truly cold regions of the Earth.

I will finish with another extract that illustrates just how easy it is to be caught out by hypothermia and how simple it is to remedy the situation.

'As he approached, I wondered what was wrong. He was moving slowly and seemed to be fiddling with his clothing, trying to undo the zip on the front of his sodden jacket. He was smiling and certainly looked happier than he had done 15 minutes back but I noticed that he stumbled a couple of times despite it being pretty flat. He drew up beside me where I stood with my back to the gale.

"Jusht a moment," he said, and then after quite a pause, "I've jusht got to get thish jacket off."

His voice was slurred and I looked at him more closely. Although he smiled, there was a strange, wild expression on his face and his eyes were slightly glazed. He wasn't shivering any more but his skin was as white as marble and I noticed that he had taken his gloves off and they were nowhere to be seen. He was also swaying as he began to almost rip at his clothing, frustrated by his fruitless attempts to pull down the zip with cold fingers.

"Are you OK?" I asked, but I got no reply, only an inane black grin as he continued with his attempts to undress. The truth began to dawn on me.

"Come on," I said, grasping him by the arm and pulling him towards the edge of the ridge. "We'll go down here and drop out of the wind."

The effect was quite spectacular. As we entered the lee of the Cwm, the noise and buffeting that we had endured all day ceased and the world became an almost silent place. It seemed so much warmer that as I hurried downward, I began to sweat, but for my companion, who I almost dragged along beside me, the move into shelter brought a different experience. Although he, too, began to warm, it only brought him back towards the normal and, with it, he began to shiver and feel miserably cold.

I could scarcely believe what I had just witnessed. It was only September on Snowdon, yet my father had been to the edge of disaster....'

Remember, always treat the cold with respect and never underestimate what even the UK weather can produce. ❧

SURVIVING THE COLD: PART 2
by Dr Richard Dawood

COLONEL JIM ADAM, the military physiologist who was, until recently, responsible for maintaining 'combat-effectiveness' of British troops under all conditions, advises observing the following steps in the event of hypothermia:

1. Stop all activity.
2. Protect those at risk by rigging a makeshift shelter from the wind, rain and snow; lay the victim on the ground, on a ground sheet or space blanket.
3. Remove wet clothing, and insulate the victim in a sleeping bag.
4. Rewarm the victim with hot drinks, followed by hot food or high-energy snacks; unconscious victims need to be rewarmed by the body warmth of a companion.
5. Observe the victim for the cessation of breathing or pulse, and start mouth-to-mouth resuscitation or cardiac massage if necessary.
6. Send for help.
7. Insist on treating the victim as a stretcher case.

Acute hypothermia

This is a medical emergency, and is almost always the result of falling into water colder than 5°C. The victim shivers violently, inhales water, panics, may have respiratory or cardiac arrest, and is dead from drowning in about five to 15 minutes. Survival is more likely if the victim is wearing a life-jacket that keeps the face out of the water and is able to keep perfectly still. Careful first aid is essential.

Following rescue from the water, do not allow the victim to move or make any physical effort. Keep the victim horizontal or slightly head-down, protect against further heat loss and arrange transportation immediately to a hospital so that rapid rewarming may begin.

The most effective way of rewarming is a bath—at 42°C or as

hot as the bare elbow can tolerate. Until normal body temperature is restored, the victim is at high risk from sudden death, partly because rewarming may actually trigger an initial further drop in body temperature; many victims of accidents at sea die after they have been removed from the water—sometimes even in hospital.

Frostbite

Localised injuries from the cold can affect the limbs of exposed skin even when core body temperature is entirely normal. This happens when insulation is not adequate or on account of other factors, such as a restricted blood supply due to clothing that is too tight. Injuries of this kind range from frostbite following freezing of the tissues of the nose, checks, chin, ears, fingers and feet, to more common problems such as frost nips and chapping of the skin, especially of the lips, nose and hands, and often compounded by sunburn.

The best way to deal with frostbite is to take careful steps to prevent it. Ensure, particularly, that gloves, socks and footwear are suitable for the conditions and the task in hand, and do not choose extreme conditions to wear any of these items for the first time. Carry a face mask to protect yourself from high wind and driving snow and carry chemical hand-warmers that can be used when needed.

Impending frostbite is usually signalled by intense pain in the part at risk, this should not be ignored and prompt rewarming is necessary. For example, hands and fingers should be slipped under the clothes and warmed in the opposite armpit. If the pain is ignored it eventually disappears, the part then becomes numb, white and hard to touch—it is frozen.

Established frostbite is a serious problem that may need lengthy hospital treatment. Once thawing has taken place, tissue is liable to much more extensive damage from even slight chilling. During evacuation, keep the affected part clean and dry, and give painkillers and antibiotics (if available) to prevent infection.

Never rub frostbite with snow or anything else, because the tissues are extremely fragile and will suffer more damage.

Some dos and don'ts:

1. Don't drink. Alcohol causes peripheral vasoldilation—it increases bloodflow through the skin—which can dramatically increase heat loss in extreme temperatures.

2. Don't smoke. Nicotine can cause vasoconstriction—reduction in blood flow to hands, fingers and toes—increasing the likelihood of frostbite.

3. Do carry high-energy carbohydrate snacks, such as glucose sweets or Mars bars.

4. Do carry extra layers of clothing.

5. Do carry chemical hand-warming sachets to put inside gloves and shoes in extreme conditions.

6. If you are on an expedition, or are looking after a large group, carry a special low-reading thermometer to measure body temperature: normal clinical thermometers are not adequate for detecting hypothermia. You may also be well advised to carry instruments for measuring high wind speed and estimating wind chill.

7. Anything that reduces activity, such as being stranded on a chair lift or being injured, can result in a rapid fall in body temperature; if this happens to you, try to maintain some muscular activity to generate warmth.

8. Children are at special risk. In particular, they are likely to need extra head protection (mechanical as well as against heat loss). Frost nip and frostbite can affect later growth.

9. In cold conditions it is easy to underestimate the need to protect skin and eyes against excessive sunlight. Take extra care. ❧

SURVIVING THE SEA
by Sir Robin Knox-Johnston

THE HEALTH OF THE CREW is the skipper's responsibility and he or she should see that the food is nourishing and sufficient, that the boat is kept clean and that the crew practise basic hygiene. A good medical kit must be carried.

There is an excellent book (published by HMSO for the British Merchant Navy) called *The Ship Captain's Medical Guide*. It is written for a ship that does not carry a doctor and includes a recommended list of medical supplies. Most doctors will supply prescriptions for antibiotics when the purpose has been explained. Two other books to recommend are *The International Medical for Ships*, published by the World Health Organisation, and *First Aid at Sea*, by Douglas Justins and Colin Berry (Adlard Coles Nautical, London).

Safety on deck

Prevention is always better than cure. Everyone on board should know their way about the deck, and know what everything is for. A good way of training is to take the boat out night sailing so that the crew get to know instinctively where everything is and what to avoid. Train the crew to squat whenever the boat lurches—it lowers the centre of gravity and makes toppling overside less likely.

In rough weather, make sure that all the crew wear their lifejackets and safety harnesses when on deck, and that they clip their harness to a strong point. A good attitude on board is that crew should wear their lifejackets at night, when told to and when they want to. If the crew have to go out from the cockpit, they should clip the harness to a wire jackstay that runs all the way from right forward to the cockpit for this purpose.

Man overboard

If someone falls overside, immediately throw a life-buoy into the water and summon the whole crew on deck. The aim is to get back and pick them up as quickly as possible, so post a look-out to keep an eye on the casualty, and the rest of the crew should assist with turning the boat around. It is worthwhile putting the boat straight in the wind, as this stops you close to the casualty, then start the engine and motor back. On one occasion in the Southern Ocean, we lost a man overside, and we ran on more than a mile before we could get the spinnaker down. Because of the large swell, the only way we could locate him when we turned round was by heading for the sea birds that were circling him. We got him back, after about 20 minutes, by which time he was unable to assist himself because of the cold.

In the upper latitudes, there is a real danger of hypothermia, so it is vital to warm the person as quickly as possible. Strip off their wet clothing and towel them dry, then put them in a warm sleeping bag. The heat is retained better if the sleeping bag can be put into a large plastic bag. If the person is very cold, it may be necessary for someone else to strip and climb into the bag with the casualty and warm them with their own body.

If the casualty is conscious, feed them hot soup or tea. Remember that it can be a nerve-shattering experience for anyone and that they may need time to get over the shock. Do *not* give them alcohol.

Abandoning the boat

When, as a last resort, it becomes necessary to leave the boat, set off the EPIRB, and, if a transmitter is carried, send out a digital selective distress call on the appropriate frequency or by satellite communications. Inflate the life-raft and pull it alongside. Put one or two of the crew on board, and, if there is time, pass over as much food, water and clothing as possible, plus the EPIRB and SART. If the boat's dinghy is available, tie it to the life-raft, as it will give extra space and also help create a larger target for rescuers. Only leave the boat if there is absolutely no alternative. Life-rafts are small and not particularly robust, and it is always preferable to keep the boat afloat if humanly possible.

The usual reason for abandoning a boat is that it has been holed. One method of improving its survivability is to fit it with water-tight bulkheads so that its volume is roughly divided into three. The Marine and Coastguard Agency insists on water-tight sub-division on yachts that take paying crew, which means that if the boat is holed the chances are that it will lose only a proportion of its buoyancy and there will still be dry, safe shelter for the crew. From the comparative safety of one of the 'safe' parts of the boat, a plan can probably be made to fix the leak.

When it is necessary to abandon the boat, having got as much food and useful equipment aboard the life-raft as possible, cut the painter and get clear. Then take stock of what you have, and post a look-out.

Ration supplies from the start. The best way to do this is to avoid food for the first day, as the stomach shrinks and the body's demand for food falls. Ration water to about a quarter of a litre a day and issue it in sips. On no account should sea water be drunk, but it can be used for washing and cooling in hot weather. Humans can last for amazingly long periods without food, but they do need water. Any rain should be trapped and saved. The canopy of the life-raft can be used for this purpose, as could the dinghy, if it has been taken along. Do not eat raw fish unless there is a plentiful water supply, as they are very rich in protein and ruin the liver unless the surplus can be washed out of the system. As a general rule, one volume of protein will require two volumes of water. Where water is plentiful, fish should be hunted. Most pelagic (open-sea) fish are edible, and quite often they will swim around a boat or dinghy out of curiosity. Inedible fish are found close to land or on reefs.

Keep movement to a minimum to conserve energy and, in cold weather, hold on to urine as long as possible to retain its heat. In hot, sunny weather, try to keep everyone in the shade. Find some mental stimulus in order to maintain morale, and remember that the crew will be looking to the skipper to set an example, so remain positive. Humans have survived for well over three months on a life-raft, but only because they had a strong will to live and were able to improvise. My book, *Seamanship* (Hodder and Stoughton), may prove useful further reading. ❧

Chapter 5 : **Disease checklist** ❧

DISEASE CHECKLIST
by Drs Sharon Welby and Nick Beeching

THIS CHAPTER CONTAINS BRIEF OUTLINES of some, but no means all, of the exotic infectious problems that travellers might encounter. They are presented in alphabetical order rather than in order of their importance, and for some diseases we felt that the details provided in the *Vaccinations* section in Chapter 1 were sufficient. Those wishing to explore the diseases in more detail can consult textbooks of tropical medicine or infectious diseases in their local library.

More user-friendly sources of information include the websites of the Centers for Disease Control and the World Health Organisation (www.cdc.gov/ and www.who.org/) or Dr Richard Dawood's book *Travellers' Health: How to Stay Healthy Abroad*.

The risk of contracting many of these infections is extremely small, and few doctors working outside specialist referral centres will have detailed knowledge of most of them. See the *Relative Risks* table in the *Directory*, which is based on a large survey of Swiss travellers.

AMOEBIASIS: Some forms of amoeba acquired via food and water can cause a severe bloody diarrhoea, often without fever. Diagnosis is by stool microscopy, followed by antibiotic treatment (metronidazole or tinidazole). Rarely, and sometimes months after travel, amoebae can cause liver abscesses, characterised by pain below the ribs on the right hand side and high fever. Diagnosis requires an ultrasound scan of the liver and special blood tests, and the condition is easily treated with antibiotics. Amoebic liver abscesses can occur in people who never had symptoms of diarrhoea.

CHOLERA: See *Vaccinations*, in Chapter 1.

CUTANEOUS LARVA MIGRANS: This occurs in the tropics and subtropics and is particularly common in people visiting the Caribbean. The worm penetrates the unbroken bare skin and causes itchy meandering skin tracks which move approximately one centimetre a day and may last for months. The lesion is very itchy and occasionally blisters. This is easily treated with topical antihelminth cream or with tablets. The worm is a hookworm which usually infects cats or dogs. The eggs are passed in the animal faeces and contaminate the soil or sand, and infect people whose skin comes into direct contact with the contaminated sand. One couple who decided to bury themselves in the sand in Jamaica ended up with a dozen or more skin tracks each.

DENGUE FEVER: A mosquito-transmitted viral infection occurring in tropical and subtropical areas. Epidemic transmission is usually during, and shortly after, the rainy season. Dengue is mainly a disease of urban areas and rarely occurs above 4,000 feet. Outbreaks have occurred with increasing frequency over the last 15 years in most countries in the tropics. The risk is greatest in the Indian subcontinent, South-East Asia, southern China, Central and South America (except Chile, Paraguay, and Argentina), the Caribbean (except the Cayman Islands), Mexico and Africa.

There is no vaccine but the risk can be reduced by taking measures to reduce mosquito bites. The mosquito that transmits dengue fever is more active during the day than at night. Dengue fever used to be known as 'breakbone fever' and typically causes a sudden onset of high fever, severe headaches, joint and muscle pain, nausea and vomiting. The fever sometimes falls temporarily after a few days and then recurs. A fine pinpoint red rash appears after three to four days of fever. The illness may last up to ten days and recovery may take two to four weeks. Paracetamol rather than aspirin should be used to relieve symptoms. The more severe forms of dengue haemorrhagic fever or dengue shock syndrome are rare among travellers. Symptoms are initially the same but the illness progresses to faintness, shock and generalised bleeding. The shock syndrome and haemorrhagic syndrome can be treated effectively with fluid replacement in hospital and the mortality is reduced to less than 1 per cent. The diagnosis is made on antibody blood tests. If fever occurs more than three weeks after leaving an endemic area it is not due to dengue.

DIPHTHERIA: Diphtheria is a bacterial infection which causes a sore throat, occasionally a skin ulcer and produces a powerful toxin. Transmission is by inhalation of infective droplets from the cough of an infected person, or by direct skin contact with infective dust. The incubation period is two to five days followed by a throat infection, often with a thick white membrane which can swell and cause breathing difficulties. The bacteria then produce a powerful toxin which affects the heart and brain (causing heart failure and paralysis, respectively). Diphtheria has reached epidemic proportions in Russia and other parts of the former Soviet Union, with over 52,000 cases and 1,700 deaths reported in 1995. A study of blood donors in the UK showed that over a third did not have immunity to diphtheria, with a trend to decreasing immunity with increasing age. Treatment consists of penicillin and antitoxin, and an effective vaccine is available. (See *Vaccinations*, in Chapter 1.)

ENCEPHALITIS (VIRAL): Viral encephalitis is a mosquito-borne viral infection which can cause a range of illnesses, from a simple fever to swelling of the brain (encephalitis) causing unconsciousness or alteration in behaviour. For every person that develops the encephalitis, there are many who have unapparent infections or only a mild fever. There is no specific treatment for viral encephalitis. The risk can be reduced by avoiding mosquito bites. Three other forms of this disease are listed below.

ENCEPHALITIS (JAPANESE): This is widespread in Asia and the Western Pacific. Many infections are unapparent, but in about 0.2 per cent of cases the infection is severe, reaching a mortality rate in elderly people of over 50 per cent. Among people who are bitten by an infected mosquito, only one in 50 to one in 1,000 people will develop the illness. The majority of people either develop no illness or a mild illness. However, among those who develop encephalitis, the consequences may be grave. The incubation period is four to 14 days followed by sudden onset of fever, and within 24 hours there are signs of acute neck rigidity, drowsiness and convulsions. After three days, coma can result; if the acute stage is survived, then recovery is slow. There is a high mortality rate of 25 per cent, and 30 per cent of those that recover have residual paralysis or brain problems. The risk to the average tourist is low—the American

Centers for Disease Control estimate the risk of this disease as less than one per million travellers annually. However, the risk is higher if travelling in the rainy season in rural areas where there is co-existing rice and pig farming, and is proportional to the length of time spent in a high risk area. There is a vaccine for Japanese encephalitis (See *Vaccinations*, in Chapter 1).

ENCEPHALITIS (ST LOUIS): This is the most important mosquito-borne virus in the USA. We receive many telephone calls from concerned tourists to Florida following periodic public health alerts about this infection, which occurs there intermittently. Most infections are unapparent in a ratio of 100 to 1. The incubation period is a few days and symptoms are usually a fever lasting a few days followed by complete recovery. In a few cases, usually the elderly, encephalitis can develop. Patients usually recover quickly and with no complications.

ENCEPHALITIS (TICK-BORNE): This viral infection occurs in the forested areas of Austria, Germany, Scandinavia, Eastern Europe and Western states of the former USSR. The incubation period is 8 to 14 days. The onset of symptoms is generally sudden and consists of fever, severe headache, nausea and photophobia (intolerance of light). The infection is often unapparent, but when overt is severe (3 per cent mortality). The risk of tick bites can be reduced in endemic areas by using insect repellents, tucking trousers into socks and inspecting your skin for ticks. If a tick is detected it should be removed as soon as possible using tweezers to pull the tick gently away from the skin intact. (See *Vaccinations*, in Chapter 1.)

FILARIASIS (BANCROFTIAN): This parasite is transmitted by the bite of an infected mosquito and occurs in Central and South America, Africa, the Indian subcontinent and Asia. It is a rare disease in travellers. The adult worms live in the lymph vessels and produce microscopic larvae (called microfilariae) which can be found periodically in the blood. Symptoms include attacks of hot swollen glands, and men may get a hydrocoel (swollen testicle). Chronic infection over a long period of time can lead to swollen limbs (elephantiasis). There is no vaccine, but the small risk of disease can be reduced by using effective insect repellents.

GIARDIASIS: Giardia is a protozoan parasite that is common everywhere, acquired through contaminated food and water. It typically causes offensive (and explosive) diarrhoea after an incubation period of at least two to three weeks. It is a common cause of prolonged diarrhoea, sometimes with marked weight loss, in travellers to the tropics. It can be diagnosed by stool examination and is treated with metronidazole or tinidazole.

HEPATITIS: 'Hepatitis' means inflammation of the liver, and may be caused by a variety of viruses that attack the liver (hepatitis A, B, C etc.), alcohol, prescribed drugs, and many other infections such as glandular fever, dengue and malaria. The symptoms are similar whatever the cause, with jaundice (yellow discolouration of the whites of the eyes, and later the skin), dark urine, pale bowel motions, feeling generally unwell and mild fever. Early symptoms in some people include severe bone and joint pains.

The precise cause of hepatitis can only be diagnosed by a variety of specific blood tests. Hepatitis A and E are both viruses that are transmitted in food and water in the tropics, with incubation periods of about two to six weeks. Neither causes any lasting liver damage once the acute illness is over. Hepatitis B is transmitted by sex, needles, transfusion etc. (see section on *Sex Abroad* in Chapter 3). Hepatitis C is mainly transmitted by blood products and needles. Both hepatitis B and C can cause continued liver problems.

Patients with hepatitis will be ill for at least several weeks, and it can take months for full recovery even after an 'uncomplicated' attack. A very small proportion can develop severe liver failure, the danger signs being progressive severe drowsiness (and coma), bleeding from the gums or spontaneous bruising of the skin. The risk of such rare problems rises with age. There is no specific treatment, but patients with hepatitis should always seek specific medical advice and should not drink any alcohol while jaundice persists. Both hepatitis A and B can be prevented by vaccination. (See *Vaccinations*, in Chapter 1.)

JIGGERS: These are fleas which are free-living and occur in South America, Africa, and India. The flea attacks man, pigs, poultry and other animals. Adult females burrow into the skin especially around the nails of the toes but any part of the body can be affected. Once in the skin, the flea swells to the size and shape of a small white pea. Only when the jigger is mature and distended with eggs will it start to irritate, approximately eight to 12 days after infection, when severe inflammation and ulceration occur so that the eggs are expelled. Eggs are discharged into the soil to form larvae and continue the life cycle. Secondary infection of the small ulcers is the chief danger. Fleas should be removed with a needle and delivered whole. To avoid the infection it is best to wear shoes at all times. We regularly see travellers after overland trips who need to have lesions dug out under sterile conditions. It is common for these lesions to get infected, and courses of antibiotics are routinely prescribed after the flea has been removed.

LEISHMANIASIS: This is caused by a parasite which is transmitted by the bite of sandflies. The disease occurs in Central and South America, the Caribbean, Africa, the Indian subcontinent, southern Europe and the USSR. Symptoms include skin sores (cutaneous leishmaniasis), prolonged fever, weakness and a swollen spleen (kalar azar). No vaccine is available but measures to prevent insect bites will reduce the risk of exposure to the parasite. Treatment is available.

LEPTOSPIROSIS: This infection is caused by a bacteria that infects rats, cows and other animals which then pass the bacteria out in their urine, contaminating fresh water. Risk areas for travellers include countries of South and Central America and Asia. Travellers are infected by contact with water, particularly when canoeing, white-water rafting and wind-surfing, or when wading through rice-paddies on military manoeuvres. Agriculturists and farmers are also at risk, and the infection is widespread in temperate countries as well as in the tropics. Symptoms vary, from mild fever with tender muscles, to severe jaundice and liver failure, or occasionally a form of meningitis. Diagnosis requires specialist expertise, and treatment with antibiotics is required. Severe cases require intensive care facilities for their management. There is no vaccine, and prevention with antibiotics is only used in specific epidemic, military or disaster situations.

LYME DISEASE: The majority of cases of Lyme disease have been reported in the north-eastern United States during the summer months, but cases have also been reported in the UK, Europe, Australia, Asia and Northern Africa. This is a bacterial infection (*Borrelia burgdorferi*) which is spread by the bite of an infected hard tick. The ticks are usually found in forests and bush areas. The bites often go unnoticed because of the small size of the tick (about the size of a pinhead). The incubation period is from three to 30 days and a range of symptoms can occur, some unapparent, others severe. A characteristic rash often occurs at the site of the lesion (*erythema chronicum migrans*) and may be associated with headache, muscle and joint aches, and a slight fever. Treatment is with antibiotics. Left untreated, neurological, joint and cardiac complications may occur. These also respond to a more intensive course of antibiotics. There is no vaccine available but the risk of disease can be reduced in high risk areas by using insect repellents, tucking trousers into socks and inspecting skin for ticks. If a tick is detected it should be removed as soon as possible using tweezers to pull the tick away intact from the skin.

MALARIA: See *Malaria* section in Chapter 3.

MENINGITIS: 'Meningitis' means inflammation of the lining of the brain and spinal cord, and can be caused by viruses and bacteria. Bacterial meningitis is a severe, life-threatening illness, characterised by the rapid onset of nausea, vomiting, fever, severe headache and, with some forms, a progressive purplish rash. The affected patient cannot bear to open their eyes in the light, and will look very ill and have a stiff neck. Untreated, the illness is often fatal, so urgent medical attention and treatment with antibiotics is required. One bacterial cause of meningitis—'meningococcal meningitis'—is common in certain parts of sub-Saharan Africa and the northern Indian subcontinent. Specific pre-travel advice should be sought if travelling to these regions. There is a vaccine to prevent some strains of meningococcal meningitis. (See *Vaccinations*, in Chapter 1.)

MYIASIS: Myiasis is a condition which looks superficially like a boil, but the boil moves and on close inspection two black eyes are looking back at you. The lesion is painful and is due to the larva of the Tumbu fly which is present in Africa. The Tumbu fly lays its eggs on washing that has been put out to dry in the shade. When the contaminated clothing is put on, the larva invades the skin and causes boil-like lesions. Eventually, when the larva has matured after eight to 12 days, it emerges and falls to the ground where it pupates and the adult fly hatches out. Rodents and dogs are the usual host. The best way to get the larva out is to suffocate it with an oily substance such as petroleum jelly; an alternative is to suffocate the larva with bacon strips— both methods have aesthetic drawbacks, but are preferable to 'digging' operations suggested by some hardier male patients. The infection can be prevented by ironing clothes (this kills the eggs): a friend once commented that the only time she ironed her underwear was when she lived in Africa.

The bot fly causes a similar condition in Central and South America. The eggs hitch a ride on the feet of flies and mosquitoes. When the mosquito takes a bite it leaves behind the egg packets, and the larvae burrow into the skin or eye. This causes a painful inflammatory swelling of 2 to 3 centimetres. The duration of larva development is about 6 to 12 weeks. The lesions are found more commonly on the head but can occur elsewhere, and the flies can penetrate clothing. Most larvae have to be removed surgically.

PLAGUE: This occurs in South-East Asia, South America, central Africa and western North America. It is a bacterial infection transmitted by the bite of an infected flea, or through exposure to plague-infected animals or their tissues, and through person-to-person spread. Classical plague symptoms include very painful swollen hot glands (bubos), fever and extreme exhaustion. Antibiotic treatment is effective. There is a vaccine against the bubonic type of plague but it is not widely available.

POLIO: This viral infection ranges in severity from unapparent infection to fever, gut symptoms, meningitis or paralysis. There are three types of polio virus, each of which can cause clinical infection. The disease is spread from person to person either directly in mucus from the nose or throat, or under poor hygienic conditions when food and drink is contaminated by faeces. The incubation period is 3 to 21 days. The symptoms occur in two phases: an initial non-specific illness of fever, headache, muscle pains, gastro-intestinal disturbance, malaise and sometimes stiffness of the neck; followed in some cases after a short interval by the return of muscle pains and the development of paralysis. The paralysis may be limited to a single limb or may spread to involve much of the body. Occasionally death may occur from paralysis of the respiratory muscles. This disease is still a problem in many parts of the tropics but can be prevented by vaccination. (See *Vaccinations*, in Chapter 1.)

RABIES: See *Vaccinations* p. 28 and *Rabies* in Chapter 3.

TETANUS: This infection is caused by bacteria which produce a toxin that damages the muscle and nervous system. The bacteria live in the guts of humans and animals where they do not cause disease, but excrete spores in the faeces which then contaminate the environment. The spores are widely distributed in dust and soil (especially if treated with manure), and can also contaminate unsterilised medical instruments. The disease is spread by contamination of wounds, burns and even trivial puncture injuries with these spores. The incubation period is from four to 21 days. The symptoms usually start with spasm of the jaw known as 'lockjaw' and progress to muscle rigidity and spasms. Death can occur during a spasm. Those that recover have a long and painful convalescence. (See *Vaccinations* p. 29.)

TRYPANOSOMIASIS: Two versions of this disease are listed below.

AFRICAN TRYPANOSOMIASIS (SLEEPING SICKNESS): African trypanosomiasis occurs in west, central and east Africa. This parasite is transmitted by the bite of an infected tsetse fly. Symptoms include a swelling at the site of the bite, followed by fever, headaches and severe illness. In west Africa, the initial infection is usually symptomless, with sleeping sickness developing after a few years and manifesting itself in daytime sleepiness and behavioural and mood changes. Travellers are rarely infected, the main risk is during safari, and the risk can be reduced by using insect repellents. No vaccine is available.

AMERICAN TRYPANOSOMIASIS (CHAGAS' DISEASE): This disease is transmitted by blood-sucking bugs (known as reduviid bug, cone-nosed or kissing bugs) or by blood transfusions, and occurs in Central and South America. These bugs live in the mud walls and thatched roofs of buildings and feed at night. The initial infection can be unapparent, or may produce swelling around the eye or lumps under the skin, followed by a fever and swollen glands a few weeks later. If people are not treated, the disease can progress after many years to cause heart disease and gut problems. Infection can be avoided by not staying overnight in buildings possibly contaminated with the bugs and, if possible, by avoiding blood transfusions in endemic countries. There is no vaccine and treatment is limited.

TUBERCULOSIS: Tuberculosis (TB) affects millions of people in the tropics and is on the increase again worldwide, particularly in HIV-positive individuals. TB affects people in many ways, but the usual illness is a progressive pneumonia, characterised by a long-lasting cough-producing sputum (sometimes blood-stained), fever, wasting and ultimately death if untreated. It was once known as 'consumption'. The disease is passed on by breathing in bacteria which have been suspended in the air by infected people coughing. Exposure to such patients in crowded, poverty-associated conditions carries a high risk. Drinking unpasteurised cow's milk is risky in the tropics, as it may harbour the bacteria. TB is not a major risk for most travellers, but health-care workers and others working in refugee situations, for example, are at some risk. Diagnosis requires medical expertise, chest X-rays and special sputum tests, followed by prolonged supervised treatment with a combination of specific antibiotics. Most British people are vaccinated at entry to secondary school (the BCG jab) but this is not an established practice in some countries, notably the USA, because the vaccine is only partially protective. (See *Vaccinations*, in Chapter 1.)

TYPHOID ('**ENTERIC FEVER**'): Typhoid and paratyphoid are similar illnesses, caused by certain salmonella bacteria that are transmitted in contaminated food and water. The infection is found worldwide, wherever water supplies are inadequate, but the most important risk area for the traveller is the Indian subcontinent and the Far East. The illness starts with non-specific, sustained fever that gets worse over a week, and is accompanied by headache, extreme lethargy and sometimes confusion. Some patients develop a pinpoint skin rash after the first week of illness, and patients may have diarrhoea or, later, constipation. Untreated, the illness lasts about three weeks and about 10 per cent of people have severe complications, especially bowel perforation. It is diagnosed by culture of blood samples, and is easily treated with appropriate antibiotics. Unfortunately, most typhoid acquired in the Indian subcontinent and in Asia is resistant to the older antibiotics, but it still responds to quinolone antibiotics such as ciprofloxacin and ofloxacin. Typhoid is preventable by immunisations and care with food and water. (See *Vaccinations*, in Chapter 1.)

TYPHUS: True typhus is very rare and presents little danger for most travellers. It is caused by small organisms known as rickettsiae which are similar to bacteria. There are many other types of typhus transmitted by different vectors (such as ticks, body lice, mites and rat fleas). The symptoms consist of fever, severe headache and skin rash, and sometimes a black scab (eschar) occurs at the site of the tick bite. The severity of illness varies between the different types of typhus. The treatment involves antibiotics and there is no vaccine available.

TYPHUS (TICK AND SCRUB): Tick typhus occurs in Africa, America, Asia and the Pacific islands; Scrub typhus occurs in Asia and the Pacific islands. Tick typhus presents a significant hazard to travellers on safari in many parts of Africa. Scrub typhus can be a severe infection, and travellers may be infected by the bite of mites which live in areas of 'scrub' vegetation, also known as areas of 'transitional' or 'secondary' vegetation. The risk of tick and mite bites can be reduced in endemic areas by using insect repellents, tucking trousers into socks and inspecting skin for ticks. If a tick is detected, it should be removed as soon as possible using tweezers to pull the tick away intact from the skin.

VIRAL HAEMORRHAGIC FEVERS (LASSA FEVER, RIFT VALLEY FEVER, EBOLA AND MARBURG DISEASE): These diseases occur in Africa, and are caused by viruses transmitted from an infected person or animal to another person, by mosquitoes or food contaminated with rat's urine. Congo-Crimean haemorrhagic fever is more widespread in Asia and the Middle East as well as in Africa. Locality-specific infections such as Bolivian and Argentinian haemorrhagic fevers affect farm workers in parts of South America. These diseases are not a significant health problem to most travellers unless they are healthcare workers or travelling rough in very rural areas, but they can cause severe illness. Treatment is limited and no vaccines are available.

WORMS: Worm infections occur world-wide but they are more common when living under poor hygienic conditions. Human faeces containing larger worm eggs contaminate the soil, food and water; another person swallows the contaminated food or water and an adult worm develops. Usually there are no symptoms and the eggs are discovered during screening tests of stool specimens, or occasionally they just surprise people and wiggle their way out of the rectum. Recently, we saw a medical student who was unimpressed by passing a large roundworm a year after working in Sri Lanka and India. In some worm life-cycles (such as hookworms), the eggs hatch in soil to produce free-living larvae that burrow through the skin to initiate new human infections. It follows that people who go barefoot are more likely to get infected, so shoes are strongly advised! Most worms are easily treated with tablets. Some worm larvae go on a safari through the body shortly after hatching in the gut, and can cause respiratory symptoms of wheezing and shortness of breath. This usually settles after a few weeks and there is no specific treatment.

YELLOW FEVER: This is a viral infection transmitted by the bite of infected mosquitoes. The disease occurs in central and west Africa, parts of South America and Panama. The incubation period is three to seven days, and the illness ranges in severity from mild symptoms to death. The mortality rate can be as much as 50 per cent. The initial symptoms are fever, vomiting and prostration, which may progress to liver failure with jaundice and haemorrhage. There is a very effective vaccination. Recently the risks of travelling without this vaccination have been highlighted by the unnecessary deaths of several travellers to West African countries or to Brazil. (See *Vaccinations*, in Chapter 1.) ❧

Chapter 6 : **Directory** ❧

COUNTRY-BY-COUNTRY HEALTH PROFILES

A checklist of health and geographical data on every country in the world.

Key to the profiles

CAPITAL is the capital city of that country.

LANG lists the official (and other) languages spoken.

GMT states the time difference relative to Greenwich Mean Time.

POP lists the population figures.

DENSITY measures the number of people per square kilometre.

LIFE EXP is the life expectancy, usually for males (M) then females (F).

SAFETY summarises political, crime and other safety factors, and is correct at time of going to press. Travellers are advised to seek up-to-date information at the time of their trip.

MED CARE analyses the quality and availability of free medical care. Travellers are advised to carry their own medical insurance, regardless of local conditions.

Afghanistan *CAPITAL* Kabul *LANG* Pashtu and Dari, some English spoken *GMT* + 4.5 *POP* 23,400,000 *DENSITY* 36 *LIFE EXP* M 45 F 46 *SAFETY* Dangerous and politically unstable. Strict Muslim regime, therefore women should not travel alone and should be totally covered. Outside Kabul in tribal areas there is very little protection *MED CARE* Very limited and up-front cash payments necessary, medical insurance strongly recommended.

Albania *CAPITAL* Tirana *LANG* Albanian but Greek also spoken *GMT* + 1 (+2 in summer) *POP* 3,400,000 *DENSITY* 124 *LIFE EXP* M 69.9 F 75.9 *SAFETY* Armed guerrilla gangs still operating in the south of the country, Tirana is calmer *MED CARE* Medical treatment to be paid for, except infectious diseases, medical insurance recommended.

Algeria *CAPITAL* Algiers (El Djezair) *LANG* Arabic and French *GMT* + 1 *POP* 27,900,000 *DENSITY* 13 *LIFE EXP* M 67.5 F 70.3 *SAFETY* High risk area, in the last three years there have been many attacks on westerners and thousands of political murders. Curfew between 23.30 and 04.00 *MED CARE* Basic in rural areas and medical insurance strongly recommended.

American Samoa (US) *CAPITAL* Pago Pago *LANG* Samoan and English *GMT* −11 *POP* 60,000 *DENSITY* 305 *LIFE EXP* M 69.3 F 73.6 *SAFETY* Safe *MED CARE* Good, but insurance recommended.

Andorra *CAPITAL* Andorra La Vella *LANG* Officially Catalan, but French and Spanish also used *GMT* +1 *POP* 65,227 (+2 in summer) *DENSITY* 139 *LIFE EXP* M 74 F 81 *SAFETY* Safe *MED CARE* Good - and covered by mutual agreements with UK.

Angola *CAPITAL* Luanda *LANG* Officially Portuguese and Bantu languages *GMT* +1 *POP* 12,000,000 *DENSITY* 10 *LIFE EXP* M 44.9 F 48.1 *SAFETY* Low-level conflict situation, many landmines, travel not recommended *MED CARE* Free but generally inadequate, medical insurance recommended for evacuation.

Anguilla (UK) *CAPITAL* The Valley *LANG* English *GMT* −4 *POP* 10,300 *DENSITY* 93.3 *LIFE EXP* M 71 F 77 *SAFETY* Safe *MED CARE* One hospital on island, free treatment for minor ailments but insurance recommended.

Antigua and Barbuda *CAPITAL* St John's *LANG* English *GMT* −4.5 *POP* 66,000 *DENSITY* 150 *LIFE EXP* 74 *SAFETY* Safe *MED CARE* One private and one public hospital, insurance recommended.

Argentina *CAPITAL* Buenos Aires *LANG* Spanish *GMT* −3 *POP* 36,100,000 *DENSITY* 13 *LIFE EXP* M 69.6 F 76.8 *SAFETY* Beware of pickpockets and petty criminals, register with British Embassy *MED CARE* Good, but no health agreements with UK so insurance recommended.

Armenia (C.I.S.) *CAPITAL* Yerevan *LANG* Armenian and Russian *GMT* +4 *POP* 3,600,000 *DENSITY* 121 *LIFE EXP* M 67.2 F 73.6 *SAFETY* Political and religious unrest, tourists are strongly advised not to go to any Trans-Causican republic, and to register with relevant embassy in Yerevan *MED CARE* Arrangement for urgent medical treatment exists for those with proof of UK citizenship but standards are low and insurance is recommended.

Aruba (The Netherlands) *CAPITAL* Oranjestad *LANG* Dutch but English and Spanish are also spoken *GMT* –4 *POP* 88,000 *DENSITY* 465 *LIFE EXP* M 71.1 F 77.1 *SAFETY* Safe *MED CARE* Good facilities at the one hospital on the island but insurance recommended.

Australia *CAPITAL* Canberra *LANG* English *GMT* +8 to +10 *POP* 18,500,000 *DENSITY* 2.3 *LIFE EXP* M 75.5 F 81.1 *SAFETY* Relatively safe *MED CARE* Free hospital treatment for UK citizens in emergencies only, insurance recommended.

Austria *CAPITAL* Vienna *LANG* German *GMT* +1 *POP* 8,200,000 *DENSITY* 99 *LIFE EXP* M 73.7 F 80.2 *SAFETY* Safe *MED CARE* Free treatment for UK citizens in emergency with nominal fee, a refund may be available for treatment in private hospitals.

Azerbaijan (C.I.S) *CAPITAL* Baku *LANG* Azerbaijani *GMT* + 5 *POP* 7,700,000 *DENSITY* 89 *LIFE EXP* M 65.5 F 74.1 *SAFETY* Although cease-fire in place since May 1994, the western area of the country is still volatile. Street crime increasing in all cities *MED CARE* Limited but free emergency treatment for a limited period only, insurance recommended.

Bahamas *CAPITAL* Nassau *LANG* English *GMT* –5 (-4 in summer) *POP* 293,000 *DENSITY* 29 *LIFE EXP* M 70.5 F 77.1 *SAFETY* Safe *MED CARE* Four hospitals where medical costs are high, insurance recommended.

Bahrain *CAPITAL* Manama *LANG* Arabic and English *GMT* +3 *POP* 594,000 *DENSITY* 874 *LIFE EXP* M 71.1 F 75.3 *SAFETY* Safe *MED CARE* Good and free emergency medical treatment.

Bangladesh *CAPITAL* Dhaka *LANG* Bengali and English *GMT* +6 *POP* 124,000,000 *DENSITY* 926 *LIFE EXP* M 58.1 F 58.2 *SAFETY* Safe if sensible, women should keep covered *MED CARE* Limited and basic, insurance strongly recommended.

Barbados *CAPITAL* Bridgetown *LANG* English *GMT* –4 (–5 in summer) *POP* 263000 *DENSITY* 61.2 *LIFE EXP* M 73.7 F 78.7 *SAFETY* Don't carry any valuables, mugging on the increase *MED CARE* UK citizens entitled to free hospital treatment but medicines for anyone other than children and the elderly must be paid for.

Belarus *CAPITAL* Minsk *LANG* Belarussian *GMT* +2 *POP* 10,300,000 *DENSITY* 50 *LIFE EXP* M 62.2 F 73.9 *SAFETY* Seek local advice *MED CARE* Free hospital treatment for UK citizens but medicines may be unobtainable, insurance recommended.

Belgium *CAPITAL* Brussels *LANG* Flemish and French *GMT* +1 *POP* 10,200,000 *DENSITY* 331 *LIFE EXP* M 73.8 F 80.6 *SAFETY* Safe *MED CARE* UK citizens with E111 certificate entitled to a 75 per cent refund on medical costs.

Belize *CAPITAL* Belmopan *LANG* English *GMT* –6 *POP* 200,000 *DENSITY* 9 *LIFE EXP* M 73.4 F 76.1 *SAFETY* Mugging and theft occur, but not as bad as South America *MED CARE* Cash payments will generally be demanded for all treatment, insurance strongly recommended.

Benin *CAPITAL* Porto Novo *LANG* French and indigenous tribal languages *GMT* +1 *POP* 5,900,000 *DENSITY* 53 *LIFE EXP* M 51.7 F 55.2 *SAFETY* Poorly lit roads make night travel hazardous. Armed robbery and muggings are on the increase *MED CARE* Very limited and cash payments expected, insurance strongly recommended.

Bermuda *CAPITAL* Hamilton *LANG* English *GMT* –4 *POP* 60,144 *DENSITY* 1,135 *LIFE EXP* M 71.1 F 77.8 *SAFETY* Safe *MED CARE* Good, but medical costs are high, insurance strongly recommended.

Bhutan *CAPITAL* Thimphu *LANG* Dzongkha *GMT* +6 *POP* 1,900,000 *DENSITY* 40 *LIFE EXP* M 59.5 F 62 *SAFETY* Safe *MED CARE* basic, insurance strongly recommended.

Bolivia *CAPITAL* La Paz *LANG* Spanish *GMT* –4 *POP* 8,000,000 *DENSITY* 7 *LIFE EXP* M 59.8 F 63.2 *SAFETY* Care should be taken, theft can be rife. The cocaine-growing areas should be avoided *MED CARE* Basic in public hospitals, insurance strongly recommended.

Bonaire (Netherland Antilles) *CAPITAL* Kralendjik *LANG* Dutch *GMT* –4 *POP* 10,187 *DENSITY* 35 *LIFE EXP* M 72.5 F 78.4 *SAFETY* Safe *MED CARE* Minor cases dealt with on the island and there is an air ambulance service to Curaçao for more serious problems, insurance recommended.

Bosnia-Herzegovina *CAPITAL* Sarajevo *LANG* Serb-Croat and Croat-Serb *GMT* +1 *POP* 4,000,000 *DENSITY* 78 *SAFETY* Extremely dangerous: despite peace agreement, land mines and violence still a hazard *MED CARE* Very limited, insurance with repatriation cover recommended.

Botswana *CAPITAL* Gaborone *LANG* English and Setswana *GMT* +2 *POP* 1,600,000 *DENSITY* 3 *LIFE EXP* M 46.2 F 48.4 *SAFETY* Safe *MED CARE* There is a nominal fee for hospital care and medicines supplied by government hospitals are free, but outside towns health facilities are basic and insurance is recommended.

Brazil *CAPITAL* Brasilia *LANG* Portuguese *GMT* from −3 to −5 *POP* 165,200,000 *DENSITY* 20 *LIFE EXP* M 63.1 F 71 *SAFETY* As with all countries in South America, beware of petty crime *MED CARE* No health agreements with UK and medical costs are high, insurance strongly recommended.

Brunei *CAPITAL* Bandar Seri Begawan *LANG* Malay and English *GMT* +8 *POP* 313,000 *DENSITY* 59 *LIFE EXP* M 73.4 F 78.1 *SAFETY* Safe *MED CARE* Good, but repatriation may be necessary for certain treatments so insurance is recommended.

Bulgaria *CAPITAL* Sofia *LANG* Bulgarian *GMT* +2 *POP* 8,427,418 *DENSITY* 76.2 *LIFE EXP* M 67.6 F 74.7 *SAFETY* Beware of bad driving habits *MED CARE* Free health care for UK citizens, some specialised treatments may not be available.

Burkina Faso *CAPITAL* Ouagadougou *LANG* French and several indigenous *GMT*: GMT *POP* 11,400,000 *DENSITY* 42 *LIFE EXP* M 43.3 F 45.2 *SAFETY* Towns can be violent after dark; avoid unnecessary travel in rural areas *MED CARE* Limited; buy basic remedies before entering the country. Insurance strongly recommended including air evacuation cover.

Burundi *CAPITAL* Bujumbura *LANG* French and Kirundi *GMT* +2 *POP* 6,600,000 *DENSITY* 257 *LIFE EXP* M 41 F 43.8 *SAFETY* Very unsafe due to ongoing civil war *MED CARE* Limited and payment will be demanded, insurance strongly recommended.

Cambodia *CAPITAL* Phnom Penh *LANG* Khmer – Chinese and Vietnamese also spoken *GMT* +7 *POP* 10,800,000 *DENSITY* 61

LIFE EXP M 51.5 F 55 *SAFETY* Currently calm after decades of guerrilla war, but drug-producing areas still hazardous for foreigners. Possibly the highest incidence of landmines and unexploded ordnance in the world, makes travel off the beaten track very dangerous *MED CARE* Limited and immediate cash payments demanded, insurance strongly recommended.

Cameroon *CAPITAL* Yaounde *LANG* French and English *GMT* +1 *POP* 14,300,000 *DENSITY* 31 *LIFE EXP* M 53.4655 *SAFETY* Douala can be dangerous after dark *MED CARE* Basic outside cities, insurance recommended.

Canada *CAPITAL* Ottawa *LANG* French and English *GMT* from −3.5 to −8 *POP* 30,200,000 *DENSITY* 3 *LIFE EXP* M 76.1 F 81.8 *SAFETY* Safe *MED CARE* Good but expensive, insurance recommended.

Cape Verde *CAPITAL* Ciudade de Praia *LANG* Portuguese *GMT* −1 *POP* 417,000 *DENSITY* 103 *LIFE EXP* M 65.5 F 71.3 *SAFETY* safe *MED CARE* Limited and expensive, insurance advised.

Cayman Islands (UK) *CAPITAL* George Town *LANG* English *GMT* −5 *POP* 35,000 *DENSITY* 135 *SAFETY* Safe *MED CARE* Good but insurance recommended.

Central African Republic *CAPITAL* Bangui *LANG* French and Sango *GMT* +1 *POP* 3,500,000 *DENSITY* 6 *LIFE EXP* M 42.9 F 46.9 *SAFETY* Potentially volatile, including banditry on country roads. Represented only by honorary British Consulate, contact French or German Embassies in emergencies *MED CARE* Limited, take own basic medical supplies and full insurance.

Chad *CAPITAL* Ndjamena *LANG* French, Arabic and 50 indigenous languages. *GMT* +1 *POP* 6,900,000 *DENSITY* 5 M 45.7 F 48.7 *SAFETY* Dangerous, contact High Commission in Abuja *MED CARE* Very limited, take own supply of basic medicines and full insurance cover.

Chile *CAPITAL* Santiago *LANG* Spanish *GMT* −5 *POP* 14,800,000 *DENSITY* 20 *LIFE EXP* M 72.3 F 78.3 *SAFETY* Safe *MED CARE* Good, but insurance necessary.

China *CAPITAL* Beijing *LANG* Mandarin Chinese *GMT* +8 *POP* 1,230,838,000 *DENSITY* 135 *LIFE EXP* M 67.9 F 72 *SAFETY* Safe

MED CARE Good but some medicines may be unavailable, insurance recommended. See also Hong Kong and Macau, below.

Hong Kong *CAPITAL* Beijing *LANG* Chinese and English *GMT* +8 *POP* 6,801000 *DENSITY* 5790 *LIFE EXP* M 75.8 F 81. *SAFETY* Safe *MED CARE* Very good, but insurance strongly recommended.

Macau *CAPITAL* Beijing *LANG* Portuguese and Chinese *GMT* +8 *POP* 466, *DENSITY* 20,482 *LIFE EXP* M 75.1 F 80.1 *SAFETY* Safe *MED CARE* Good, but insurance recommended.

Colombia *CAPITAL* Santa Fe de Bogotá *LANG* Spanish *GMT* –5 *POP* 37,700,000 *DENSITY* 36 *LIFE EXP* M 67.3 F 74.3 *SAFETY* Violence and kidnapping remain a serious problem. Do not accept food, sweets or drinks from strangers, they may be drugged. Large areas of the country subject to low-level conflict or banditry *MED CARE* Limited outside cities.

Comoros *CAPITAL* Moroni *LANG* French and Arabic *GMT* +3 *POP* 672,000 *DENSITY* 301 *LIFE EXP* M 57.4 F 60.02 *SAFETY* Safe *MED CARE* Full insurance recommended.

Congo (Brazzaville) *CAPITAL* Brazzaville *LANG* French *GMT* +1 *POP* 2,800,000 *DENSITY* 8 *LIFE EXP* M 48.3 F 50.8 *SAFETY* Currently calm following coup, but politically volatile at any time. *MED CARE* Limited, insurance strongly recommended. See also Democractic Republic of Congo, below.

Congo (Democratic Republic of Congo, formerly Zaire) *CAPITAL* Kinshasa *LANG* Officially French, many African languages used *GMT* +1 and +2 depending on region *POP* 49,200,000 *DENSITY* 22 *LIFE EXP* M 49.2 F 52.3 *SAFETY* Highly unstable, politically and militarily, currently involved in a wide-ranging civil war. Large areas have no access to law enforcement or communications of any kind *MED CARE* Very limited and there is a shortage of supplies, insurance with repatriation cover recommended.

Cook Islands (New Zealand) *CAPITAL* Avarua *LANG* Maori, English also spoken *GMT* –10.5 *POP* 20,200 *DENSITY* 85 *LIFE EXP* M 70 F 73 *SAFETY* Safe *MED CARE* Good, but check with tourist office to see if free medical care agreement between UK and NZ applies here.

Costa Rica *CAPITAL* San Jose *LANG* Spanish *GMT* −6 *POP* 3,700,000 *DENSITY* 72 *LIFE EXP* M 74.3 F 78.9 *SAFETY* Beware of tides while swimming *MED CARE* Good and free hospital treatment in emergencies, but insurance recommended.

Côte d'Ivoire (Ivory Coast) *CAPITAL* Yamoussoukro *LANG* French *GMT* GMT *POP* 14,600,000 *DENSITY* 45 *LIFE EXP* M 46.1 F 47.3 *SAFETY* Generally safe, though recently subject to a palace coup. Has its full share of street crime after dark *MED CARE* Fair, but insurance recommended.

Croatia *CAPITAL* Zagreb *LANG* Croat-Serb and Serb-Croat *GMT* +1 *POP* 4,500,000 *DENSITY* 80 *LIFE EXP* M 68.8 F 76.5 *SAFETY* Seek official/local advice at time of trip *MED CARE* Free hospital care for UK citizens, some payment for medication may be demanded.

Cuba *CAPITAL* Havana *LANG* Spanish *GMT* −5 *POP* 11,100,000 *DENSITY* 100 *LIFE EXP* M 74.2 F 78 *SAFETY* Be aware of bag snatchers *MED CARE* Limited, insurance recommended in case of need for repatriation.

Curaçao (Netherlands Antilles) *CAPITAL* Willemstad *LANG* Dutch *GMT* −4 *POP* 144,097 *DENSITY* 324.5 *LIFE EXP* M 72.5 F 78.4 *SAFETY* Safe *MED CARE* Good but expensive, so insurance recommended.

Cyprus *CAPITAL* Nicosia *LANG* Greek *GMT* +2 *POP* 766,000 *DENSITY* 84 *LIFE EXP* M 75.5 F 80 *SAFETY* Safe *MED CARE* Good, but insurance recommended.

Czech Republic *CAPITAL* Prague *LANG* Czech *GMT* +1 *POP* 10,200,000 *DENSITY* 129 *LIFE EXP* M 70.3 F 77.4 *SAFETY* Safe *MED CARE* Free for UK citizens.

Denmark *CAPITAL* Copenhagen *LANG* Danish *GMT* +1 (+2 in summer) *POP* 5,300,000 *DENSITY* 125 *LIFE EXP* M 73 F 78.5 *SAFETY* Safe *MED CARE* Very good and free for UK citizens.

Djibouti *CAPITAL* Djibouti *LANG* Arabic and French *GMT* +3 *POP* 652,000 *DENSITY* 28 *LIFE EXP* M 48.7 F 52 *SAFETY* Areas in the country remain closed. Risk of banditry at night *MED CARE* Insurance highly recommended.

Dominica *CAPITAL* Roseau *LANG* English *GMT* −4 *POP* 74,000

Density 99 *Life Exp* 72 *Safety* Safe *Med Care* Cash payments demanded, insurance strongly recommended.

Dominican Republic *Capital* Santo Domingo *Lang* Spanish *GMT* –4 *Pop* 8,200,000 *Density* 169 *Life Exp* M 68.9 F 73.1 *Safety* Safe *Med Care* Insurance recommended.

Ecuador *Capital* Quito *Lang* Spanish *GMT* –5 (Galapagos Islands –6) *Pop* 12,200,000 *Density* 44 *Life Exp* M 67.3 F 72.5 *Safety* One of the safest countries in South America *Med Care* Good but expensive, insurance recommended.

Egypt *Capital* Cairo *Lang* Arabic *GMT* +2 *Pop* 65,700,000 *Density* 66 *Life Exp* M 64.7 F 67.9 *Safety* Government claims that terrorist attacks on tourists are over. Otherwise fairly safe, but women should beware sexual harassment or worse *Med Care* Insurance strongly recommended.

El Salvador *Capital* San Salvador *Lang* Spanish *GMT* –6 *Pop* 6,100,000 *Density* 294 *Life Exp* M 66.5 F 72.5 *Safety* Robbery and murder are not uncommon, for advice contact an embassy in San Salvador *Med Care* Cash payments demanded, insurance strongly recommended.

Equatorial Guinea *Capital* Malabo *Lang* Spanish *GMT* +1 *Pop* 430,000 *Density* 15 *Life Exp* M 48.4 F 51.6 *Safety* Exercise caution. There is no British Consular presence: if in difficulties seek assistance from the French or Spanish embassies *Med Care* Limited, insurance cover for repatriation recommended.

Eritrea *Capital* Asmara *Lang* Arabic and Tigrinya *GMT* +3 *Pop* 3,500,000 *Density* 37 *Life Exp* M 49.3 F 52 *Safety* Currently embroiled in border war with Ethiopia, otherwise relatively safe. Avoid Sudanese and Ethiopan borders. Don't travel after dark. Register with the Consulate in Asmara if travelling outside the capital *Med Care* Adequate, but insurance strongly recommended.

Estonia *Capital* Tallinn *Lang* Estonian *GMT* +2 (+3 in summer) *Pop* 1,476,301 *Density* 33.3 *Life Exp* M 64.1 F 75 *Safety* Safe *Med Care* Limited, cash payments demanded, insurance recommended.

Ethiopia *CAPITAL* Addis Ababa *LANG* Amharic *GMT* +3 *POP* 62,100,000 *DENSITY* 56 *LIFE EXP* M 42.4 F 44.3 *SAFETY* Sudanese, Eritrean and Somali border areas should be avoided. Do not travel after dark and register with an embassy if travelling outside the capital by road *MED CARE* Limited, repatriation cover recommended.

Falkland Islands (UK) *CAPITAL* Stanley *LANG* English *GMT* –4 (–3 in winter) *POP* 2,564 *DENSITY* 0.21 *LIFE EXP* M 68.2 F 73.8 *SAFETY* Safe, except there are marked unexploded mines, seek local advice *MED CARE* Free for UK residents.

Fiji *CAPITAL* Suva *LANG* Fijian and Hindi *GMT* +12 *POP* 822,000 *DENSITY* 45 *LIFE EXP* M 70.6 F 74.9 *SAFETY* Usually safe, currently uncertain with attempted coup *MED CARE* Adequate, but insurance recommended.

Finland *CAPITAL* Helsinki *LANG* Finnish *GMT* +2 *POP* 5,200,000 *DENSITY* 17 *LIFE EXP* M 72.9 F 80.6 *SAFETY* Safe *MED CARE* UK citizens eligible for refund on most medical expenses.

France *CAPITAL* Paris *LANG* French *GMT* +1 *POP* 58,700,000 *DENSITY* 107 *LIFE EXP* M 74.2 F 82 *SAFETY* Safe *MED CARE* UK citizens eligible for a refund on some medical expenses.

French Guiana (France) *CAPITAL* Cayenne *LANG* French *GMT* –3 *POP* 152,300 *DENSITY* 2 *LIFE EXP* M 62.3 F 67.6 *SAFETY* Safe *MED CARE* As for France, but more limited.

Gabon *CAPITAL* Libreville *LANG* French *GMT* +1 *POP* 1,200,000 *DENSITY* 5 *LIFE EXP* M 51.1 F 53.8 *SAFETY* Generally stable *MED CARE* Very limited, insurance strongly recommended.

The Gambia *CAPITAL* Banjul *LANG* English *GMT* GMT *POP* 1,260,000 *DENSITY* 119 *LIFE EXP* M 45.4 F 48.6 *SAFETY* Calm since military coup of 1994 *MED CARE* Adequate, but insurance advised, take supplies of basic medicines.

Georgia *CAPITAL* Tbilisi *LANG* Georgian, Russian *GMT* +4 *POP* 5,471,000 *DENSITY* 78.5 *LIFE EXP* M 68.5 F 76.8 *SAFETY* Avoid travel at night outside Tbilisi *MED CARE* Limited but free emergency care for UK citizens.

Germany *CAPITAL* Berlin *LANG* German *GMT* +1 *POP* 82,400,000 *DENSITY* 236 *LIFE EXP* M 73.9 F 80.2 *SAFETY* Safe

MED CARE Free to UK citizens, with charge for prescribed medicines.

Ghana *CAPITAL* Accra *LANG* English *GMT* GMT *POP* 18,900,000 *DENSITY* 82 *LIFE EXP* M 58.3 F 56.1 *SAFETY* Generally safe apart from petty crime. Precautions should be taken, travel after dark not recommended *MED CARE* Adequate, but insurance recommended.

Gibraltar *CAPITAL* Gibraltar *LANG* English and Spanish *GMT* +1 *POP* 28,051 *DENSITY* 4,315.5 *LIFE EXP* M 73.4 F 80.4 *SAFETY* Safe *MED CARE* Free to UK citizens.

Greece *CAPITAL* Athens *LANG* Greek *GMT* +2 *POP* 10,600,000 *DENSITY* 81 *LIFE EXP* M 75.6 F 80.6 *SAFETY* Safe *MED CARE* Refunds for hospital care can be obtained from IKA offices in Greece, but it will not be for more than 50 per cent at the most, insurance strongly recommended.

Greenland *CAPITAL* Nuuk *LANG* Greenlandic *GMT* –4 *POP* 56,076 *DENSITY* 0.03 *LIFE EXP* M 58.8 F 68.1 *SAFETY* Safe *MED CARE* Can be difficulties in obtaining supplies, but care is free for UK citizens.

Grenada *CAPITAL* St Georges *LANG* English *GMT* –4 *POP* 98,600 *DENSITY* 290 *LIFE EXP* 71 *SAFETY* Safe *MED CARE* Adequate, but insurance advised because relocation to mainland may be necessary and payment is demanded for all treatment.

Guadeloupe *CAPITAL* Basse-Terre (admin) Pointe-a-Pitre (comm) *LANG* French *GMT* –4 *POP* 419,500 *DENSITY* 236 *LIFE EXP* M 73.6 F 80.9 *SAFETY* Safe *MED CARE* Generally as for France, but check with embassy.

Guam (US) *CAPITAL* Agana *LANG* English and Chamorro *GMT* +10 *POP* 149,249 *DENSITY* 273.2 *LIFE EXP* M 72.9 F 77.4 *SAFETY* Safe *MED CARE* Limited, and as for USA, insurance strongly recommended.

Guatemala *CAPITAL* Guatemala City *LANG* Spanish *GMT* –6 *POP* 11,600,000 *DENSITY* 107 *LIFE EXP* M 61.4 F 67.2 *SAFETY* Possible low-level conflict between guerrillas and government *MED CARE* Limited outside capital and all healthcare has to be paid for; insurance recommended.

Guinea Republic *CAPITAL* Conakry *LANG* French *GMT* GMT *POP* 7,700,000 *DENSITY* 31 *LIFE EXP* M 46 F 47 *SAFETY* High levels of violent street crime. Leave valuables in secure place *MED CARE* Limited, and all health treatments must be paid for, insurance recommended.

Guinea-Bissau *CAPITAL* Bissau *LANG* Portuguese *GMT* GMT *POP* 1,100,000 *DENSITY* 39 *LIFE EXP* M 43.5 F 46.4 *SAFETY* Check with Foreign Office at time of trip *MED CARE* Limited, and immediate payment expected, insurance strongly recommended.

Guyana *CAPITAL* Georgetown *LANG* English *GMT* –3 *POP* 856,000 *DENSITY* 4 *LIFE EXP* M 61.1 F 67.9 *SAFETY* Violent crime common in Georgetown *MED CARE* Limited supplies and hospital care, insurance recommended.

Haiti *CAPITAL* Port-au-Prince *LANG* French and Creole *GMT* –5 *POP* 7,500,000 *DENSITY* 272 *LIFE EXP* M 51.4 F 56.2 *SAFETY* Highly unstable, subject to political violence and serious crime *MED CARE* Unreliable, insurance strongly recommended.

Honduras *CAPITAL* Tegucigalpa *LANG* Spanish *GMT* –6 *POP* 6,100,000 *DENSITY* 55 *LIFE EXP* M 67.5 F 72.3 *SAFETY* Take normal precautions for Latin America, especially regarding street crime *MED CARE* Limited, insurance strongly recommended.

Hong Kong (see China)

Hungary *CAPITAL* Budapest *LANG* Hungarian *GMT* +1 *POP* 10,276,968 *DENSITY* 110.5 *LIFE EXP* M 66.8 F 74.9 *SAFETY* Safe *MED CARE* Free health care for UK citizens.

Iceland *CAPITAL* Reykjavik *LANG* Icelandic *GMT* +1 *POP* 277,000 *DENSITY* 3 *LIFE EXP* M 76.8 F 81.3 *SAFETY* Safe *MED CARE* Very good, insurance recommended.

India *CAPITAL* New Delhi *LANG* English *GMT* +5.5 *POP* 976,000,000 *DENSITY* 328 *LIFE EXP* M 62.3 F 62.9 *SAFETY* Safe if sensible, including for women. Certain areas (e.g. Kashmir, Bihar) are volatile and Westerners have been targetted for kidnapping or murder *MED CARE* Good in some places, limited in others, insurance strongly recommended.

Indonesia *CAPITAL* Jakarta *LANG* Bahasa Indonesian *GMT* +7 to +9 *Pop* 206,500,000 *Density* 114 *Life Exp* M 63.3 F 67 Seriously volatile due to political and ethnic tensions. Muslim-Christian rioting and provincial separatism have sometimes spilled over into mainstream tourist islands. Kidnap of Westerners by separatists is a real risk in Irian Jaya and several Western journalists were killed in the East Timor crisis. Seek official/local advice at time of trip *Med Care* Limited outside cities, insurance with repatriation cover recommended.

Iran *Capital* Tehran *Lang* Persian (Farsi) *GMT* +3.5 *Pop* 73,100,000 *Density* 42 *Life Exp* M 63.3 F 70 *Safety* Generally welcoming and safe. Take sensible precautions for a Muslim country (women should be completely covered up) and note that there is a total ban on video cameras *Med Care* Very limited outside capital, insurance recommended.

Iraq *Capital* Baghdad *Lang* Arabic *GMT* +3 *Pop* 21,800,000 *Density* 50 *Life Exp* M 60.9 F 63.9 *Safety* The Foreign Office do not recommend any visits to Iraq *Med Care* Limited and insurance cover with repatriation strongly recommended.

Ireland *Capital* Dublin *Lang* English and Gaelic *GMT* GMT *Pop* 3,600,000 *Density* 52 *Life Exp* M 73.6 F 79.2 *Safety* Safe *Med Care* Free to UK citizens.

Israel *Capital* Jerusalem *Lang* Hebrew and Arabic *GMT* +2 *Pop* 5,900,000 *Density* 290 *Life Exp* M 75.7 F 79.7 *Safety* Mainly safe, but political unrest in certain areas, take local advice *Med Care* Very good but insurance recommended.

Italy *Capital* Rome *Lang* Italian *GMT* +1 *Pop* 57,268,578 *Density* 188.4 *Life Exp* M 75 F 81.2 *Safety* Safe *Med Care* Good, but free treatment for emergencies only, insurance recommended.

Jamaica *Capital* Kingston *Lang* English *GMT* −5 *Pop* 2,500,000 *Density* 231 *Life Exp* M 72.9 F 76.8 *Safety* High murder rate, but generally safe for tourists. Be vigilant, do not walk at night or use public transport *Med Care* Adequate, but insurance recommended.

Japan *Capital* Tokyo *Lang* Japanese *GMT* +9 *Pop* 125,900,000 *Density* 334 *Life Exp* M 76.8 F 82.9 *Safety* Safe *Med Care* Very good but expensive, insurance strongly recommended.

Jordan *CAPITAL* Amman *LANG* Arabic *GMT* +2 *POP* 6,000,000 *DENSITY* 67 *LIFE EXP* M 68.9 F 71.5 *SAFETY* Safe *MED CARE* Good, but insurance recommended.

Kazakhstan *CAPITAL* Astana *LANG* Kazakh *GMT* +5 (+6 in summer) *POP* 16,900,000 *DENSITY* 6.2 *LIFE EXP* M 62.8 F 72.4 *SAFETY* Some reports of banditry on roads and railways, seek local advice *MED CARE* Variable, supplies may be limited, insurance with repatriation cover recommended.

Kenya *CAPITAL* Nairobi *LANG* Swahili and English *GMT* +3 *POP* 29,292,000 *DENSITY* 36.9 *LIFE EXP* M 55.9 F 59.9 *SAFETY* Recent official attempts may reduce soaring levels of violent crime, principally carjackings and muggings. Tourist routes on the coast and railways have been targetted by thieves. Nairobi is known as 'Nairobbery' because of frequent muggings of tourists. *MED CARE* Adequate but insurance recommended.

Korea (North) *CAPITAL* Pyongyang *LANG* Korean *GMT* +9 *POP* 23,483,000 *DENSITY* 191.3 *LIFE EXP* M 68.9F 75.1 *SAFETY* Unknown due to government block on foreign visitors *MED CARE* Generally good, but supplies may be limited, insurance recommended.

Korea (South) *CAPITAL* Seoul *LANG* Korean *GMT* +9 *POP* 46,100,000 *DENSITY* 467 *LIFE EXP* M 68 F 76 *SAFETY* Safe *MED CARE* Adequate, but payment demanded, insurance advised.

Kuwait *CAPITAL* Kuwait City *LANG* Arabic and English *GMT* +3 *POP* 1,800,000 *DENSITY* 101 *LIFE EXP* M 74.16 F 78.2 *SAFETY* The border with Iraq should be avoided, and care should be taken in more remote spots for unexploded ordnance *MED CARE* Free emergency treatment at state medical centre but otherwise very expensive, insurance strongly recommended.

Kyrgyzstan (C.I.S.) *CAPITAL* Bishkek *LANG* Kyrgyz *GMT* +5 *POP* 4,500,000 *DENSITY* 23 *LIFE EXP* M 64.3 F 72.4 *SAFETY* Mostly safe, theft a problem *MED CARE* Limited, and cash payments demanded, insurance essential.

Laos *CAPITAL* Vientiane *LANG* Laotian *GMT* +7 *POP* 5,400,000 *DENSITY* 23 *LIFE EXP* M 52 F 54.5 *SAFETY* Safe, but be wary in drug-producing areas *MED CARE* limited and cash payments demanded, insurance strongly recommended.

Latvia *CAPITAL* Riga *LANG* Latvian *GMT* +2 *POP* 2,529,500 *DENSITY* 39.7 *LIFE EXP* M 62.4 F 74.4 *SAFETY* Safe *MED CARE* Limited and expensive, insurance strongly recommended.

Lebanon *CAPITAL* Beirut *LANG* Arabic *GMT* +2 *POP* 3,855,000 *DENSITY* 271.5 *LIFE EXP* M 68.1 F 71.7 *SAFETY* Unstable: Israeli withdrawal may stabilise the situation or may spark territorial competition between political groupings. Check with Foreign Office at time of trip *MED CARE* Adequate, but insurance recommended.

Lesotho *CAPITAL* Maseru *LANG* Sesotho and English *GMT* +2 *POP* 2,200,000 *DENSITY* 72 *LIFE EXP* M 55.5 F 60.5 *SAFETY* Generally safe, but travel with caution *MED CARE* Cash payments, insurance recommended.

Liberia *CAPITAL* Monrovia *LANG* English *GMT* GMT *POP* 2,700,000 *DENSITY* 27 *LIFE EXP* M 46 F 48 *SAFETY* Highly unsafe due to ongoing guerrilla conflict, unsafe frontiers and frequent attempted coups. The British Embassy in Liberia was closed in 1991 and the Foreign Office do not advise travel. *MED CARE* Very limited, insurance with repatriation cover recommended.

Libya *CAPITAL* Tripoli *LANG* Arabic *GMT* +1 *POP* 6,000,000 *DENSITY* 3 *LIFE EXP* M 68.3 F 72.2 *SAFETY* Unknown quantity because only just opening to travellers. Harsh penalties are imposed for the possession or use of alcohol or drugs and for criticising the country, its leadership or religion. Avoid internal air flights. Register with the British Interests Section of the Italian Embassy on arrival *MED CARE* Limited outside capital, insurance strongly recommended.

Liechtenstein *CAPITAL* Vaduz *LANG* German *GMT* +1 *POP* 31,000 *DENSITY* 195 *LIFE EXP* M 78 F 84 *SAFETY* Safe *MED CARE* Very good and free for UK citizens.

Lithuania *CAPITAL* Vilnius *LANG* Lithuanian *GMT* +2 *POP* 3,717,700 *DENSITY* 57 *LIFE EXP* M 64.3 F 75.6 *SAFETY* Safe *MED CARE* Free emergency treatment, but insurance recommended.

Luxembourg *CAPITAL* Luxembourg-ville *LANG* German *GMT* +1 *POP* 422,000 *DENSITY* 168 *LIFE EXP* M 73.3 F 79.9 *SAFETY*

Safe *MED CARE* Good, and refunds can be obtained for all but medical basic costs.

Macau (see China)

Macedonia *CAPITAL* Skopje *LANG* Macedonian *GMT* + 1 *POP* 2,200,000 *DENSITY* 86 *LIFE EXP* M 71 F 75.3 *SAFETY* Potentially unstable due to regional tensions: seek advice from Foreign Office at time of trip *MED CARE* Emergency treatment free but repatriation insurance cover recommended.

Madagascar *CAPITAL* Antananarivo *LANG* Malagasy and French *GMT* + 3 *POP* 16,300,000 *DENSITY* 28 *LIFE EXP* M 56 F 59 *SAFETY* Be aware of mugging danger. Register presence at the Embassy *MED CARE* Limited, repatriation insurance cover recommended.

Malawi *CAPITAL* Lilongwe *LANG* English *GMT* +2 *POP* 10,400,000 *DENSITY* 111 *LIFE EXP* M 44.6 F 46.2 *SAFETY* Generally safe. Avoid travelling after dark, especially outside the main towns *MED CARE* Very basic, take supplies with you, insurance with repatriation cover recommended.

Malaysia *CAPITAL* Kuala Lumpur *LANG* Bahasa Malaysia *GMT* +8 *POP* 21,500,000 *DENSITY* 65 *LIFE EXP* M 69.9 F 74.3 *SAFETY* Safe, though recently compromised by kidnapping of tourists in area bordering on the Philippines (this may be a one-off). *MED CARE* Good, but insurance recommended.

Maldives *CAPITAL* Malé *LANG* Dhivehi *GMT* +5 *POP* 282,000 *DENSITY* 940 *LIFE EXP* M 66.2 F 63.3 *SAFETY* Safe *MED CARE* Adequate but repatriation insurance cover recommended.

Mali *CAPITAL* Bamako *LANG* French *GMT* GMT *POP* 11,800,000 *DENSITY* 10 *LIFE EXP* M 52 F 54.6 *SAFETY* Ethnic tensions between government and tribespeople may affect area north of Bamako—seek local advice. Otherwise safe for travellers including women *MED CARE* Very limited, take medical supplies with you, insurance with repatriation cover strongly recommended.

Malta *CAPITAL* Valletta *LANG* Maltese *GMT* +1 *POP* 374,000 *DENSITY* 1,169 *LIFE EXP* M 74.9 F 79.3 *SAFETY* Safe *MED CARE* Good and free for UK citizens.

Martinique (France) *CAPITAL* Fort-de-France *LANG* French *GMT* –4 *POP* 381,200 *DENSITY* 342 *LIFE EXP* M 75.5 F 82 *SAFETY* Safe *MED CARE* Generally as for France but check with embassy.

Mauritania *CAPITAL* Nouakchott *LANG* Arabic and French *GMT* GMT *POP* 2,500,000 *DENSITY* 2 *LIFE EXP* M 51.9 F 55.1 *SAFETY* Fairly safe except in disputed border areas *MED CARE* Limited, and insurance with repatriation cover recommended.

Mauritius *CAPITAL* Port Louis *LANG* English *GMT* +4 *POP* 1,200,000 *DENSITY* 649 *LIFE EXP* M 67.9 F 75.1 *SAFETY* Safe *MED CARE* Good, but insurance recommended.

Mexico *CAPITAL* Mexico City *LANG* Spanish *GMT* –6 to –8 *POP* 95,800,000 *DENSITY* 50 *LIFE EXP* M 69.5 F 75.5 *SAFETY* Central Chiapas remains tense, seek local advice. High levels of violence, murder and other crimes relating to drugs and illegal border-crossings, but these tend not to affect foreign travellers. *MED CARE* Good, but insurance recommended.

Moldova *CAPITAL* Chisinau *LANG* Romanian *GMT* +2 *POP* 4,500,000 *DENSITY* 134 *LIFE EXP* M 63.5 F 71.3 *SAFETY* Seek advice from the Foreign Office before travelling *MED CARE* Free emergency treatment but supplies may be limited, insurance recommended.

Monaco *CAPITAL* Monaco-ville *LANG* French *GMT* +1 *POP* 32,000 *DENSITY* 16,410 *LIFE EXP* M 73.1 F 81.3 *SAFETY* Safe *MED CARE* Good but expensive, insurance strongly recommended.

Mongolia *CAPITAL* Ulan Bator *LANG* Mongolian Khalkha *GMT* +8 *POP* 2,600,000 *DENSITY* 2 *LIFE EXP* M 62.4 F 67.3 *SAFETY* Safe *MED CARE* Limited, insurance with repatriation cover recommended.

Montserrat (UK) *CAPITAL* Plymouth *LANG* English *GMT* –4 *POP* 12,850 *DENSITY* 109 *LIFE EXP* M 70.1 F 77.1 *SAFETY* Safe, depending on volcanic activity *MED CARE* Limited facilities, free emergency care for those under 16 or over 65, otherwise insurance recommended.

Morocco *CAPITAL* Rabat *LANG* Arabic *GMT* GMT *POP*

28,000,000 *Density* 63 *Life Exp* M 64.8 F 68.5 *Safety* Safe for tourists, beware of drugs being offered, for which penalties are harsh *Med Care* Good in cities and free for emergency treatment, otherwise insurance recommended.

Mozambique *Capital* Maputo *Lang* Portuguese *GMT* +2 *Pop* 18,700,000 *Density* 24 *Life Exp* M 43.9 F 46.6 *Safety* Recovering from devastating floods, but otherwise fairly safe for travellers. Beware unexploded landmines *Med Care* Limited, insurance with repatriation cover recommended.

Myanmar (Burma) *Capital* Yangon (Rangoon) *Lang* Burmese *GMT* +6.5 *Pop* 47,600,000 *Density* 72 *Life Exp* M 58.5 F 61.8 *Safety* Tourists may be required to keep to officially designated areas. Southern borders subject to separatist guerrilla conflict *Med Care* Adequate but no free facilities, insurance recommended.

Namibia *Capital* Windhoek *Lang* English *GMT* +2 *Pop* 1,700,000 *Density* 2 *Life Exp* M 51.8 F 53 *Safety* Safe, except possibly the Caprivi Strip which has been affected by cross-border war in Angola: check with Foreign Office if transiting through Caprivi *Med Care* Adequate but no free treatment, insurance recommended.

Nepal *Capital* Kathmandu *Lang* Nepali *GMT* + 5.45 *Pop* 23,200,000 *Density* 170 *Life Exp* M 57.6 F 57.1 *Safety* Usually safe, but some recent reports of low-level Maoist insurgency affecting even tourist areas: check with Foreign Office *Med Care* Adequate in capital but no free treatment, insurance recommended.

The Netherlands *Capital* Amsterdam *Lang* Dutch *GMT* +1 *Pop* 15,700,000 *Density* 463 *Life Exp* M 75 F 80.7 *Safety* Safe *Med Care* Good and free for UK citizens.

New Caledonia (France) *Capital* Noumena *Lang* French *GMT* +11 *Pop* 196,836 *Density* 10 *Life Exp* M 69.2 F 76.3 *Safety* Safe *Med Care* Adequate, insurance recommended.

New Zealand *Capital* Wellington *Lang* English *GMT* +12 *Pop* 3,700,000 *Density* 14 *Life Exp* M 74.1 F 79.7 *Safety* Safe *Med Care* Good and free state emergency medical treatment.

Nicaragua *CAPITAL* Managua *LANG* Spanish *GMT* –6 *POP* 4,500,000 *DENSITY* 37.4 *LIFE EXP* M 65.8 F 70.6 *SAFETY* Political stability and safety can not be guaranteed, but currently quiet *MED CARE* Limited, insurance recommended.

Niger *CAPITAL* Niamey *LANG* French *GMT* +1 *POP* 10,100,000 *DENSITY* 8 *LIFE EXP* M 46.9 F 50.1 *SAFETY* Potentially unstable: check with Foreign Office *MED CARE* Very limited, bring own supplies, insurance with repatriation cover recommended.

Nigeria *CAPITAL* Abuja *LANG* English *GMT* +1 *POP* 109,000,000 *DENSITY* 134 *LIFE EXP* M 48.7 F 51.5 *SAFETY* High incidence of street crime and business fraud. Political violence and rioting in many areas. Avoid the Niger delta. Travelling outside cities after dark is unsafe *MED CARE* Very limited except for a few private hospitals in cities, insurance essential.

Norway *CAPITAL* Oslo *LANG* Norwegian *GMT* +1 *POP* 4,400,000 *DENSITY* 14 *LIFE EXP* M 75.2 F 81.1 *SAFETY* Safe *MED CARE* Good, mostly free, total refunds for all medical treatment unlikely, insurance advisable.

Oman *CAPITAL* Muscat *LANG* Arabic and English *GMT* +4 *POP* 2,500,000 *DENSITY* 12 *LIFE EXP* M 68.9 F 73.3 *SAFETY* Safe *MED CARE* Good but expensive, insurance recommended.

Pakistan *CAPITAL* Islamabad *LANG* Urdu and English *GMT* +5 *POP* 147,500,000 *DENSITY* 192 *LIFE EXP* M 62.9 F 65.1 *SAFETY* Safe if sensible in northern areas, but central and south Pakistan are unsafe and advice should be taken *MED CARE* Limited, cash payments demanded, insurance strongly recommended.

Panama *CAPITAL* Panama City *LANG* Spanish *GMT* –5 *POP* 2,800,000 *DENSITY* 37 *LIFE EXP* M 71.8 F 76.4 *SAFETY* Do not visit the Colombian border. Beware muggings in tourist areas *MED CARE* Free emergency treatment, but insurance recommended.

Papua New Guinea *CAPITAL* Port Moresby *LANG* English and Pidgin English *GMT* +10 *POP* 4,600,000 *DENSITY* 10 *LIFE EXP* M 57.2 F 58.7 *SAFETY* Extremely dangerous – take local advice. Westerners have been kidnapped for propaganda purposes. Port Moresby has gangland violence *MED CARE* Very limited, cash payments demanded, it may be worthwhile getting a visa for Australia in case of medical emergencies, so that you can be evacuated to decent medical facilities, insurance strongly recommended.

Paraguay *CAPITAL* Asuncion *LANG* Spanish and Guarani *GMT* –4 *POP* 5,200,000 *DENSITY* 13 *LIFE EXP* M 67.5 F 72 *SAFETY* Safe with usual South American provisos, *MED CARE* Insurance strongly recommended.

Peru *CAPITAL* Lima *LANG* Spanish and Quechua *GMT* –5 *POP* 24,800,000 *DENSITY* 19 *LIFE EXP* M 65.9 F 70.9 *SAFETY* Guerrilla activities mainly suppressed and therefore relatively safe for travellers. Many reports of street theft *MED CARE* Cash payments demanded, insurance strongly recommended.

Philippines *CAPITAL* Manila *LANG* Filipino *GMT* +8 *POP* 72,200,000 *DENSITY* 242 *LIFE EXP* M 66.5 F 70.2 *SAFETY* Some areas unstable, with clashes between Christians and Muslims, take local advice. Southern areas currently volatile, including kidnappings of tourists or locals, and parcel-bombings *MED CARE* Adequate three-tier system, but insurance recommended.

Poland *CAPITAL* Warsaw *LANG* Polish *GMT* +1 *POP* 38,700,000 *DENSITY* 127 *LIFE EXP* M 68.2 F 76.9 *SAFETY* Safe *MED CARE* Free to UK citizens, except for a charge for 30 per cent of prescribed medicines.

Portugal *CAPITAL* Lisbon *LANG* Portuguese *GMT* GMT *POP* 9,902,200 *DENSITY* 107 *LIFE EXP* M 71.8 F 78.8 *SAFETY* Safe *MED CARE* Good and free for UK citizens.

Puerto Rico (USA) *CAPITAL* San Juan *LANG* Spanish *GMT* -4 *POP* 3,800,000 *DENSITY* 424 *LIFE EXP* M 69.4 F 78.5 *SAFETY* Beware of pickpockets *MED CARE* Good but expensive, insurance strongly recommended.

Qatar *CAPITAL* Doha *LANG* Arabic *GMT* +3 *POP* 600,000 *DENSITY* 136 *LIFE EXP* M 66.9 F 71.8 *SAFETY* safe *MED CARE* Good but expensive, insurance recommended.

Réunion (France) *CAPITAL* Saint-Denis *LANG* French *GMT* +4 *POP* 697,000 *DENSITY* 278 *LIFE EXP* M 70.9 F 79.8 *SAFETY* Safe *MED CARE* As for France.

Romania *Capital* Bucharest *Lang* Romanian *GMT* +2 *Pop* 22,730,622 *Density* 98 *Life Exp* M 66.6 F 73.1 *Safety* Bad reputation for petty crime, beware of bogus policemen *Med Care* Limited, free for UK citizens except for medicine from chemist.

Russian Federation *Capital* Moscow *Lang* Russian *GMT* +3 to +12 *Pop* 148,000,000 *Density* 9 *Life Exp* M 60.6 F 72.8 *Safety* Unsafe. Murder for political or commercial reasons, high levels of theft and alcoholism. Kidnapping endemic in Caucasus areas including Chechnya and Ingushetya. AIDS and tuberculosis increasing *Med Care* Free emergency treatment, but very expensive if further treatment is needed, insurance strongly recommended.

Rwanda *Capital* Kigali *Lang* Kinyarwanda and French Kiswahili *GMT*+2 *Pop* 6,500,000 *Density* 261 *Life Exp* M 39.4 F 41.7 *Safety* Apparently returning to normal, and some reports that travel is easy and safe. Potentially volatile, given continuing ethnic clashes in neighbouring states. *Med Care* Extremely limited, insurance with repatriation cover strongly recommended.

Saba (Netherlands Antilles) *Capital* The Bottom *Lang* English and Dutch *GMT* –4 *Pop* 1,130 *Density* 86.9 *Life Exp* M 71.1 F 75.8 *Safety* Safe *Med Care* One hospital on the island, insurance recommended with evacuation cover.

St Eustatius *Capital* Oranjestad *Lang* English *GMT* –4 *Pop* 1,839 *Density* 87.6 *Life Exp* M 72.5 F 78.4 *Safety* Safe *Med Care* Only one hospital, insurance with evacuation cover recommended.

St Kitts and Nevis *Capital* Basseterre *Lang* English *GMT* –4 *Pop* 41,000 *Density* 114 *Life Exp* M 67.4 F 70.4 *Safety* Safe *Med Care* Adequate, but insurance recommended with evacuation cover.

St Lucia *Capital* Castries *Lang* English *GMT* –4 *Pop* 142,000 *Density* 233 *Life Exp* M 69.3 F 74 *Safety* Safe *Med Care* Adequate but expensive, insurance recommended with evacuation cover.

St Maarten *Capital* Philipsburg *Lang* English *GMT* –4 *Pop*

32,221 *DENSITY* 785.9 *LIFE EXP* M 72.5 F 78.4 *SAFETY* Safe *MED CARE* Good, but insurance recommended, with evacuation cover.

St Vincent and Grenadines *CAPITAL* Kingstown *LANG* English *GMT* –4 *POP* 111,000 *DENSITY* 327 *LIFE EXP* M 69.3 F 74 *SAFETY* Safe *MED CARE* Adequate, but insurance recommended with evacuation cover.

São Tomé e Príncipe *CAPITAL* São Tomé *LANG* Portuguese *GMT* GMT *POP* 131,000 *DENSITY* 137 *LIFE EXP* 67 *SAFETY* Safe *MED CARE* Poor, insurance with evacuation cover strongly recommended.

Saudi Arabia *CAPITAL* Riyadh *LANG* Arabic *GMT* +3 *POP* 20,200,000 *DENSITY* 8 *LIFE EXP* M 69.9 F 73.4 *SAFETY* Safe *MED CARE* Very high standard but expensive, insurance recommended.

Senegal *CAPITAL* Dakar *LANG* French and Wolof *GMT* GMT *POP* 9,000,000 *DENSITY* 47 *LIFE EXP* M 50.5 F 54.2 *SAFETY* Some unrest, take local advice *MED CARE* Basic in rural areas, insurance recommended.

Seychelles *CAPITAL* Victoria (Mahé) *LANG* Creole *GMT* +4 *POP* 75,000 *DENSITY* 279 *LIFE EXP* M 65.3 F 74.1 *SAFETY* Safe *MED CARE* Adequate but insurance recommended.

Sierra Leone *CAPITAL* Freetown *LANG* English *GMT* GMT *POP* 4,600,000 *DENSITY* 64 *LIFE EXP* M 35.8 F 38.7 *SAFETY* Extremely dangerous, continued fighting between government and rebel forces, atrocities enacted on civilians, kidnapping of Westerners. Country outside of Freetown entirely unstable. Contact the Foreign Office before departing *MED CARE* Non-existent, insurance with repatriation cover recommended.

Singapore *CAPITAL* Singapore *LANG* Chinese *GMT* +8 *POP* 3,500,000 *DENSITY* 5,738 *LIFE EXP* M 74.9 F 79.3 *SAFETY* Safe *MED CARE* Good but expensive, insurance recommended.

Slovak Republic *CAPITAL* Bratislava *LANG* Slovak *GMT* +1 *POP* 5,400,000 *DENSITY* 110 *LIFE EXP* M 69.1 F 76.7 *SAFETY* Relatively safe *MED CARE* Free emergency treatment for UK citizens.

Slovenia *CAPITAL* Ljubljana *LANG* Slovene *GMT* +1 *POP*

1,989,477 *DENSITY* 98.2 *LIFE EXP* M 70.6 F 78.2 *SAFETY* Safe *MED CARE* Good and free emergency treatment for UK citizens.

Solomon Islands *CAPITAL* Honiara *LANG* English *GMT* +11 *POP* 417,000 *DENSITY* 15 *LIFE EXP* M 69.9 F 73.9 *SAFETY* Usually very safe, but currently (2000) undergoing an attempted military coup d'etat. Contact Foreign Office for latest advice. *MED CARE* Adequate, but insurance advised with evacuation cover.

Somalia *CAPITAL* Mogadishu *LANG* Somali and Arabic *GMT* +3 *POP* 10,700,000 *DENSITY* 17 *LIFE EXP* M 45.4 F 48.6 *SAFETY* Highly volatile, little diplomatic representation, seek official advice at time of trip *MED CARE* Very limited, take own medical supplies and insurance with repatriation cover.

South Africa *CAPITAL* Pretoria *LANG* Afrikaans and English *GMT* +2 *POP* 41,244,000 (including the homelands) *DENSITY* 33.1 *LIFE EXP* M 57.5 F 63.5 *SAFETY* Variable: cities experiencing high crime rates, especially carjackings and gang-rape, and especially Johannesburg; rural areas and Cape Town calmer *MED CARE* Good and free for pregnant women and children, otherwise insurance recommended.

Spain *CAPITAL* Madrid *LANG* Spanish *GMT* +1 *POP* 44,300,000 *DENSITY* 77.5 *LIFE EXP* M 74.5 F 81.5 *SAFETY* Safe, except for some terrorist activities in Basque region *MED CARE* Good, limited free emergency treatment service, insurance recommended.

Sri Lanka *CAPITAL* Colombo *LANG* Sinhala, Tamil and English *GMT* +5.5 *POP* 18,500,000 *DENSITY* 274 *LIFE EXP* M 70.9 F 75.4 *SAFETY* Mainly safe, despite low-level conflict between Tamil Tigers and government which mainly affects the north *MED CARE* Free emergency treatment at government hospitals.

Sudan *CAPITAL* Khartoum *LANG* Arabic *GMT* +2 *POP* 28,500,000 *DENSITY* 12 *LIFE EXP* M 53.6 F 56.4 *SAFETY* Ongoing civil war in south. Do not travel in south or on Ethiopian or Eritrean borders – contact Foreign Office *MED CARE* Limited outside capital, insurance strongly recommended.

Surinam *CAPITAL* Paramaribo *LANG* Dutch *GMT* –3 *POP* 442,000 *DENSITY* 3 *LIFE EXP* M 67.5 F 72.7 *SAFETY* Safe *MED CARE* Good but expensive, insurance recommended.

Swaziland *CAPITAL* Mbabane *LANG* English and Siswati *GMT* +2 *POP* 900,000 *DENSITY* 54 *LIFE EXP* M 57.9 F 62.5 *SAFETY* Generally stable *MED CARE* Good private health care, insurance recommended.

Sweden *CAPITAL* Stockholm *LANG* Swedish *GMT* +1 *POP* 8,900,000 *DENSITY* 22 *LIFE EXP* M 76.3 F 80.8 *SAFETY* Safe *MED CARE* Very good and free to UK citizens.

Switzerland *CAPITAL* Bern *LANG* German *GMT* +1 *POP* 7,300,000 *DENSITY* 184 *LIFE EXP* M 75.4 F 81.8 *SAFETY* Safe *MED CARE* Good but very expensive, insurance strongly recommended.

Syria *CAPITAL* Damascus *LANG* Arabic, French and English *GMT* +2 *POP* 15,300,000 *DENSITY* 83 *LIFE EXP* M 66.7 F 71.2 *SAFETY* Generally welcoming, but take care to behave appropriately for a Muslim country. Photography near military bases and government installations is prohibited *MED CARE* Emergency treatment free to those who cannot afford to pay, insurance recommended.

Taiwan *CAPITAL* Taipei *LANG* Mandarin Chinese and English *GMT* +8 *POP* 21,500,000 *DENSITY* 666 *LIFE EXP* M 72 F 77.4 *SAFETY* Safe *MED CARE* Good but expensive, insurance recommended.

Tajikistan *CAPITAL* Dushanbe *LANG* Tajik *GMT* +5 *POP* 6,200,000 *DENSITY* 43 *LIFE EXP* M 64.2 F 70.2 *SAFETY* Politically unstable but travel is possible, given local knowledge or information *MED CARE* Limited, take medical supplies and insurance with you.

Tanzania *CAPITAL* Dodoma *LANG* Swahili and English *GMT* +3 *POP* 32,200,000 *DENSITY* 36 *LIFE EXP* M 46.8 F 49.1 *SAFETY* Fairly safe, but watch for street crime after dark *MED CARE* Adequate supplies and care at private or religious hospitals but can be expensive, insurance strongly recommended.

Thailand *CAPITAL* Bangkok *LANG* Thai *GMT* +7 *POP* 59,600,000 *DENSITY* 117 *LIFE EXP* M 65.8 F 72 *SAFETY* Safe, apart from border with Myanmar *MED CARE* Good but insurance recommended.

Togo *CAPITAL* Lomé *LANG* French *GMT* GMT *POP* 4,400,000 *DENSITY* 81 *LIFE EXP* M 47.6 F 50.1 *SAFETY* Quiet but potentially unstable *MED CARE* Limited, bring own medical supplies and insurance with repatriation cover.

Tonga *CAPITAL* Nuku'alofa *LANG* Tongan and English *GMT* +13 *POP* 97,000 *DENSITY* 135 *LIFE EXP* 68 *SAFETY* Safe *MED CARE* Adequate for minor problems, but insurance with evacuation cover strongly recommended.

Trinidad and Tobago *CAPITAL* Port of Spain *LANG* English *GMT* –4 *POP* 1,300,000 *DENSITY* 253 *LIFE EXP* M 71.5 F 76.2 *SAFETY* safe *MED CARE* Free and adequate on Trinidad, but limited on Tobago so insurance recommended.

Tunisia *CAPITAL* Tunis *LANG* Arabic *GMT* +1 *POP* 9,500,000 *DENSITY* 61 *LIFE EXP* M 68.4 F 70.7 *SAFETY* Relatively safe *MED CARE* Adequate, but all medical supplies to be paid for and they are expensive, consider taking supplies with you; insurance recommended.

Turkey *CAPITAL* Ankara *LANG* Turkish *GMT* +2 *POP* 63,800,000 *DENSITY* 83 *LIFE EXP* M 66.5 F 71.7 *SAFETY* Safe, except for some eastern and south-eastern areas affected by ongoing Kurdish war *MED CARE* Good, but no free health provision, insurance recommended.

Turkmenistan *CAPITAL* Ashgabat *LANG* Turkmen *GMT* +5 *POP* 4,483,300 *DENSITY* 9 *LIFE EXP* M 61.9 F 68.9 *SAFETY* Check with Foreign Office *MED CARE* Limited, take own supplies with you as well as insurance with repatriation cover.

Turks and Caicos (UK) *CAPITAL* Cockburn Town *LANG* English *GMT* –5 *POP* 13,800 *DENSITY* 32 *SAFETY* Safe *MED CARE* Free to UK citizens under 16 or over 65 and free prescribed medicine and ambulance travel to all UK citizens, otherwise insurance recommended.

Tuvalu *CAPITAL* Fongafale *LANG* Tuvalaun and English *GMT* +12 *POP* 9,000 *DENSITY* 377 *LIFE EXP* M 68.3 F 72.5 *SAFETY* Safe *MED CARE* Good but insurance recommended with evacuation cover.

Uganda *CAPITAL* Kampala *LANG* English *GMT* +3 *POP*

21,300,000 *DENSITY* 107 *LIFE EXP* M 38.9 F 40.4 *SAFETY* Potentially safe, despite murders of safari-tourists visiting mountain gorillas. Be very vigilant in border areas, especially the northwest, haunt of bandits and insurgents. Do not travel at night *MED CARE* Limited, bring medical supplies with you and insurance with repatriation cover.

Ukraine *CAPITAL* Kiev *LANG* Ukrainian *GMT* +2 *POP* 51,200,000 *DENSITY* 85 *LIFE EXP* M 63.8 F 73.7 *SAFETY* Be wary of carjackings and muggings *MED CARE* Limited, take supplies with you and full insurance.

United Arab Emirates *CAPITAL* Abu Dhabi *LANG* Arabic *GMT* +4 *POP* 2,400,000 *DENSITY* 29 *LIFE EXP* M 73.9 F 76.5 *SAFETY* Safe *MED CARE* Good and free emergency treatment, but any other kind of treatment is very expensive, so insurance advised.

United Kingdom *CAPITAL* London *LANG* English *GMT* GMT *POP* 58,200,000 *DENSITY* 241 *LIFE EXP* M 74.5 F 79.8 *SAFETY* Safe *MED CARE* Free emergency treatment for travellers.

United States of America *CAPITAL* Washington DC *LANG* English *GMT* –5 to –11 *POP* 273,800,000 *DENSITY* 30 *LIFE EXP* M 73.4 F 80.1 *SAFETY* Generally safe, but depends on the area, especially in big cities. Take local advice, especially in Florida *MED CARE* Good but expensive; insurance strongly recommended as some hospitals will not treat patients without proof of insurance cover.

Uruguay *CAPITAL* Montevideo *LANG* Spanish *GMT* –3 *POP* 3,300,000 *DENSITY* 18 *LIFE EXP* M 70.4 F 78 *SAFETY* generally safe, but check with Foreign Office *MED CARE* Good, but insurance recommended.

Uzbekistan *CAPITAL* Tashkent *LANG* Uzbek *GMT* +5 *POP* 24,100,000 *DENSITY* 54 *LIFE EXP* M 64.3 F 70.7 *SAFETY* Dress down and avoid travelling at night *MED CARE* Limited, but free for emergency treatment, insurance with repatriation cover strongly recommended.

Vanuatu *CAPITAL* Port Vila *LANG* Bislama *GMT* +11 *POP* 200,000 *DENSITY* 16 *LIFE EXP* M 65.5 F 69.5 *SAFETY* Safe *MED CARE* Adequate but insurance strongly recommended.

Venezuela *CAPITAL* Caracas *LANG* Spanish *GMT* –4 *POP* 23,200,000 *DENSITY* 26 *LIFE EXP* M 70 F 75.7 *SAFETY* Beware violent crime in cities, register with British Embassy in Caracas *MED CARE* Good and free emergency treatment for travellers.

Vietnam *CAPITAL* Hanoi *LANG* Vietnamese *GMT* +7 *POP* 77,900,000 *DENSITY* 239 *LIFE EXP* M 64.9 F 69.6 *SAFETY* Increasingly safe *MED CARE* Generally limited, insurance with repatriation cover strongly recommended.

Virgin Islands (UK) *CAPITAL* Road Town *LANG* English *GMT* –4 *POP* 17,896 *DENSITY* 117 *LIFE EXP* M 72.9 F 74.9 *SAFETY* Safe *MED CARE* Free for UK citizens.

Virgin Islands (US) *CAPITAL* Charlotte Amalie *LANG* English *GMT* –4 *POP* 101,809 *DENSITY* 293 *SAFETY* Safe *MED CARE* As for USA, insurance strongly advised

Yemen *CAPITAL* Sana'a *LANG* Arabic *GMT* +3 *POP* 16,900,000 *DENSITY* 32 *LIFE EXP* M 57.4 F 58.4 *SAFETY* Variable, security improved but westerners can still be subjects of kidnappings, check with relevant embassy *MED CARE* Adequate, but insurance recommended.

Yugoslavia (Montenegro and Serbia) *CAPITAL* Belgrade *LANG* Serbo-Croat *GMT* +1 *POP* 10,482,000 *DENSITY* 102 *LIFE EXP* M 70.2 F 75.5 *SAFETY* Highly unstable. Political assassinations and gangland crime increasing *MED CARE* Poor and limited supplies, cash payments demanded, insurance with repatriation cover essential.

Zambia *CAPITAL* Lusaka *LANG* English *GMT* +2 *POP* 8,700,000 *DENSITY* 12 *LIFE EXP* M 39.5 F 40.6 *SAFETY* Relatively safe *MED CARE* Limited, and cash payments demanded, take own supplies, insurance with repatriation cover strongly recommended.

Zimbabwe *CAPITAL* Harare *LANG* English *GMT* +2 *POP* 11,900,000 *DENSITY* 31 *LIFE EXP* M 43.6 F 44.7 *SAFETY* Currently very volatile, political unrest at elections, seek advice from Foreign Office at time of trip *MED CARE* Good, but insurance recommended.

QUALITY OF HEALTHCARE WORLDWIDE

(Source: World Health Organisation, 2000)

1 France
2 Italy
3 San Marino
4 Andorra
5 Malta
6 Singapore
7 Spain
8 Oman
9 Austria
10 Japan
11 Norway
12 Portugal
13 Monaco
14 Greece
15 Iceland
16 Luxembourg
17 Netherlands
18 United Kingdom
19 Ireland
20 Switzerland
21 Belgium
22 Colombia
23 Sweden
24 Cyprus
25 Germany
26 Saudi Arabia
27 United Arab Emirates
28 Israel
29 Morocco
30 Canada
31 Finland
32 Australia
33 Chile
34 Denmark
35 Dominica
36 Costa Rica
37 United States of America
38 Slovenia
39 Cuba
40 Brunei
41 New Zealand
42 Bahrain
43 Croatia
44 Qatar
45 Kuwait
46 Barbados
47 Thailand
48 Czech Republic
49 Malaysia
50 Poland

51 Dominican Republic
52 Tunisia
53 Jamaica
54 Venezuela
55 Albania
56 Seychelles
57 Paraguay
58 South Korea
59 Senegal
60 Philippines
61 Mexico
62 Slovakia
63 Egypt
64 Kazakhstan
65 Uruguay
66 Hungary
67 Trinidad and Tobago
68 St Lucia
69 Belize
70 Turkey
71 Nicaragua
72 Belarus
73 Lithuania
74 St Vincent and the Grenadines
75 Argentina
76 Sri Lanka
77 Estonia
78 Guatemala
79 Ukraine
80 Solomon Islands
81 Algeria
82 Palau
83 Jordan
84 Mauritius
85 Grenada
86 Antigua and Barbuda
87 Libya
88 Bangladesh
89 FYR Macedonia
90 Bosnia-Herzegovina
91 Lebanon
92 Indonesia
93 Iran
94 Bahamas
95 Panama
96 Fiji
97 Benin

98 Nauru
99 Romania
100 St Kitts and Nevis
101 Moldova
102 Bulgaria
103 Iraq
104 Armenia
105 Latvia
106 Yugoslavia
107 Cook Islands
108 Syria
109 Azerbaijan
110 Surinam
111 Ecuador
112 India
113 Cape Verde
114 Georgia
115 El Salvador
116 Tonga
117 Uzbekistan
118 Comoros
119 Samoa
120 Yemen
121 Niue
122 Pakistan
123 Micronesia
124 Bhutan
125 Brazil
126 Bolivia
127 Vanuatu
128 Guyana
129 Peru
130 Russian Federation
131 Honduras
132 Burkina Faso
133 São Tomé and Principe
134 Sudan
135 Ghana
136 Tuvalu
137 Côte d'Ivoire
138 Haiti
139 Gabon
140 Kenya
141 Marshall Islands
142 Kiribati
143 Burundi
144 China
145 Mongolia

146 Gambia
147 Maldives
148 Papua New Guinea
149 Uganda
150 Nepal
151 Kyrgyzstan
152 Togo
153 Turkmenistan
154 Tajikistan
155 Zimbabwe
156 Tanzania
157 Djibouti
158 Eritrea
159 Madagascar
160 Vietnam
161 Guinea
162 Mauritania
163 Mali
164 Cameroon
165 Laos
166 Congo (Brazaville)
167 North Korea
168 Namibia
169 Botswana
170 Niger
171 Equatorial Guinea
172 Rwanda
173 Afghanistan
174 Cambodia
175 South Africa
176 Guinea-Bissau
177 Swaziland
178 Chad
179 Somalia
180 Ethiopia
181 Angola
182 Zambia
183 Lesotho
184 Mozambique
185 Malawi
186 Liberia
187 Nigeria
188 Democratic Republic of the Congo
189 Central African Republic
190 Burma
191 Sierra Leone

WORLDWIDE VACCINATIONS GUIDE

THIS TABLE SHOWS IMMUNISATIONS that are recommended for each country. No immunisations are recommended for countries that are not listed here.

Long term travellers should also consider having the following vaccinations: BCG, diphtheria, hepatitis B, Japanese encephalitis (if travelling in Asia), rabies, tick-borne encephalitis (forests of Europe). See *Vaccinations* in Chapter 1.

YELLOW FEVER: In some countries, yellow fever vaccination is an essential entry requirement. This is noted below with a superscript [1]. In other countries, it is an essential entry requirement only if the traveller has come from an infected area. This is noted with a superscript [2]. In either case, the immigration authorities will require documentary proof, such as a vaccination certificate, before allowing the traveller to enter their country. The superscript [3] indicates countries where we recommend yellow fever vaccination for all travellers, although officials require a certificate only for travellers from infected areas.

CHOLERA: At some borders, officials may request a cholera certificate. This is an outdated requirement, since the international medical community no longer recognises cholera vaccines as significantly effective. Currently there is no cholera vaccine available in the UK. See *Vaccinations*, in Chapter 1.

MENINGITIS: This refers to meningococcal meningitis, for which vaccination is usually recommended only for long-stay travellers or during epidemics.

MALARIA: In many of these countries, malaria may only be present in certain localities.

Local disease conditions may vary and it is always useful to ask your travel clinic for the latest advice.

Afghanistan	*Hep. A, Polio, Typhoid, Malaria, Y. Fever*[2]
Albania	*Hep. A, Polio, Typhoid, Y. Fever*[2]
Algeria	*Hep. A, Polio, Typhoid, Y. Fever*[2]
Angola	*Hep. A, Polio, Typhoid, Malaria, Y. Fever*[1]
Antigua & Barbuda	*Hep. A, Typhoid, Y. Fever*[2]
Argentina	*Hep. A, Typhoid, Malaria*
Armenia	*Hep. A, Polio, Typhoid, Malaria*

Australia	*Y. Fever²*
Azerbaijan	*Hep. A, Polio, Typhoid, Malaria, Diphtheria*
Bahamas	*Hep. A, Typhoid, Y. Fever²*
Bahrain	*Hep. A, Polio, Typhoid*
Bangladesh	*Hep. A, Polio, Typhoid, Malaria, Y. Fever²*
Barbados	*Hep. A, Typhoid, Y. Fever²*
Belarus	*Hep. A, Polio, Typhoid, Diphtheria*
Belize	*Hep. A, Typhoid, Malaria, Y. Fever²*
Benin	*Hep. A, Polio, Typhoid, Malaria, Y. Fever¹, Meningitis*
Bermuda	*Hep. A, Typhoid*
Bhutan	*Hep. A, Polio, Typhoid, Malaria, Y. Fever², Meningitis*
Bolivia	*Hep. A, Typhoid, Malaria, Y. Fever³*
Borneo (see Malaysia or Indonesia)	
Bosnia Herzegovina	*Hep. A, Polio, Typhoid*
Botswana	*Hep. A, Polio, Typhoid, Malaria*
Brazil	*Hep. A, Typhoid, Malaria, Y. Fever³*
British Virgin Islands	*Hep. A, Typhoid*
Brunei	*Hep. A, Polio, Typhoid, Y. Fever²*
Bulgaria	*Hep. A, Polio, Typhoid*
Burkina Faso	*Hep. A, Polio, Typhoid, Malaria, Y. Fever¹, Meningitis*
Burundi	*Hep. A, Polio, Typhoid, Malaria, Y. Fever³, Meningitis*
Cambodia	*Hep. A, Polio, Typhoid, Malaria, Y. Fever²*
Cameroon	*Hep. A, Polio, Typhoid, Malaria, Y. Fever¹, Meningitis*
Cape Verde	*Hep. A, Polio, Typhoid, Malaria, Y. Fever²*
Cayman Islands	*Hep. A, Typhoid*
Central African Republic	*Hep. A, Polio, Typhoid, Malaria, Y. Fever¹, Meningitis*
Chad	*Hep. A, Polio, Typhoid, Malaria, Y. Fever, Meningitis*
Chile	*Hep. A, Typhoid*
China	*Hep. A, Polio, Typhoid, Malaria, Y. Fever²*
China (Hong Kong)	*Hep. A, Polio, Typhoid*
China (Macau)	*Hep. A, Polio, Typhoid*
Colombia	*Hep. A, Typhoid, Malaria, Y. Fever*
Comoros	*Hep. A, Polio, Typhoid, Malaria*
Congo (Brazzaville)	*Hep. A, Polio, Typhoid, Malaria, Meningitis, Y. Fever¹*
Congo (DRC)	*Hep. A, Polio, Typhoid, Malaria, Y. Fever¹*
Cook Islands	*Hep. A, Polio, Typhoid*

Costa Rica	*Hep. A, Typhoid, Malaria*
Côte d'Ivoire	*Hep. A, Polio, Typhoid, Malaria, Y. Fever[1], Meningitis*
Croatia	*Hep. A, Polio, Typhoid*
Cuba	*Hep. A, Typhoid*
Czech Republic	*Hep. A, Polio, Typhoid*
Djibouti	*Hep. A, Polio, Typhoid, Malaria, Y. Fever[2], Meningitis*
Dominica	*Hep. A, Typhoid, Y. Fever[2]*
Dominican Republic	*Hep. A, Typhoid, Malaria*
Ecuador	*Hep. A, Typhoid, Malaria, Y. Fever[3]*
Egypt	*Hep. A, Polio, Typhoid, Malaria , Y. Fever[2]*
El Salvador	*Hep. A, Typhoid, Malaria, Y. Fever[2]*
Equatorial Guinea	*Hep. A, Polio, Typhoid, Malaria, Y. Fever[3], Meningitis*
Eritrea	*Hep. A, Polio, Typhoid, Malaria, Y. Fever[2], Meningitis*
Estonia	*Hep. A, Polio, Typhoid, Diphtheria*
Ethiopia	*Hep. A, Polio, Typhoid, Malaria, Y. Fever[3], Meningitis*
Falkland Islands	*Hep. A, Polio, Typhoid*
Fiji	*Hep. A, Polio, Typhoid, Y. Fever[2]*
French Guiana	*Hep. A, Typhoid, Malaria, Y. Fever[1]*
French Polynesia	*Hep. A, Polio, Typhoid, Y. Fever*
Gabon	*Hep. A, Polio, Typhoid, Malaria, Y. Fever[1]*
The Gambia	*Hep. A, Polio, Typhoid, Malaria, Y. Fever[3], Meningitis*
Georgia	*Hep. A, Polio, Typhoid, Diphtheria, Malaria*
Ghana	*Hep. A, Polio, Typhoid, Malaria, Y. Fever[1], Meningitis*
Greece	*Y. Fever[2]*
Grenada	*Hep. A, Typhoid, Y. Fever[2]*
Guadeloupe	*Hep. A, Typhoid, Y. Fever[2]*
Guam	*Hep. A, Typhoid*
Guatemala	*Hep. A, Polio, Typhoid, Malaria, Y. Fever[2]*
Guinea Republic	*Hep. A, Polio, Typhoid, Malaria, Y. Fever[3], Meningitis*
Guinea-Bissau	*Hep. A, Polio, Typhoid, Malaria, Y. Fever[3], Meningitis*
Guyana	*Hep. A, Typhoid, Malaria, Y. Fever[3]*
Haiti	*Hep. A, Typhoid, Malaria, Y. Fever[2]*
Honduras	*Hep. A, Typhoid, Malaria, Y. Fever[2]*
India	*Hep. A, Polio, Typhoid, Malaria, Y. Fever[2], Meningitis*
Indonesia	*Hep. A, Polio, Typhoid, Malaria, Y. Fever[2]*
Iran	*Hep. A, Polio, Typhoid, Malaria*
Iraq	*Hep. A, Polio, Typhoid, Malaria, Y. Fever[2]*
Israel	*Hep. A, Polio, Typhoid*

Jamaica	*Hep. A, Typhoid, Y. Fever[2]*
Japan	*Polio, Typhoid*
Jordan	*Hep. A, Polio, Typhoid, Y. Fever[2]*
Kazakhstan	*Hep. A, Polio, Typhoid, Y. Fever[2], Diphtheria*
Kenya	*Hep. A, Polio, Typhoid, Malaria, Y. Fever[3], Meningitis*
Kiribati	*Hep. A, Polio, Typhoid, Y. Fever[2]*
Korea (North)	*Hep. A, Polio, Typhoid, Malaria*
Korea (South)	*Hep. A, Polio, Typhoid*
Kuwait	*Hep. A, Polio, Typhoid*
Kyrgyzstan	*Hep. A, Polio, Typhoid, Diphtheria*
Laos	*Hep. A, Polio, Typhoid, Malaria, Y. Fever[2]*
Latvia	*Hep. A, Polio, Typhoid, Diphtheria*
Lebanon	*Hep. A, Polio, Typhoid, Y. Fever[2]*
Lesotho	*Hep. A, Polio, Typhoid, Y. Fever[2]*
Liberia	*Hep. A, Polio, Typhoid, Malaria, Y. Fever[1], Meningitis*
Libya	*Hep. A, Polio, Typhoid, Y. Fever[2], Malaria*
Lithuania	*Hep. A, Polio, Typhoid, Diptheria*
Macedonia	*Hep. A, Polio, Typhoid*
Madagascar	*Hep. A, Polio, Typhoid, Malaria, Y. Fever[2]*
Madeira	*Y. Fever[2]*
Malawi	*Hep. A, Polio, Typhoid, Malaria, Y. Fever[2], Meningitis*
Malaysia	*Hep. A, Polio, Typhoid, Malaria, Y. Fever[2]*
Maldives	*Hep. A, Polio, Typhoid, Y. Fever[2]*
Mali	*Hep. A, Polio, Typhoid, Malaria, Y. Fever[1], Meningitis*
Malta	*Y. Fever[2]*
Martinique	*Hep. A, Typhoid*
Mauritania	*Hep. A, Polio, Typhoid, Malaria, Y. Fever[1]*
Mauritius	*Hep. A, Polio, Typhoid, Y. Fever[2], Malaria*
Mexico	*Hep. A, Typhoid, Malaria, Y. Fever[2]*
Moldova	*Hep. A, Polio, Typhoid, Diphtheria*
Mongolia	*Hep. A, Polio, Typhoid*
Monserrat	*Hep. A, Polio, Typhoid*
Morocco	*Hep. A, Polio, Typhoid, Malaria*
Mozambique	*Hep. A, Polio, Typhoid, Malaria, Y. Fever[2], Meningitis*
Myanmar (Burma)	*Hep. A, Polio, Typhoid, Malaria, Y. Fever[2]*
Namibia	*Hep. A, Polio, Typhoid, Malaria, Y. Fever[2]*
Nauru	*Hep. A, Polio, Typhoid, Y. Fever[2]*
Nepal	*Hep. A, Polio, Typhoid, Malaria, Y. Fever[2], Meningitis*

Netherlands Antilles	*Hep. A, Typhoid, Y. Fever[2]*
New Caledonia	*Hep. A, Polio, Typhoid, Y. Fever[2]*
Nicaragua	*Hep. A, Typhoid, Malaria, Y. Fever[2]*
Niger	*Hep. A, Polio, Typhoid, Malaria, Y. Fever[1], Meningitis*
Nigeria	*Hep. A, Polio, Typhoid, Malaria, Y. Fever[3], Meningitis*
Niue	*Hep. A, Polio, Typhoid, Y. Fever[2]*
Oman	*Hep. A, Polio, Typhoid, Malaria, Y. Fever[2]*
Pakistan	*Hep. A, Polio, Typhoid, Malaria, Y. Fever[2]*
Panama	*Hep. A, Polio, Typhoid, Malaria, Y. Fever[3]*
Papua New Guinea	*Hep. A, Polio, Typhoid, Malaria, Y. Fever[2]*
Paraguay	*Hep. A, Typhoid, Malaria, Y. Fever[2]*
Peru	*Hep. A, Typhoid, Malaria, Y. Fever[3]*
Philippines	*Hep. A, Polio, Typhoid, Malaria, Y. Fever[2]*
Pitcairn Island	*Hep. A, Polio, Typhoid, Y. Fever[2]*
Portugal	*Y. Fever[2]*
Puerto Rico	*Hep. A, Typhoid*
Qatar	*Hep. A, Polio, Typhoid*
Réunion	*Hep. A, Polio, Typhoid, Y. Fever[2]*
Romania	*Hep. A, Polio, Typhoid*
Russian Federation	*Hep. A, Polio, Typhoid, Diphtheria*
Rwanda	*Hep. A, Polio, Typhoid, Malaria, Y. Fever[1], Meningitis*
St. Helena	*Hep. A, Polio, Typhoid, Y. Fever[2]*
St Kitts & Nevis	*Hep. A, Typhoid, Y. Fever[2]*
St. Lucia	*Hep. A, Typhoid, Y. Fever[2]*
St. Maarten	*Hep. A, Polio, Typhoid, Y. Fever[2]*
St. Vincent & Grenada	*Hep. A, Typhoid, Y. Fever[2]*
Samoa (American)	*Hep. A, Polio, Typhoid, Yellow Fever[2]*
Samoa (Western)	*Hep. A, Polio, Typhoid, Y. Fever[2]*
São Tomé & Principe	*Hep. A, Polio, Typhoid, Malaria, Y. Fever[1]*
Saudi Arabia	*Hep. A, Polio, Typhoid, Malaria, Meningitis, Y. Fever[2]* *([1] for pilgrims)*
Senegal	*Hep. A, Polio, Typhoid, Malaria, Y. Fever[3], Meningitis*
Seychelles	*Hep. A, Polio, Typhoid, Y. Fever[2]*
Sierra Leone	*Hep. A, Polio, Typhoid, Malaria, Y. Fever[3], Meningitis*
Singapore	*Hep. A, Polio, Typhoid, Y. Fever[2]*
Slovak Republic	*Hep. A, Polio, Typhoid*

Slovenia	Hep. A, Polio, Typhoid
Solomon Islands	Hep. A, Polio, Typhoid, Malaria, Y. Fever[2]
Somalia	Hep. A, Polio, Typhoid, Malaria, Y. Fever[3], Meningitis
South Africa	Hep. A, Polio, Typhoid, Malaria, Y. Fever[2]
Sri Lanka	Hep. A, Polio, Typhoid, Malaria, Y. Fever[2]
Sudan	Hep. A, Polio, Typhoid, Malaria, Y. Fever[3], Meningitis
Surinam	Hep. A, Polio, Typhoid, Malaria, Y. Fever[3]
Swaziland	Hep. A, Polio, Typhoid, Malaria, Y. Fever[2]
Syria	Hep. A, Polio, Typhoid, Malaria, Y. Fever[2]
Taiwan	Hep. A, Polio, Typhoid, Y. Fever[2]
Tajikistan	Hep. A, Polio, Typhoid, Malaria, Diphtheria
Tanzania	Hep. A, Polio, Typhoid, Malaria, Y. Fever[3], Meningitis
Thailand	Hep. A, Polio, Typhoid, Malaria, Y. Fever[2]
Togo	Hep. A, Polio, Typhoid, Malaria, Y. Fever[1], Meningitis
Tonga	Hep. A, Polio, Typhoid, Y. Fever[2]
Trinidad & Tobago	Hep. A, Typhoid, Y. Fever[2]
Tunisia	Hep. A, Polio, Typhoid, Y. Fever[2]
Turkey	Hep. A, Polio, Typhoid, Malaria
Turkmenistan	Hep. A, Polio, Typhoid, Malaria, Diphtheria
Tuvalu	Hep. A, Polio, Typhoid
Uganda	Hep. A, Polio, Typhoid, Malaria, Y. Fever[3], Meningitis
Ukraine	Hep. A, Polio, Typhoid, Diphtheria
United Arab Emirates	Hep. A, Polio, Typhoid, Malaria
Uruguay	Hep. A, Typhoid
Uzbekistan	Hep. A, Polio, Typhoid, Diphtheria
Vanuatu	Hep. A, Polio, Typhoid, Malaria
Venezuela	Hep. A, Typhoid, Malaria, Y. Fever
Vietnam	Hep. A, Polio, Typhoid, Malaria, Y. Fever[2]
Virgin Islands	Hep. A, Typhoid
Yemen	Hep. A, Polio, Typhoid, Malaria, Y. Fever[2]
Yugoslavia	Hep. A, Polio, Typhoid
Zambia	Hep. A, Polio, Typhoid, Malaria, Y. Fever
Zimbabwe	Hep. A, Polio, Typhoid, Malaria, Y. Fever[2]

VACCINATION AND INFORMATION CENTRES

In the uk, most vaccinations can be given by the traveller's own doctor. Yellow fever vaccine can be given by some general practitioners, or this and other unusual vaccines can be obtained from the centres listed below. It is best to consult your own doctor before ringing any of the hospital-based clinics.

It is also worth looking at the list of British Airways travel clinics that follows this section.

Vaccination requirements are listed in the *Worldwide Vaccination Guide*. Please note these are only guidelines as inoculations can change with new outbreaks of diseases, so please check with your own doctor or with a travel clinic as far in advance as possible.

Official information sources

British Foreign Office
Travel Advice Unit
Consular Division
Foreign & Commonwealth
Office
1 Palace Street
London SW1E 5HE
Tel: 020 7238 4503/4504
Fax: 020 7238 4545
Website: www.fco.gov.uk/
travel/countryadvice.asp

US State Department
Website: www.travel.state.gov/

World Health Organisation
Website: www.who.org
Useful Publication:
*International Travel and
Health (WHO publication/
IBSN 92 4 1580259,$15.30).
This annual guide, updated each
January, issues authoritative
advice on the medical and
personal precautions needed
to protect the health of
international travellers.*

Publication available online at:
www.who.org (link to
www.who.int/dsa/)

United Nations
Website: www.un.org/Depts/
unsd/social

Medical advice at Heathrow

Health Control Unit
Terminal 3 Arrivals
Heathrow Airport
Hounslow
Middlesex TW6 1NB
Tel: 020 8745 7209
*At any time, can give up-to-date
information on compulsory and
recommended immunisations
for different countries.*

In London

MASTA
London School of Hygiene and
Tropical Medicine
Keppel Street
London WC1E 7BR

Tel: 020 7631 4408
Health Brief: 0891 224 100
Markets a wide range of products. For detailed advice on all health requirements for your intended destination(s), ring the Health Brief phoneline; calls typically take 3-4 minutes and, following this, your health brief arrives by first class post (covered by the cost of the call).

Fleet Street Travel Clinic
29 Fleet Street
London EC4Y 1AA
Tel: 020 7353 5544
Run by Dr. Richard Dawood, health columnist of TRAVELLER magazine.

West London Designated Vaccination Centre
53 Great Cumberland Place
London W1H 7HL
Tel: 020 7262 6456
Open 8.45am-5pm Monday-Friday, no appointment necessary.

Hospital for Tropical Diseases
4 St. Pancras Way
London NW1 0PE
Tel: 020 7637 6099
(Travel clinic)
Comprehensive range of pre-travel immunisations and advice, and post–travel check-ups in travel clinic and large travel shop. Pre-recorded healthline gives country-specific health hazards — you will be asked to dial the international dialling code of the relevant country, so have it ready. Centre

for investigation and treatment of tropical illness.

Ross Institute Malaria Advisory Service
London School of Hygiene and Tropical Medicine
Keppel Street
London WC1E 7HT
Tel: 020 7636 7921
24-hour taped advice.

Central Public Health Laboratory
61 Colindale Avenue
London NW9 5HT
Tel: 020 8200 4400
Provides advice and supplies of rabies vaccines and gammaglobulin to general practitioners for immunisation against hepatitis A.

UK Department of Health
Public Enquiries Office
Richmond House
79 Whitehall
London SW1A 2NS
Tel: 020 7210 4850
Also publish a free booklet Health Advice for Travellers (order from 0800-555777).

In Birmingham

Department of Infectious Diseases & Tropical Medicine
Birmingham Heartlands Hospital
Bordesley Green East
Birmingham B9 5SS
Tel: 0121 766 6611
Pre-travel telephone advice and expertise in investigation and treatment of tropical illness.

In Glasgow

Department of Infectious Diseases and Tropical Medicine/Travel Information
Ruchill Hospital
Glasgow G20 9NB
Tel: 0141 946 7120
Together with Communicable Disease (Scotland) Unit, provides telephone advice for general practitioners and other doctors and maintains 'Travax', a computerised database on travel medicine that may be accessed remotely by modem. Pre- and post-travel clinics and limited travel health supplies. Enquiries/referrals to clinics are best initiated by your general practitioner.

In Liverpool

Liverpool School of Tropical Medicine
Pembroke Place
Liverpool L3 5QA
Tel: 0151-708 9393
www.liv.ac.uk/lstm/travelmed.html.
Clinic open 1pm-4pm Monday-Friday, no appointments necessary. Pre-recorded travel health, vaccination and malaria advice on 0891 172111 (costs 50p per minute).
Regular immunisation and post-travel clinic with a range of travellers' health supplies. An international centre of expertise and research on venoms and snake bites, and investigation and management of tropical diseases.

In Manchester

Department of Infectious Diseases and Tropical Medicine
North Manchester General Hospital
Delaunays Road
Manchester M8 5AB
Tel: 0161 795 4567

UK phone-based services

Travellers' Healthline
Tel: 0891 224 100
This is a regularly updated advice line (with inter-active technology) for travellers seeking information about vaccinations etc.

Malaria Reference Laboratory
Tel: 020 7636 7921/8636
Advice on malaria prophylaxis and prevention.

Biting Insects and How to Avoid Getting Bitten Advice Line
Tel: 0891 600 270
Calls cost 50p per minute.

WEXAS healthline
Tel: 0906 1337730
(50p per minute)
WEXAS club members' exclusive traveller's health information service.

In the USA

Centers for Disease Control
Traveller's Health section
101 Marietta Street
Atlanta
GA 30323
USA

Tel: 404 332 4559
*Based in Atlanta, Georgia
(USA), CDC runs a 24-hour
automated system giving advice
by region and on special
problems such as malaria, food,
water precautions and advice for
pregnant travellers.*

Convenience Care Centers
Suite 10010301
East Darvey Armani
CA 91733
USA
*Undertakes all necessary
vaccinations.*

**International Association for
Medical Assistance to
Travelers**
417 Center Street
Lewiston NY 14092
USA
Tel: 716 754 4883
www.sentex.net/~iamat
*Non-profit organisation
dedicated to the gathering and
dissemination of health and
sanitary information world-
wide. Publishes a directory of
English-speaking medical
centres world-wide and many
leaflets on world climates,
immunisation, malaria and
other health risks world-wide.
(Also at 40 Regal Road Guelph,
Ontario N1K 1B5, Canada,
tel: 519-836 0102.)*

BRITISH AIRWAYS TRAVEL CLINICS

These clinics provide a
comprehensive vaccination
and travellers' health
information service to anyone,
regardless of whether they
travel by BA. Please ring first to
make an appointment. WEXAS
members are entitled to a
discount of £5, if they spend
more than £10, at these clinics.

For further information,
check their website at
**www.british-airways.com/
travelqa/fyi/health/docs/
clinfone.shtml**

London

BMI HealthLinx
46 Wimpole Street, W1M 7DG
020 7569 5000

British Airways
101 Cheapside, EC2V 6DT
020 7606 2977

British Airways
156 Regent Street, W1R 6DA
020 7439 9584
*(Regent Street branch operates a
no-appointment, walk-in centre)*

British Airways
Gatwick London Terminal
SW1W 9SJ
020 7233 6661

Flightbookers
177 Tottenham Court Road
W1P 0LX
020 7637 8999

Hampstead Group Practice
75 Fleet Road, NW3 2QU
020 7433 1331

Unilabs
79 Harley Street, W1N 1AE
020 7908 7220

Aberdeen
RGIT Limited
338 King Street, AB 2 3BJ
01224 624669

Birmingham
110 Church Lane
Handsworth Wood, B20 2ES
0121 523 2522

Brighton
30-36 Oxford Street, BN1 4AL
01273 606636

Bristol
Staple Hill Surgery
14 Staple Hill, BS16 5DN
0117 975 5500

Cambridge
1 Huntingdon Road, CB3 0DB
01223 313969

Cardiff
The Medical Centre
Taff's Well, CF4 7YG
02920 811425

Chester
PHLS
Countess of Chester
Health Park,
Liverpool Road, CH2 1BA
01244 377844

Edinburgh
Davidsons Mains
Medical Centre
5 Quality Street, EH4 5BP
0131 336 3038

Harrow
The Harrow
Health Care Centre
84-88 Pinner Road, HA1 4LF
020 8861 1181

Hemel Hempstead
Bennetts End Surgery
Gatecroft, HP3 9LY
01442 236733

Manchester
6 St. Ann's Square, M2 7HN
0161 832 3019

Newcastle-upon-Tyne
University Medical Centre,
Claremont Road, NE1 7RU
0191 230 3721

Newport Pagnell
Queen's Avenue Medical
Centre, MK16 8QT
01908 211035

Plymouth
Lisson Grove Medical Centre
Mutley, PL4 7DL
01752 205556

Purley
Claremont House
Woodcote Valley Road
CR8 3AG
020 8763 1372

Reading
Grovelands Medical Centre
701 Oxford Road, RG3 1HG
0118 958 5101

Shenfield
The Surgery
Mount Avenue, CM13 2NL
01277 200169

Stoke Poges
The Lanes Practice
Plough Lane, SL2 4JW
01753 662243

Tonbridge
Warders Medical Centre
East Street, TN9 1LA
01732 772815

York
Lavender Grove Practice
Boroughbridge Road
Y024 3DX
01904 784484

South Africa

Cape Town	021 419 3172
Durban	031 303 2423
East London	043 743 7471
Johannesburg	011 807 3132

MEDICAL KIT SUPPLIERS

Homeway Ltd
Fighting Cocks, West Amesbury
Salisbury, Wilts SP4 7BH
Tel: 01980 626361
*Provides a Travel With Care
package and also sells sterile
medical packs.*

**Medical Advisory Services
for Travellers (MASTA)**
London School of Hygiene and
Tropical Medicine,
Keppel Street, London WC1
Tel: 020 7837 5540.
*MASTA has helped to design the
Travel-Well personal water
purifiers. This removes partic-
ulate matter, bacteria, protozoa
and viruses from contaminated
water. They also sell Sterile
Medical Equipment Packs and
Emergency Dental Packs.*

Nomad Travellers Stores
40 Bernard Street, Russell
Square, London WC1N 1LS
Tel: 0207 833 411
Fax: 0207 833 4470

3-4 Wellington Terrace, Turn-
pike Lane, London N8 0PX
Tel: 0208 889 7014
Fax: 0208 889 9529

4 Potters Road, New Barnet
Herts EN5 5HW
Tel: 0208 441 7208
Fax: 0208 440 2340

43 Queens Road, Clifton
Bristol BS8 1QH
Tel: 0117 922 6567
Fax: 0117 922 7789

*For catalogue/mail order,
tel 0208 889 7014, e-mail
nomad.travstore@virgin.net,
www.nomadtravel.co.uk.
Travel Health Information Line:
09068 633414
(calls cost 60p per minute).
Full medical centre, vaccination
service and pharmacy. Wide
range of medical and non-
medical equipment, including
mosquito nets. Mail order
available.*

Oasis
High Street, Stoke ferry
King's Lynn, Norfolk PE33 9SP
Tel: 0403 257299
*Sells mosquito nets and provides
a free malaria advice sheet. Sells
sterile medical kits.*

Safety and First Aid (SAFA)
59 Hill Street, Liverpool L8 5SB
Tel: 0151 708 0397
*Provides general medical kits
and also prevention kits for
AIDS and Hepatitis B.*

MEDICAL KIT CHECKLIST
by Dr Richard Dawood

THIS IS A CHECKLIST of the main essentials to consider. Some of the items listed require a doctor's prescription: they are intended for use in circumstances where skilled medical care is not available. Clearly, such medication needs to be prescribed for you by a doctor who has given you careful (and, ideally, written) instructions about its use, and about any side effects and possible problems.

Make sure all medicines are easily identifiable: keep them in their original container. When possible, ask your pharmacist to dispense drugs in blister packs—these travel best and are easiest to identify. They also save space, and can be kept in small, resealable plastic bags or pouches.

ALLERGIES: antihistamine tablets are sometimes useful for treating allergic skin reactions; Piriton or Clarityn (less likely to cause drowsiness) are suitable choices. People suffering from severe or potentially life-threatening allergies should carry their own emergency supply of adrenaline.

ALTITUDE SICKNESS: some experts advise using the drug acetazolamide (Diamox) to prevent mountain sickness. For emergency use, it may also be worth carrying a supply of dexamethasone tablets to buy time in the treatment of acute mountain sickness.

ANTIBIOTICS: for longer or high-risk trips, I also advise taking a broad-spectrum, prescription antibiotic for treatment of more troublesome intestinal infections. The most suitable drug is ciprofloxacin, which can be taken either as a single dose, or as a more conventional course. In more remote places, medication for treatment of amoebic dysentery and giardia (such as Fasigyn) may also be worth carrying, in case skilled medical care can't be found.

ANTIBIOTICS AND ANTI-FUNGAL DRUGS: for long-term travellers venturing far from the beaten track, a supply of broad-spectrum antibiotics may also be worthwhile. An antibiotic like co-amoxiclav can be used to treat a variety of infections, including common infections of the skin, sinuses, and chest. Fungal infections such as athlete's foot, groin infections and thrush, are common in tropical conditions—so it is also worth taking an anti-fungal preparation, such as Canesten.

ANTI-DIARRHOEAL DRUGS: travellers' diarrhoea is seldom a medically serious condition, but can turn a long bus journey into a remarkably sophisticated form of torture. For troublesome symptoms, it is strongly advisable to travel with a supply of loperamide (sold as Imodium or Arret), which is fast-acting and safe.

ANTI-MALARIALS: the best choice of malaria medication for a particular trip is a matter for discussion at your travel clinic, prior to departure. Do allow plenty of time in advance of your trip—some anti-malarials need to be started between two and three weeks before you leave. If you need rabies vaccine, that course may need to be completed before you start taking the tablets. Besides taking preventive medication, we strongly recommend travelling with insect repellents, mosquito killers and mosquito nets.

BITE CREAMS: Take a tube of Eurax cream to relieve itching from insect bites (avoid anti-histamine creams—they may cause sensitisation). If you suffer from severe reactions to insect bites, your doctor may prescribe a more powerful, steroid cream if you need one.

BLOOD AND INTRAVENOUS FLUIDS: these are often talked about, but are quite impractical to travel with. Accidents are the commonest reason for travellers to need a transfusion, and taking precautions to avoid accidents the most effective measure to avoid the necessity of a blood transfusion. Knowing your blood group can make it easier to find a donor in an emergency—embassies keep a record of screened donors willing to help. Alternatively, join the Blood Care Foundation, a charity that undertakes to supply blood for transfusion in an emergency.

COLD SORES: these are often triggered by strong sunlight, cold and wind. If you are prone to them, use high-factor sunblock on the lips, and consider taking acyclovir cream (Zovirax) for treatment.

COLDS AND SINUSITIS: travel with a decongestant spray (e.g. Sinex) to avoid discomfort caused by pressure changes during air travel.

CONSTIPATION: dehydration, jet lag, dietary changes (including low-fibre airline food) and an initial reluctance to use dirty toilets all add to this common problem. It may be worth travelling with a small supply of natural bran (or bran tablets).

DENTAL EMERGENCY KITS: these often seem appealing, but are in fact of very limited value. Any likely problems should be dealt with at a check-up prior to travel, and the best person to advise on the likelihood of DIY repairs becoming necessary is your own dentist.

EYE INFECTIONS: minor eye infections are common in travellers to tropical countries and contact lens wearers. It is worth travelling with antibiotic drops in case of trouble (gentamicin drops do not need refrigeration, and can also be used as ear drops for infections caused by swimming).

FIRST AID KIT: minor injuries are common, and need much more care in hot climates than they normally would at home in order to avoid infection. It's worth buying a small pack of Band-aids and dressings, plus a small bottle of liquid antiseptic, such as betadine. A supply of non-adherent dressings can also be helpful for dealing with slightly larger wounds. The other essential is something capable of holding together the edges of a clean, gaping wound if medical care cannot be obtained: Steristrips and similar adhesive tapes are extremely useful.

'FLU: depending on the nature of your trip, consider travelling with a supply of Relenza, the new anti-viral 'flu medication, which can be used to abort an attack of the disease. Research has shown that it may also be of value in preventing 'flu.

INSECT REPELLENTS: insects don't just spread malaria, but also dengue fever, many forms of encephalitis (such as the variety that last year caused such havoc in New York) and other diseases not easily preventable with vaccines or medication. Repellents dramatically reduce the risk. DEET is the chemical repellent most widely used, and comes as a liquid, spray, gel, on wipes and in sticks; high concentrations are more economical and long-lasting, but should be used carefully. DEET can be applied to exposed skin and also sprayed or impregnated onto clothing. In addition, the insecticide permethrin can be applied to clothing and mosquito nets; it lasts weeks or months (and survives washing) and it kills mosquitoes, rather than merely re-directing them towards somebody not using repellent. An alternative choice is a lemon eucalyptus preparation sold as Mosi-guard. Some people prefer the smell of this, though it is not as effective as DEET.

Mosquito killers: Use a mosquito killer at night—mosquito coils are suitable for use outdoors, or where there is no electricity. Otherwise, use the plug-in variety. Mosquito nets are increasingly important, with the continuing spread of drug-resistant malaria. Ideally, use a net that has been impregnated with permethrin—this means taking your own rather than buying a net of unknown origin on arrival at your destination.

Motion sickness: the best choice of medication is largely a matter of individual preference. There is very little objective difference in effectiveness between the many products available. Many products have side-effects such as drowsiness. Whatever your choice, take the medication well in advance of trouble—most tablets are useless once vomiting starts.

Oral rehydration solutions: sachets containing oral rehydration powder (which is added to water to make the solution) are ideal for prompt treatment of dehydration caused by diarrhoea, which is the most important consequence especially in children and older travellers. You should also know how to make your own ORS.

Painkillers: the choice is between a milder type, such as paracetamol, and something a little more powerful, such as ibuprofen.

Salt: anyone travelling to extreme hot climates should increase salt intake to reduce the risk of heat illness. Take a small supply of ordinary table salt (rather than salt tablets, which may cause stomach irritation and do not always dissolve) to add to drinking water during acclimatisation: a quarter teaspoon per pint (just below the taste threshold) should be added to all drinking water.

Sterile needle kits: in many developing countries, there is a high potential for the spread of HIV and hepatitis B through non-sterile needles, syringes and other medical items. These simple, basic supplies may not be widely available; and even if they can be found in the capital city, don't expect them to be available in a poor, rural clinic at the moment you might need them. Most travellers to developing countries should take their own: the best way to do this is to buy a ready-made commercial kit rather than to attempt buying the items individually.

SUNBURN: a good supply of high-factor sunscreens (SPF 15 or higher) is essential for almost any outdoor activity, especially at altitude. Water-resistant sunscreens are also available, and last longer on the skin. Choose a brand that gives protection against UVA as well as UVB.

WATER PURIFICATION SUPPLIES: my own preference is either for iodine tablets (such as Potable Aqua) or for solution (the dose is four drops of two per cent tincture of iodine per litre of water—wait 20 minutes before drinking). There is also a wide choice of water purification gadgets that are effective and simple to use, such as the PentaPure Travel Cup, if you have enough room in your luggage. ❧

USEFUL READING

THE TRAVELLER'S GOOD HEALTH GUIDE
by Ted Lankester
£6.99 paperback, 224 pages,
Sheldon Press 1999
ISBN 0859698270
A guide to health and wellbeing for anyone planning a long trip overseas. It contains information on preparations, including immunisation, possible problems and precautions for life abroad, how to recognise and treat common illnesses, and returning home (health checks and reverse culture shock).

TRAVELLERS' HEALTH : HOW TO STAY HEALTHY ABROAD
by Richard Dawood (Editor)
Oxford University Press
(1993 edition)
Comprehensive collection of international medical experts write about every conceivable health problem abroad. Perhaps too much detail for most, but very useful for expeditions or prolonged travel off the beaten track.

HAVE BABY WILL TRAVEL
by Sarah Tucker
£12.99, 174 pages,
Lennard Publishing
ISBN 1852911433
Excellent first-hand advice on travelling with a new young child.

BUGS, BITES AND BOWELS : TRAVEL HEALTH
by Jane Wilson-Howarth
£7.99 paperback, 256 pages,
Cadogan Books 1999
ISBN 186011914X
Practical general guide about health hazards of travel.

TRAVEL IN HEALTH
by Graham Fry
£6.99 paperback, 158 pages,
Gill and Macmillan 2000
ISBN: 0717129888
A popular general guide to travel health, recently updated

ARE WE NEARLY THERE ?
by Samantha Gore-Lyons
£8.99 paperback, 288 pages,
Virgin Books 2000
ISBN 0753503999
A comprehensive and practical guide to travelling with babies, toddlers and children. Very down to earth and easy reading.

YOUR CHILD'S HEALTH ABROAD, A MANUAL FOR TRAVELLING PARENTS
by Jane Wilson-Howarth and Matthew Ellis
£8.95 paperback, 208 pages,
BRADT Publications 1998
ISBN 1898323631
Written by medical parents of children reared in remote parts of the world, useful and practical guide for the worried expat parent.

Nothing Ventured: Disabled People Travel the World

by Alison Walsh
£7.99 paperback, 560 pages,
Rough Guides 1992
ISBN 0747102082
A collection of over 100 tales by disabled travellers, describing their adventures, their setbacks and ultimately—more often than not—their triumphs.

Comprehensive Guide to Wilderness & Travel Medicine

by Eric A. Weiss
$6.05 paperback, 198 pages,
Adventure Medical Kits 1998
ISBN: 0965976807
For the mountain men out there

International Travel and Health

$15.30, World Health Organization
IBSN 92 4 1580259
*This annual guide, updated each January, issues authoritative advice on the medical and personal precautions needed to protect the health of international travellers.
It is available online at:*
www.who.org (link to www.who.int/dsa/)

HIV/AIDS INFORMATION

National AIDS Helpline

Tel: 0800 567 123
24-hour free helpline providing advice on all aspects of HIV infection.

Terence Higgins Trust

Tel: 020 7242 1010
Confidential phoneline for detailed information about travel restrictions, insurance etc. for HIV-positive individuals.

Positive Discounts

PO Box 347
Twickenham TW1 2SN
Tel: 020 8891 2561
www.positive-discounts.org.uk
Travel insurance whether or not you are HIV-positive.

ALTERNATIVE MEDICINE SOURCES

The Society of Homoeopaths
4 Artisan Road
Northhampton NN1 4HU
Tel: 01604 621400

The Chinese Herbal Medicine Centre
34 Knight Hill
London SE27 0HY
Tel: 020 8670 7477

Herbline UK
Tel: 01323 834 803
Open Tuesday, Wednesday, and Friday from 9am-3pm.

Hambledon Herbs
Court Farm, Milverton,
Somerset TA4 1NS
Tel: 01823 401104
Cannot give advice over the telephone but they will send a mail-order catalogue on request.

Neal's Yard Remedies Hotline
will answer any queries
General enquiries
tel: 020 7498 1686
Customer services
tel: 020 7627 1949
e-mail:
mail@nealsyardremedies.com
or
cservices@nealsyardremedies.com
Mail order: Neal's Yard Remedies, 26-34 Ingate Place, Battersea, London SW8 3NS

Helios Homeopathic Pharmacy
97 Camden Road, Tunbridge Wells, Kent TN1 2QR
Tel: 01892 536393 and 537254

Centre for the Study of Complementary Medicine
14 Harley House
Upper Harley St
London NW1 4PR
Tel: 020 7935 7848
Fax: 020 7224 4519
www.complemed.co.uk
e-mail:
enquiries@complemed.co.uk

Council for Complementary and Alternative Medicine (CAM)
Tel: 020 8735 0632

FURTHER READING

The World Travellers Manual of Homoeopathy by Dr. Colin B Lessell (£16.95, The C.W. Daniel Company)
A Handbook of Homeopathic Alternatives to Immunisation by Susan Curtis (£5.99, Winter Press)
Prescription for Nutritional Healing by James F. Balch and Phyllis A Balch (\$6.95, Avery Publishing Group)
Nature's Pharmacy by Lynne Paige-Walker (£9.49, Macmillan)
Neal's Yard Remedies: Homeopathy by Rebecca Wells (£9.99, Arum Press)

THE RELATIVE RISKS...

This table details the percentage risk of infection for various diseases during a one-month stay in a developing country.

Diarrhoea	50%
Malaria (no tablets, visiting West Africa)	2.4%
Malaria (no tablets, visiting East Africa)	1.5%
Acute respiratory tract infection	1.3%
Giardiasis	0.7%
Hospitalised abroad	0.4%
Viral hepatitis (all types)	0.4%
Amoebiasis	0.4%
Gonorrhoea	0.3%
Air evacuation	0.06%
Syphilis	0.04%
Typhoid fever (India or north Africa)	0.03%
HIV infection	0.01%
Died abroad	0.001%
Cholera	0.0003%

SOURCES: Steffen, R. Lobel, H.O. 'Travel Medicine' in Cook, G.C. (ed.), *Manson's Tropical Diseases* (20th edition, 1996, London).

'A survey of 7,886 Swiss travellers to developing countries', by Steffen, R. et al., in *The Journal of Infectious Diseases* 1987, 156:1:84-91.

'A survey of 42,202 European tourists visiting tropical Africa', by Steffen, R. et al. *Bulletin of the World Health Organisation* 1990, 68 (3): 313-322.

'A review of 34 studies on travellers' diarrhoea', by Black, R.E., *Reviews of Infectious Diseases* 1990, 12: s73-s79

NOTES ON CONTRIBUTORS

JACK BARKER is a freelance travel writer and editor of the online *Travelmag* e-zine. He is a regular contributor to *Traveller* magazine.

DR NICK BEECHING is a Senior Lecturer at the Liverpool School of Tropical Medicine, and is Clinical Director of the Infectious Disease Unit at University Hospital Aintree in Liverpool. He has travelled widely and he has worked in India, Australia, New Zealand and the Middle East. He continues active teaching and research collaborations with colleagues in many parts of the tropics.

COL. JOHN BLASHFORD-SNELL is the founder of Operation Drake and Operation Raleigh, and a fearless leader of countless expeditions world-wide.

HILARY BRADT is the founder of Bradt Guides and a frequent lecturer on travel topics.

INGRID CRANFIELD is a freelance writer and broadcaster and a former editor of *The Traveller's Handbook* (WEXAS).

SHEILA CRITCHLEY is a Canadian journalist now based in London, and has run an airline in-flight magazine.

ADRIAN FURNHAM is a lecturer in psychology at London University. He is the co-author with Prof. F. Bochner of *Culture Shock: psychological consequences of geographic movement* (Methuen).

ROBIN HANBURY-TENISON has led many expeditions in South America, Africa and Asia. He is the founder of Survival International and a campaigner for the preservation of tribal peoples.

IAN IRVINE is a registered insurance broker, specialising in insurance for adventure and overland travellers.

Jack Jackson is an experienced expedition leader and overland traveller. He is co-author of *The Asian Highway*.

Dr Saye Khoo is a Senior Lecturer in the Department of Pharmacology and Therapeutics of the University of Liverpool and a Consultant in general medicine and infectious diseases. He was medical officer on the 1997 Malaysian Everest Expedition.

Sir Robin Knox-Johnston was the first man to sail single-handed non-stop around the world. He has also set the world record for sailing round the world on a catamaran. He has written numerous books on sailing.

Jonathan Lorie is the Editor of *Traveller* magazine and has travelled widely in Africa, Indochina and Europe. Previously he worked in the international aid and arts sectors.

Julian McIntosh has lived in Africa and travelled extensively. His overland experiences prompted him to set up his own specialist tropical equipment firm.

Paul Pratt has been a ship's radio officer in the British Merchant Navy and an electronics engineer in Britain and Scandinavia.

Melissa Shales is a freelance travel writer. She is a former editor of *The Traveller's Handbook* (WEXAS).

Mike Stroud has been the medical advisor on Sir Ranulph Fiennes's polar expeditions. He specialises in the effects of physical extremes on the human body, and is based at the Army Personnel Research Establishment at Farnborough.

Sarah Thorowgood is an editor for Footprint Handbooks.

Dr Sharon Welby is a Lecturer in Travel Medicine at the Liverpool School of Tropical Medicine, where she runs the travel clinic and organises travel medicine courses for other health professionals.

Ian Wilson is the founder and Chairman of WEXAS International.

FREE TRIAL TRAVEL CLUB MEMBERSHIP

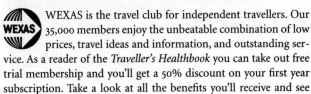 WEXAS is the travel club for independent travellers. Our 35,000 members enjoy the unbeatable combination of low prices, travel ideas and information, and outstanding service. As a reader of the *Traveller's Healthbook* you can take out free trial membership and you'll get a 50% discount on your first year subscription. Take a look at all the benefits you'll receive and see how you'll save your subscription many times over.

■ Discount rates on airfares, hotels and car hire worldwide
■ Annual travel insurance from as little as £59 per year (2000 rates)
■ FREE subscription to *Traveller* – the highly acclaimed travel magazine
■ Expert services from experienced travel consultants and access to our members-only phone numbers
■ Privileged access to VIP airport lounges
■ Currency & travellers cheques available by post, commission-free
■ Special rates for airport parking
■ Discounts at British Airways Travel Clinics
■ £50,000 free Flight Accident Insurance with every flight booking
■ Bagtag lost luggage retrieval service
■ Free international assistance 24 hours a day
■ Discounts on local tours and sightseeing worldwide
■ Additional benefits for business travellers
■ Access to WEXASonline (members-only website)
■ Customised round-the-world itineraries
■ Quarterly Update newsletter on special offers and discounts

 Complete this form and post today for full details of WEXAS membership and the free trial offer.

WEXAS International, FREEPOST, London SW3 1BR.

Name (Mr/Mrs/Miss/Ms) ....

Address ....

....

Postcode ....

Telephone ....

Email ....

T250